TEMPTING FATE

TEMPTING FATE
A CAUTIONARY TALE OF POWER AND POLITICS

PATTI STARR

Stoddart

Copyright © 1993 by Patricia Starr

All rights reserved. No part of this publication may be repoduced or transmitted in any form or by any means, electronic or mechanical, including photocopying, recording, or any information storage and retrieval system, without permission in writing from the publisher.

First published in 1993 by
Stoddart Publishing Co. Limited
34 Lesmill Road
Toronto, Canada
M3B 2T6
(416) 445-3333

Canadian Cataloguing in Publication Data is available from the National Library.

ISBN 0-7737-2761-2

Typesetting by Tony Gordon Ltd.

Printed and bound in the United States of America

*To my husband Jerry and our children,
David, Evan, Brooke, Stuart, and Randy,
who asked that this story be told:
with love, all things are possible*

Contents

Preface   xi

CHAPTER ONE	"An Example Must Be Made" *1*
CHAPTER TWO	Born to Fight *13*
CHAPTER THREE	A Houswife Volunteers *25*
CHAPTER FOUR	Movers and Shakers *32*
CHAPTER FIVE	Out of the Cocoon *42*
CHAPTER SIX	"Keep Your Options Open" *67*
CHAPTER SEVEN	A 7:00 a.m. Phone Call *81*
CHAPTER EIGHT	Chairman of the Board *109*
CHAPTER NINE	In the Maelstrom *134*
CHAPTER TEN	On the Waterfront *140*
CHAPTER ELEVEN	The Housing Battle *157*
CHAPTER TWELVE	A Visit from the *Globe* *169*
CHAPTER THIRTEEN	The Daggers Are Unsheathed *184*
CHAPTER FOURTEEN	"I'm Through Sneaking" *198*
CHAPTER FIFTEEN	"They'll Never See Me Cry" *204*
CHAPTER SIXTEEN	Scapegoat *220*
CHAPTER SEVENTEEN	Timberlea, June-July 1991, Vanier Centre for Women *237*
CHAPTER EIGHTEEN	Ingleside Cottage, July-August 1991, Vanier Centre for Women *261*
CHAPTER NINETEEN	Ingleside Cottage, August 1991, Vanier Centre for Women *276*
CHAPTER TWENTY	Time to Move On *282*

Epilogue   288
Index   307

Preface

In September 1991, a week after I was released from the Vanier Centre for Women, I met Rosemary Aubert, who was then the director of public relations for the Elizabeth Fry Society. As a successful author and editor in her own right, Rosemary began urging me to consider writing this book and offered to edit my first attempts. Her expertise, sensitivity, and encouragement were invaluable. Without her, it might not have happened.

In January 1992, I met John Honderich, editor of the *Toronto Star*. I was anxious to provide some assistance to the women still in prison, and he thought the "written word" would have the most impact. He offered to publish an article I was thinking of writing, providing it was appropriate and of interest to his readers. His reaction when I handed it in to him was most enthusiastic, and his decision to print it verbatim encouraged me to take seriously his suggestion that I write a book on the Starr Affair. I'm grateful for the constructive suggestions he made.

Fortunately for me, John Pollock, Q.C., an expert in the publishing field, undertook to represent me and sell my manuscript. John's encouragement and support were so important in keeping things on track and in helping to overcome my initial reluctance to proceed with this project.

My good fortune continued when John introduced me to Jack Stoddart, president of Stoddart Publishing, who had the guts to publish what he knew would be a very controversial book. My trust in Jack was reinforced when I began working with some of his key staff — Angel Guerra, director of marketing, and Don Bastian, managing editor. Don, in particular, was able to take my words and make them compelling. I am grateful to the entire Stoddart Publishing team.

During this past year, Zelda Young, local television and radio talk show host on CHIN, extended her hand in support by inviting me on her programs to give some political commentaries, and I thank her.

My friend, walking partner, and sometime critic, Nancy Kumer, provided another perspective on the manuscript. She softened a lot of the edges and added new dimensions.

I want to acknowledge and thank some others for their unwavering loyalty and support of me and my family during the three-year nightmare of the Starr Affair. Dino Chiesa, Betty Disero, Jerry Friedman, Mario Giampietri, Ruth Gold, Jerry Gold, Barbara Graff, Marilyn Guttman, Ray Hoffman, Bonnie Lee, David Michener, Brenda Netkin, Rochelle Reingold, Arlene Resnick, Linda Richman, Marty Richman, Lyla Satok, Irving Starr, Joey Stern, May Stern, Michael Stern, Barry Swadron, Marshall Swadron, Fran Tishman, Fran Walderman, Donna Zener, and their families.

The events of this book have been recounted to the best of my ability, using notes and documentation (1975-1991) in my possession. Although quotation marks are sometimes used for dramatic effect, many of the conversations reported are intended to give a sense of what was said, and are not always meant to be the exact words spoken. In the descriptions of the Vanier Centre for Women, the names of all guards and inmates have been changed, with the exception of Lori Pinkus.

PATRICIA STARR
TORONTO,
JULY 1993

TEMPTING FATE

CHAPTER ONE

"An Example Must Be Made"

Friday, June 27, 1991. After three years of defiance, fear, anguish, and disillusionment, I was pleading guilty to one charge of fraud and one charge of breach of trust relative to my volunteer activities. The University Avenue courtroom in Toronto was packed — my daughter, friends, the press, and the investigating police officers were all there. It felt as though everyone was looking at me — awaiting my sentence and my reaction. I looked at no one.

Speaking to the court on my behalf were Les Scheininger, president, Canadian Jewish Congress; Frank Diament, executive vice-president of B'nai Brith Canada; Rabbi Jordan Pearlson of Temple Sinai; and two friends who had also volunteered with me over the years, Barbara Graff and Marilyn Aarons. More than fifty letters of support were submitted to the court by other community leaders, friends, and family.

As soon as Mr. Justice Ted Wren started talking about my outstanding achievements and referred to me as a remarkable woman, I knew I was gone. I took off my earrings and steeled myself for what was coming: jail, for signing a grant in June of 1987 on behalf of the Council House of the National Council of Jewish Women, Canada, Toronto Section (NCJW).

"Notwithstanding there was no personal financial benefit to Mrs. Starr, and her colleagues were surely aware of her activities on their behalf, an example must be made as a general deterrent to the public because of the high profile of this case," ruled the judge. Crown prosecutor Peter Griffiths was in agreement. They barely mentioned the other charge of breach of trust.

Back on June 23, 1989, after several months of press allegations and innuendoes about my political connections and activities, Premier David Peterson of Ontario called a judicial inquiry, forever to be known as the Patricia Starr Inquiry. Its hearings began on September 18, 1989. After months of appeals, the Supreme Court of Canada ruled that the Starr Inquiry was unconstitutional, based on the fact that it was tantamount to a criminal investigation with none of the built-in protections under the Canadian Charter of Rights and Freedoms. They ended the inquiry on April 5, 1990. On April 20, 1990, criminal charges were laid against me by the provincial Crown prosecutor, which then allowed the investigation to continue under his jurisdiction. And this is where it wound up.

In light of what was coming, I became two people — one actually there, the other, outside, watching. It was on this other self that I concentrated.

"Don't think, just observe," I warned myself. To that end, I tried to wipe my husband's and children's faces from my mind, to turn a deaf ear to the groans of the friends and supporters who had stood by me in court for two days, and to forever erase the memory of twenty-five years of volunteerism with NCJW. In that moment I believed, and still do, that my former volunteer colleagues, more than anyone or anything else, had betrayed me by their "leaks" to the press and the "I can't remember" statements given to the police. Precisely when the truth would have saved me, they pretended ignorance and allowed me to be sacrificed.

Some justified their silence — or so they told me when I got out of the Vanier Centre for Women in Brampton, Ontario — by telling me that someone I trusted had given them the advice that "as long as you girls didn't know anything you won't get in trouble — Patti will only get a slap on the wrist ... nobody goes to jail for a first offence, especially when no money was taken — and given her record of community service."

The judge's sentence proved them wrong. He gave me six months in jail. The same judge who in 1992 gave a suspended sentence to a male nurse who had given a lethal overdose to one of his terminally ill patients.

I don't know where I got the strength to get up, hold my head high, and walk silently out of the courtroom into the handcuffs held by two police officers outside. The hallways were absolutely empty, a consideration no doubt of some sensitive official, which I appreciated. I was taken into an elevator with bars, which descended into the basement of the courthouse.

There I was greeted by the screams and shouting of other people in custody, some in an awful state of dishevelment. I was taken to a cell, there to be kept until the paddy wagon arrived to take me to the Metro Toronto West Detention Centre.

"Concentrate on what you see, observe everything and everybody," my other self kept screaming silently. "Don't start to cry. Think how happy your enemies will be and how they will smile."

Two female officers took my purse and jewellery. They asked me what must have been the usual questions, but I could barely answer, I was so terrified. By now, reality was starting to set in, and the enormity of what had happened started to hit. I wanted to scream and cry and beg them to let me go home. I started to shake.

The Metro police assigned to the courthouse were professional, kind, and sensitive. Those in charge told me, "Hang on, don't be afraid, hold your head high." They also told me how much they admired my achievements, especially at Ontario Place. "This too shall pass," they said.

While I was sitting on an uncomfortable bench waiting to be processed, several other young policemen came over to speak to me, and gradually I stopped shaking. Finally I was uncuffed and put in a cell with several other women. One of them was lying on the cement bench, wearing only a thin nightgown with nothing underneath. She was filthy.

"She's stoned on drugs," I was told. The others had been there before and seemed like old hands. Feeling totally conspicuous, I cringed in the corner, hoping no one would notice me. No such luck.

Several guards came over to the cell and looked in, obviously at me. One was quite happy because he had won a bet that I would be jailed rather than getting a suspended sentence. There had been a betting pool going on since the day before, and he thanked me for the dinner he and his girlfriend were going to have that night. As if sensing I was about to shoot back a snarky response, the obvious leader of our cell, Isobel, a Jamaican, grabbed my arm and told me to keep my mouth shut.

"You're Patti Starr, aren't you?" she asked. "I've seen you on TV. You're not as fat as you look in the papers, or did you lose weight?" She didn't wait for an answer. "So your political friends let you take the fall? Well, you're okay in my book. You didn't rat on nobody. I heard you were Mafia. Boy, those Jewbroads really fucked you, after all the money you got them. Jews already have all the money. I hate Jews. But you, you shouldn't be here. I'll look after you. Stick with me, kid."

I was trying to ignore the fact that I had to go to the bathroom. There was an open toilet in the cell. Ten other women present. Outside, guards — both male and female — walked back and forth. I couldn't do it. Then my other self said, "If you don't do exactly what the others do, if you act as though you think you're better, they'll get hostile. Remember all the movies you've seen about women in prison."

So I walked over to the toilet, with everyone watching me, and I tried to use it. Nothing happened.

Isobel walked over to the tap and turned it on. Magic.

After that, all the girls gathered around asking me questions and commenting about my case. Some were quite aware of the Starr Affair, including the inquiry. They talked about some of the judges they knew, and several women had very insightful opinions on how my case had been "handled."

Before being sent away, I was led off towards a glassed-off cubicle to see one of my two lawyers, Peter West, of Cooper, Sandler

& West, who looked like he was going to break down. My cousin Rick Stern, who is also a criminal lawyer, was with him. At that point, I almost lost it. What could I say to Peter? I knew in my heart of hearts that at the end he had fought for me to the limits of any human being's ability to do so, but it was too late.

Austin Cooper had been retained in July of 1989. He was regarded as one of the best criminal lawyers in Canada. Even though he was involved at the time with the Joe Burnett case (the longest-running fraud case in Canada's history), he assured me he would have time for me and that when he was tied up, his associates would be there. He felt that his high-profile experience on the Susan Nelles case (the nurse accused of murdering several babies, who was exonerated after a horrendous media and public attack) would serve him well in an inquiry bound to be as public as mine.

At our first meeting, I had stressed that politics is different from anything else. People get more intense about political scandal and corruption than they do about murder. Politicians live or die by the press, and along with their staff, would dump their own grandmothers rather than risk being booted out of office. I had told Austin about all my activities and those of my colleagues. He seemed to be as angry and bewildered as I was by the abandonment of my community and certain politicians.

For the next two years, on their instructions, nothing had been said publicly about my side of the story. Now it was too late to explain anything — and my silence was perceived as arrogance. What might have been explainable, understandable, and usually forgiveable, became unthinkable, outrageous, and criminal.

I begged Peter and Rick to tell my husband Jerry not to come to visit me in jail. The thought of his seeing me in such a place was unbearable. Peter tried to rationalize what had happened, but I cut him off. I knew it sounded cold, but I just couldn't help it.

"Twenty-five years of my life, everything I've worked for, all my accomplishments, in the garbage can," I said. "It's finished!"

My other self cried, "What the hell did I fight for three years about, go before the Supreme Court about, and spend nearly $300,000 for?

If I'm guilty today, I was guilty back then. No one ever suggested I give up, or plea bargain, or ask for mercy until it was too late."

Both Peter and Rick looked close to tears. I felt completely alone, but stronger. I got up without a word and left.

When the van was ready to take us to the Metro Toronto West Detention Centre, the girls lined up as if they knew what was coming. I, of course, did not. Isobel had pushed me to the end of the line. Everyone was to be handcuffed together, so being at the end meant having one hand free. I was grateful for that.

Being herded down the hall handcuffed to other people, in full view of others, was the most humiliating experience yet.

"No," I kept screaming silently to myself, "let me go. I want to go home. I want my babies. I'm so afraid. Mommy, Daddy, where are you?" I was shocked at the depth of my fear.

The van was overloaded and underventilated. Several women were on the floor, some totally out of it. Their language was shocking, but funny at the same time. My fellow prisoners all knew who I was. These women were also more knowledgeable about the criminal justice system and its loopholes than I had ever been about government grants. They knew which judge did what, how to delay, when to get a remand, when to plead, when to ask for bail, how to avoid "dead" time, and so much else. I was fascinated listening to them. During the two-hour ride through the streets of Toronto as our van picked up more inmates from different courts, they kept me distracted. I had once ridden through these same streets in a limousine. But I stopped myself from thinking about that as I shared the van with women who had been in jail at least once before — most several times.

Despite my fear and discomfort, I was getting angry. "What kind of way is this to treat human beings?" I thought. Herded like cattle into a van, no ventilation, women falling over each other when the van turned sharply, two of them pregnant.

"That's it, Patti girl," I thought. "Concentrate on what's wrong, and think about how to make it right."

We arrived at last and got out of the wagon, still handcuffed together.

"An Example Must Be Made"

The Metro Toronto West Detention Centre, located near the Lester B. Pearson International Airport on the outskirts of Toronto, is known simply as "The West." It was originally built as a holding facility, where people were to be kept for a few hours or days until they had their bail hearing or trial or until they were sent to their final destination. Unfortunately, because of the backlog in the courts, some are kept there for weeks, or as in Lawrie Bemebenek's case, months. It is overcrowded, and its facilities are stretched to the limit.

Lawrie Bemebenek was a former Milwaukee, Wisconsin, police officer who had been convicted of murdering her ex-husband's first wife despite the overwhelming evidence of a cover-up by the Milwaukee police. Her case was covered extensively in the media over the years and she was often referred to as a former Playboy Bunny, which she resented, because it wasn't true. It helped to reinforce the negative image of her in the media at the beginning of her trial. Over the years, however, as the questions about her innocence grew stronger, she was then portrayed as a caring and intelligent woman (which she is), and this helped in having her case reviewed. After eleven years in jail, with no hope of parole, she escaped from prison and fled with her lover to Thunder Bay, Ontario, in 1991. She was caught some months later and transferred to the Metro Toronto West Detention Centre in Toronto, where she was kept while arguments went on over her legal status.

Lawrie and I began a correspondence from the time of her imprisonment in the West and her eventual return and imprisonment in Wisconsin until she was paroled earlier this year as a result of plea bargaining. Our dialogue came to an end at this point, since under parole regulations, a parolee cannot associate with anyone who has a criminal record.

✦ When I saw the grim walls of the West, all my terror returned. Now I was in real shock, unable to believe this was really happening. Isobel sidled up to me and whispered a reminder: "Answer only if you're spoken to. Never talk back to anyone, guard or inmate."

Along with women from another van, we were all put into a holding cell just inside the entrance. By now I was soaking wet from perspiration. Inside, the noise was unbelievable. Men and women were being brought in, load after load of them, from all over Metro and beyond. Most of the prisoners were screaming and swearing at the guards.

During the several hours I was in that cell, I never heard one guard say anything impolite or threatening in response to the abuse they were getting from the newly arrived prisoners. Their self-control and professional demeanour were impressive.

Like an animal in the zoo, I kept trying to hide in the corner, but every so often a group would walk by and comment on my presence. "Hey, there's Patti Starr! Hi Patti, how do you like jail?" I fought back my tears and tried to act nonchalant.

After a little while, a new group of women arrived. The leader of this group was Coco, also a Jamaican. It was easy to see why everyone was afraid of her. She was tall and muscular, and her hair was in long curls — very intimidating. She had been arrested again, I learned, for trafficking and assault with a deadly weapon (a gun). As she worked her way through the cell, shoving girls to the side, she saw me and stopped dead in her tracks, staring. I sensed Isobel starting to edge her way towards me when Coco said, "Hey, you're Patti Starr, mon. What happened to your Peterson friends? Left you, eh? I saw you on TV wearing that suit. How much did it cost? You fucking Jews! Where are they now? Well, at least you never ratted on no one, so you can stay."

Where the hell was I going to go?

"But I'm the boss," Coco said. "Here's your first lesson." She moved closer.

By this time I was ready to fight. The time had come to stop cowering in the corner. As my mother had always told me, "If you don't stand up for yourself, no one else will. Cowards never win." Coco sensed that Isobel was trying to get between us. "Fuck off," she said to my new protector and kept walking towards me. All of a sudden about six women blocked the entrance and the visibility into the cell. No guards could help me now. I was on my own.

But I wasn't afraid anymore. I was ticked off. What the hell was I doing in a jail cell with drug traffickers and armed robbers? So be it! I'd have to make the best of it, but for sure no one was going to push me around.

Coco shoved her face into mine and asked if I had ever gotten off with another woman. I kept the stone face I had on in the courtroom and didn't flinch, or answer. She kept on. Her language was more disgusting than any I'd ever heard. She taunted and teased.

Then she made a mistake. She grabbed my arm and tried to twist it. All the while the other girls were talking loudly and making noise so no one outside could hear or see anything. With a silent prayer to whoever was up there listening, I grabbed her hair, twisted her around, put my arm across her neck, and pulled it back towards my body, with my knee shoved in the small of her back.

"Didn't you know Jesus was a Jew?" I snarled in her ear. "Didn't anyone ever tell you that Jews eat you people for lunch? Didn't you know Jewish mothers are invincible? Touch me again, you bitch, and I'll kill you!" With that, I shoved her away as hard as I could. Then I stood there, watching and waiting.

There was absolute silence in the cell. No one moved. Then Coco walked over to the cell door and yelled out at the guard, "Hey, out there, Mrs. Starr hasn't eaten nothing all day."

The guards brought over an apple, which Coco proceeded to rinse in the sink, dry with the paper towels, and hand to me.

I hate red apples.

I took it, and thanked her. As soon as I bit into it, the tension was gone and everyone sat down to gossip and talk. My insides were twisting and turning, but I was exhilarated. You were right again, Ma, I said silently. Bullies never go after anyone who will fight back. If only my former friends and colleagues had stood their ground and fought back with me.

During those hours at the West, my cellmates talked about prison life — especially about the sexual abuse and harassment many of them had endured at the hands of COs (the prison guards, who were officially called corrections officers) and each other.

Some spoke of their lesbian relationships. Others gave vivid descriptions of the sexual favours they had exchanged for cigarettes, drugs, and good reports. Most of them went both ways, depending on the circumstances. To many, sex, no matter how unsatisfying, was the only human warmth they had, especially during long stays in prison. "After a couple of years behind bars, another woman becomes appealing," several commented.

Many of these women were mothers, and of particular concern to them were the overtures and seductions of young offenders by other inmates and some COs. Katherine, a native Canadian, had been sexually assaulted with a nightstick wielded by three male guards when she was arrested the first time in Saskatchewan. She had been to Kingston Penitentiary, Canada's only federal women's prison, and there she had developed a relationship with another inmate. Her crime was armed robbery — she had helped her boyfriend, who beat her regularly. Her life on the reserve had been wretched. This time she was in the West for prostitution and drug possession, which had become her way of life. She was going back to P4W in Kingston. She was pregnant.

Mrs. Li, a tiny Oriental woman, in jail for assault with a deadly weapon (she had knifed her abusive husband), spoke eloquently about the ethnic barriers that prevented so many new Canadians from accepting a woman's role in society as anything more than being an object for sexual and physical abuse.

The girls tried to prepare me for rough treatment "upstairs" and gave me suggestions on how to behave. I believed everything they told me.

"Starr, get over here for processing" was the next thing I heard.

Two guards took me into a cubicle. Despite my earlier bravado, I started to shake again. Joining us was a medical technician. I was shocked when they closed the door, pointed to the ceiling with their fingers over their lips, and proceeded to talk to me very softly.

"Mrs. Starr, we rarely get someone like you here. Please listen carefully. Some of us have been trying to get some changes in the system, especially here at the West. We can't really speak out, and no one listens to the inmates. Of course, most of them deserve to be here. Don't be fooled by the way they'll talk to you. They know who you are. Don't discuss your personal life or your family. Being Jewish will be a problem. Most of them would have already assaulted you if not for fear of reprisals.

"The press is camped outside in full force, with TV cameras — the works. The bureaucrats are really getting edgy. They want you moved out of here tonight.

"Most of the staff do care about this place. We're worried because the West is overcrowded to the point of danger. Some cells have six women, two sleeping on the floor. Some of the prisoners are psychotic and should be in a hospital. The allocation of funds for the women is pathetic.

"Listen and watch closely, but don't take any notes. Wherever you are, your cell will be searched regularly. Never talk back, no matter what happens. Trust no one. Sometimes snitches are put into cell blocks to spy. Don't complain. You'll see drug smuggling and sexual activity. Never, and we repeat, never, report it to anyone. There are inmates who rat for privileges. If the other inmates find out before we can move them — well, you don't want descriptions. Rats are the lowest form of life.

"The word is already out that you have an Italian connection. Say nothing to change that opinion. It will probably help you. Try to help the girls when you get out. Good luck."

Still stunned by all that had happened, I was then taken in handcuffs and shackles in another van, alone, to the Vanier Centre for Women in Brampton. I was totally drained.

Once there, the female staff in charge of processing me politely asked me to strip, spread my legs, and bend over. "Don't be embarrassed," said one of the COs, "we've seen so many bare asses, it doesn't even register anymore."

Well, it registered with me. I can understand the concerns about drug smuggling, but many inmates are not drug users or alcoholics. The humiliation and degradation of this kind of inspection with more than one person watching is overwhelming. It is done regularly.

When I got to my "cottage," Timberlea, a maximum security unit, I was assigned a room and allowed to make a phone call. I called home. Many of our friends were there, comforting my husband Jerry. When he got on the line, I broke down and begged him to come and take me home. He broke down too. I heard crying in the background.

I was taken back to my cell by a very sweet young guard who tried to console me. Then I was startled by the sound of the automatic locks closing on my cell door, a grinding and clanging noise that will haunt my dreams forever.

Four years earlier I was welcoming Prince Andrew and Fergie to Ontario Place, Ontario's waterfront showplace and park. David Peterson, premier of Ontario, who was escorting them around town, knew how excited I was about meeting them in person.

In the presence of the Prince and Princess, he kept making jokes about the new boss (me), aggressive women (who, me?), and the overhaul going on at Ontario Place under my guidance. I was trying to concentrate on the rules of protocol, but he kept trying to muddle me up.

When I shook their hands first and curtsied second (not the right way), he yelled, "Off with her head!" Everyone laughed, Prince Andrew the loudest.

And now I was in jail.

I thought of my husband and children, buried my head in my pillow, and cried myself to sleep.

The next morning I woke up disoriented, with a sick feeling in the pit of my stomach, not quite realizing where I was. But then reality set in and I remembered. Instead of giving in to the urge to start crying and pounding on the locked door, I resolved instead to get on with it, to try to find something positive in the experience I was about to live, to try not to cry again and to never forgive or forget those who had so gleefully sent me here.

My old life was over. I tried to muster all my courage to face the new life I was about to begin.

CHAPTER TWO

Born to Fight

I was born in Toronto. In 1947 when I was five years old, my family lived with my grandparents next to St. Alban's Anglican Church and park in the Bloor-Bathurst area of Toronto, which was not a Jewish neighbourhood. I used to play with two girls who lived around the corner and didn't realize I was different until the other kids started to call me a dirty Jew. My mother said I should beat up anyone who did that. So I did. Pretty soon I could take on more than one kid at a time and sometimes I didn't even wait till they called me *the name*; I just attacked if they looked at me funny.

I had two brothers — Michael, who was older, and Joey, who was younger. My mother said I had to take care of them. If anyone looked at either of them crosswise, I would beat them up. The good news is that kids rarely picked on my brothers. The bad news is that I was always in fights.

When I was seven, I joined the Brownies group associated with St. Alban's Church, since there were no similar programs within the Jewish community at the time. I tried to pretend I wasn't Jewish because I wanted to have friends and not fight all the time, so I went to the church services with the rest of the Brownie pack. I remember that when everyone kneeled during the service, I panicked. It was unthinkable for me to kneel, since Jews *never* kneeled before statues. So I faked a sore knee and never went back. After all, we Jews spent forty years wandering in the desert for worshipping idols!

When I was eight, I started to take singing lessons at the Loretto Abbey, a Roman Catholic convent, after my regular classes at Associated Hebrew School. The abbey was on Brunswick Avenue, around the corner from our house on Howland Avenue, where we all lived with my maternal grandparents, David and Dora Book. My mother took me over to meet the nuns in the hope that they would accept me into their music classes even though I was Jewish. We had very little money, and when they heard me sing, they took me at no charge to my parents. I had to wear a tunic and follow all their regulations.

Since I had a very good voice, I was soon representing them in competition at the Kiwanis Festivals — in fact, I came first and second in two festivals. I was dark haired and looked Italian, so no one ever suspected I wasn't Catholic. I used to cross my fingers whenever I said I was from the abbey. I can still sing Ave Maria in perfect Latin.

All the nuns were warm and caring, but the two I remember best were Sister St. Germaine and Mother Dorothy, who used to travel with me. The irony of a Jewish girl attending parochial school and representing a Catholic abbey in music competitions was not lost on them. They said I was their special cross to bear, and they were right. They kept trying to teach me not to fight all the time and be more ladylike, but I was only ten years old and didn't know how.

I have never forgotten those wonderful women and how kind they were to me. Often in my loneliest moments, I have remembered, with great affection, Sister St. Germaine, who was rather portly but who had soft, soft eyes, and who used to lecture me, ever so quietly, about the good things in life and the importance of keeping one's faith.

We lived on the second floor of my grandparents' house. My grandfather (my mother's father) was the thirteenth child and first son of Russian parents, a violent, vicious man who I am told beat his first and second wives — ultimately, to their deaths.

When he met my grandmother (his third wife), he neglected to tell her that he had three daughters (aged one and a half to four years) and that their mother (his second wife) was in an institution as a result of his beatings.

My mother was born in Brooklyn, where my grandparents had gone for a short time, and was brought back to Toronto shortly thereafter, where her three half-sisters (my beloved aunts Sadie, Tillie, and Doreen) were introduced to my grandmother Dora.

My grandparents were married in the religious and not the legal sense, since at least one of his former wives was still alive when my mother was born. In those days it was common for religious Jews to be married in the eyes of the Rabbis only, and not under Canadian law. Of course this reduced even more any legal protection these women had from abuse or financial deprivation. Their only recourse for help was the Beth Din, a religious body of Rabbis (all males, of course), whose view of women wasn't very high.

My grandfather owned a men's pant factory on Spadina Avenue, in the heart of Toronto's garment district. My mother worked for him as a bookkeeper. He was tyrannical to his employees, and on one occasion my mother, eighteen years old, challenged him for his abusive treatment of his workers. Zaidy (the Jewish name for grandfather) grabbed her by the hair and dragged her up the aisle of sewing machines, along the floor, to give her a beating in his office. A man who worked there and witnessed it told me that Mother, all five feet of her, grabbed a pair of scissors and proceeded to stab him in self-defence. My grandfather was so shocked and impressed with her courage that he let her go and strutted around the shop bragging about his tough little *maidele* (little girl).

I don't know why my grandfather didn't like girls, but maybe it was because he had twelve sisters back in Russia and four daughters. When my older brother Michael was born, he and my grandmother were in ecstasy. At last, a boy in his life! After that, nothing else mattered. My younger brother Joey and I were totally ignored or slapped around. When my grandparents went on trips, they'd always come home with presents for Michael, including an electric car, but they never had anything for Joey and me, though we'd always wait in the hall hoping. We never felt any resentment towards Michael, however, because we knew it wasn't his fault and often he'd share his spoils with us anyway.

My grandfather used to break chairs over my grandmother's head, but since he was somewhat afraid of my mother, he only pushed me a little. Just once he left bruise marks on my neck from squeezing.

When my grandmother (wife number three) was dying in hospital in 1953 following a heart attack, she kept crying her heart out for my grandfather, who never even came to see her.

"This is what happens when you love a man," she cried to me. "Don't ever care about anyone so much that they can make you suffer this way. I have nothing to live for!" And then she died.

In 1954 Zaidy's fourth wife tried to kill him by putting ground glass in his food. He divorced her.

In 1956, well into his seventies, Zaidy sold his pant business for $100,000 cash and moved to Arizona because of his asthma. He carried the cash sewn into his underwear when he left. About six months later he met and married a young nurse, his fifth wife. She eventually shot him in the head, claiming self-defence. Given my grandfather's history of abuse towards his wives, she was never charged when he died. None of his money was ever recovered.

As my mother had a serious heart condition, I went to the funeral parlour to identify Zaidy's body when it was sent back to Toronto for burial. I was only fifteen years old. The bullet had gone through his ear and out the top of his head. It was interesting and I felt nothing.

In later years I tried to understand how my father could have put up with living in Zaidy's house. Why didn't he rescue us by moving out? I also wondered why he allowed my grandparents to bring presents home for Michael, but never Joey and me. He tried to explain that life was different in those days, and even though he had a job, the most important thing for him was to save money on rent by living on the second floor of my grandparents' house.

However, in adulthood I came to understand and appreciate my father's qualities. Abusive treatment was quite common in those days, and parents didn't understand the depth of a child's trauma in those circumstances, at least not as they do today. My father never borrowed money, never gambled or ran around the way many of his contemporaries did, always worked hard to try to support us, and tried to be nice to everyone.

How difficult it must have been for him in his youth, the third child of nine, with only a grade three education, in a very religious home where my grandfather (his father) worked as a *mashgiech* (ritual slaughterer of kosher meat) in a butcher shop. During his early twenties, he was an organizer for the International Fur Workers' Union. My mother told the story of seeing my father's name in the newspaper for getting shot in the rear end by union busters.

Mother, who weighed only ninety-five pounds, never lost her quick temper, her drive, or her will to win. I probably inherited these qualities from her. She had a hysterectomy at the age of twenty-seven during a time when doctors had none of the knowledge of estrogen therapy that they have today. She had a major coronary at the age of thirty-six and died at forty-six.

Like many Jewish families, most of our relatives were slaughtered in the gas chambers of Poland during the Second World War. My parents worked so hard to bring survivors to Canada, and a wonderful young orphaned boy, "Sammy," lived with us after the war. He became a successful jeweller and now has a wonderful family and a good life here in Canada.

However, my family also sponsored the immigration of two of our cousins from Poland, one of whom became a mega-developer. When my world came apart in 1990, these cousins and their families disappeared from my life; it was as if they had never known me. If there is another world, I know what my mother will say to them when and if they ever get there.

I went to Camp B'nai Brith in Haliburton, Ontario, when I was a pre-teen. It was a community camp, funded by private donations from well-off contributors to the United Jewish Welfare Fund. There were two kinds of campers in those days: the payers and the charity cases. My brothers and I were the latter. I still remember so clearly the girls in my cabin who had stacks of sweaters and jeans — especially my rich cousin's Levis and cashmere sweaters, which were "in." I had two pairs of jeans, four wool sweaters, and two blouses, plus four pairs of shorts and one skirt. I still cringe inside, remembering the sneers of some of the other girls when they saw my hand-me-downs and outdated clothing. I resolved never to forget what peer pressure meant when I had children of my own.

When I got my first part-time job at Eaton's, the first things I bought were *real* Levis and white buck shoes. I was fifteen years old.

We used to visit our relatives on Sundays during the nice weather, especially if they were renting a cottage, usually in Belle Ewart, about forty minutes outside Toronto. I hated the looks on their faces when all five of us would arrive, unannounced, for a visit. We would sit around waiting to be invited for lunch or dinner, which usually didn't happen. I hated being unwelcome. I'll never know what possessed my parents to believe we would be welcome, but my father kept insisting that we visit.

◆ I was in a special class of only ten kids during the years I was at Associated Hebrew School from age five to twelve. Today it would be called a gifted class. My mother worked in the school office as a bookkeeper in order to pay for my brothers and me to go to this school, and for me to take piano and singing lessons at the Royal Conservatory of Music on College Street, across from Queen's Park. The nuns at Loretto Abbey had encouraged Mother to continue my musical training, since they had taught me as much as they could. So my mother enrolled me at a cost of seven dollars a lesson. (Mother had wanted to be a concert pianist herself, but her marriage to my father had ended that.)

Every week I gave an envelope with the money to my teacher, Miss McGavin, a tall and very masculine-looking woman. But I really wasn't interested in a music career, and to my mother's great disappointment, soon stopped my lessons.

By the time I was twelve, I was in grade nine at Bathurst Heights Collegiate, since I had skipped a grade twice in primary school. It was a non-parochial school, with options I had never had before. There was, however, one common theme in those days — the mid-fifties. My brothers and I were still called dirty Jews.

We had by then moved to our own house in North Toronto, in the Avenue Road–Lawrence Avenue area, and on my way to and from school, I still had to fight an average of three times a week. My mother told me that the way to handle the *goyim* (non-Jews) was to attack — or at least to never run away. "As soon as you cringe or show fear, they'll jump all over you. They are mostly cowards who are only brave ganging up on someone, so you make them afraid of you."

And so I did. Pretty soon I had my own gang of warriors (all boys), and I specialized in carrying a bag full of pennies so when I slugged they could really feel the pain.

When I was thirteen, in grade ten, I went after three creeps who had cornered my brother Joey in an empty lot behind our street and roughed him up. One wound up in the hospital. The other two had some serious pain. I was hauled into the principal's office and suspended for three days because of unladylike behaviour. My science teacher referred to the incident as another example of those "dirty little Jewish brats" acting up — and he said it in the classroom, right in front of everybody. In those days, everyone was afraid to speak out, including my parents, and nothing was ever done.

By the next year, however, our recently developed neighbourhood had become more built-up, and the number of Jewish kids had increased dramatically — which meant less fighting.

When I was twelve I looked twenty, so there was the added

dynamic of awakening sexuality, which of course, was inappropriate for a Jewish girl in those days. "Why buy the cow if you can get the milk for free?" was my parents' daily lecture. I believed it, I really did. Any guy who wasn't afraid of me to begin with was certain to develop strong fears if he ever tried to reach past my waistband.

Unless you have lived it, you can't imagine how important it is to a teenager to be "one of the group" and not stand out like an old shoe. I still didn't have the right clothes or live in the kind of house the other kids had. But because I was well developed, by the time I was fourteen, I was dating university guys, lying about my age and getting away with it because I was in grade eleven. I was also invited to join a high school sorority, which was very important for status in those days.

I didn't have the material things, but I had the boys, and the girls didn't want to miss an opportunity to get some new guys into our club parties. It was a lesson in opportunism I never forgot. None of those girls was ever really my friend. They lived in Forest Hill and were all rich. My mother was always sick and couldn't clean very well, while these girls all had maids. I tried so hard to get the girls to like me, but I learned many years later that they used to make jokes about my house and clothes.

Sex was still mysterious and forbidden in the late fifties. There were no birth control pills, and condoms (called "safes") were whispered about — but certainly never seen up close. Besides, the thought was so gross. Since I never trusted anyone anyway, the chances of my ever letting go enough to even be at risk of "going all the way" were slim to none. I clung to my virtue for dear life, believing some prize awaited me at the end of the rainbow.

✦ I met my first husband at the Beta Sigma Rho fraternity house, on the campus of the University of Toronto in 1958. It was a party hosted by the frat for grade thirteen girls they wanted to show around the campus. I was sixteen, still lying about my age; he was twenty-five. I was wearing a red skin-tight dress and had long, dark brown hair. I liked him right away, and when we started to date, I saw him as the way to escape from my unhappy home.

The previous summer — having lied about my age, naturally — I had landed a job as a counsellor at the very same Camp B'nai Brith where I had gone as a kid.

I was very sensitive to the feelings of my own campers that year, especially since there were so many underprivileged ones there. I volunteered to develop a choir program for some of the campers, and they turned out to be quite good. As I was fluent in Hebrew, I taught them how to sing the traditional songs for festive occasions and Shabbat (Friday night), which they performed every Friday night and on visitors' days — much to the delight of their parents. I had all the kids wear white shirts and shorts, so no one would feel, as I had once, that they stuck out like a sore thumb if they had shabby clothes.

The kids were so pleased with themselves, and I was very proud. So were the camp brass. They had already found out that I was only fifteen but decided not to fire me because of the choir.

In 1959, my first husband and I became engaged. He thought I was nineteen. When I told him I was really only seventeen, he almost fainted, especially since my mother had to go with us to get a marriage licence.

Jewish girls rarely lived on their own before they got married and certainly weren't ever supposed to "do it." That's too bad, because so many of us got married for the wrong reasons — especially me. I hung onto unrealistic expectations of romance, life, and men for another twenty-five years before I finally grew up.

But during our wedding reception, I was giggling with my friends (most of whom had already "tried it") about how I was finally going to do it. It all put unbelievable pressure on my new husband, who found himself married to a teenaged wife with expectations beyond the realm of reality and with the maturity of a baby.

✦ In those days most Jewish girls didn't have careers, other than perhaps being a teacher or secretary to support their husbands while they finished school and developed their own careers. Which is exactly what happened to me. I went to work for an insurance company president so my husband could finish his schooling as a chartered accountant, fulfilling the dream of many Jewish mothers for their sons. By then I was eighteen.

My new boss was "old" — forty-one. After three months, I found myself not only managing his office but running three regional offices. Despite my age, I found a niche for myself in administration and did a good job during the two years I stayed with the company. But since I had absolutely no "worldly" experience, his ulterior motive passed right over my head — at first.

He taught me how to read financial statements and how to anticipate trends. He showed me how insurance risks are calculated and taught me all about the inside operations of a mega-million-dollar business. I loved the challenge.

We began travelling to the branch offices and he kept giving me more and more responsibility. In hindsight I can see that he knew what would be my turn-on. His experience with women told him the way to my heart. Sure enough, one evening after dinner, music, and a detailed discussion of an expansion program and its financing strategy, I found myself in bed with him. Not quite like the movies, but almost.

It was wonderful. It should have happened before I got married. It was an unrealistic fantasy about romance come true for me. I thought this was the way it was supposed to be. I didn't understand then that it's easy to live in a cocoon of tenderness and ecstasy when one doesn't share a bathroom and the everyday problems of life.

When the heavens didn't open up and no invisible hand came down to stamp a bright red "A" on my forehead, I pushed my guilty conscience aside. For several months our affair continued, until one day he arrived at my door announcing that he was leaving his wife for me.

I panicked. I was only twenty years old. My mother would kill me. I didn't want him to leave his wife. I didn't want to leave my husband, who was my best friend. My boss and I had never talked about anything beyond business and the silly things lovers say to each other. I had given no thought to the repercussions of our relationship. I didn't understand that one cannot always control the direction of an affair, especially when the chemistry is right.

Fate stepped in.

During a trip to the Kitchener office, my car skidded off the road in a sleet storm, and I had to be cut out of it. My only injury was a crushed collarbone, but I was lucky to get out alive. My lover came rushing to the hospital along with my husband and mother, both of whom had no idea what was going on. He was upset, and my mother became suspicious. I think she said something to him. When I got out of the hospital, he and his family moved to the company's head office in California. I never saw or heard from him again.

In 1963 my mother died and left me $7,500. At that time, I was working for the CEO of another insurance company, with offices on Bay Street. Each time the elevator doors opened on the third floor I could see and hear the ticker tape flashing across the lounge area of Bache & Co. stockbrokers. The sight fascinated me, so I decided to take the $7,500 and spend my lunch hour, every day, playing the penny stocks with the old guys. I would sit in the reception room learning to read the Board, since I had never played the stock market before. They would tell me their strategy and why they made the moves they did. Stock promoters were a dime a dozen, but the really good ones could make gold from garbage.

"Watch their eyes," the men would tell me. "If they won't look at you, they're lying. That's okay — everyone lies in penny stocks. It's how well they lie that counts. Never be greedy. Sell whenever you have a profit. Don't wait till it goes up just a little more. That's how you go bankrupt. Short sell, very carefully. Read the trends in similar stocks. In and out — quick and sharp."

No, not an obscene act but the way to make money.

I loved the action. It seemed to me that researching these stocks and then gambling on when to sell and which promoter could push them up was part of the brains required to be a successful wheeler dealer. At one point I had made, on paper, more than $100,000. Since most of the money went into my first husband's business, he didn't mind my activities. It also motivated him to take more chances because I could always be counted on to do my bit, when necessary, to find the money he needed. It never occurred to me that it was "unseemly" for a woman to love the action.

Our first business promoted vacation properties, which I used to buy at tax sales for my husband and his partner, since they were still working full-time for someone else. We would describe the land in a glamorous way in the sports magazines and try to re-sell them. I would dress like a local and try to outbid and outmanoeuvre the "land developers," who were picking up huge parcels of land for tax arrears. (This would happen when farmers couldn't pay their land taxes and the government seized their property to sell at auction. In those days, parcels were picked up for only the back taxes — sometimes as little as $1,200 for several acres of land. Today the land would be worth millions of dollars.)

I could never sit still and keep quiet at these auctions. I wanted everything and kept trying to "beat" some of these guys at their own game. I'd forget what I was there for and get carried away by the action.

Unrealistic for a twenty-one-year-old, but I wanted to try.

CHAPTER THREE

A Housewife Volunteers

In 1963 I joined the National Council of Jewish Women, Toronto Section. The president of the organization was Eleanor Appleby and a couple of the senior officers were Helen Marr and Gloria Strom, all of whom went on to become national members of NCJW. The secretary-bookkeeper was Betty Stone.

The volunteers I met at Council House were like me — enthusiastic but bored. My husband was successful and expected me to stay home and care for our house and young son. He was no longer interested in my input in his business, which was true for most men in those days. For many of us, staying at home was not offering us the challenges we wanted, and the options available were very limited. So most of us took up volunteerism and joined study groups. We played mah jong, a popular Chinese tile game, walked through plazas with the kids, went to antique shows (my friends taught me how to set a proper table), and fantasized about escape (divorce was still not an option for most Jewish girls). I learned to play bridge, became good at it, and spent many hours in tournaments, distracting myself from boredom.

I was also trying to push away the thoughts that were filling my head more and more — a longing for freedom from the restrictions of marriage. But I wouldn't give up my children, and unless my husband cooperated, I had no way of supporting us. So from 1964 until 1969, I held on, hoping that I was just going through a stage in my life that would soon pass.

I became a driver for Meals On Wheels, taking my infant son and my paternal grandfather with me to deliver hot food to shut-ins. I also used to go to the mental health centre at 999 Queen Street on Sunday mornings to volunteer in the canteen for psychiatric patients.

One day I got a call from Betty Stone, who asked if I would volunteer in the office at Council House, doing some typing and general odd jobs. I agreed, and became the unpaid bookkeeper for NCJW's Thrift Shop, which collected nearly new clothing from members and generous suppliers and sold them to raise funds for NCJW programs. This formed the basis of the Boutique Wearhouse project that developed when the Thrift Shop closed in the late 1970s.

I was also the dues treasurer, before computers and electronic mail equipment had come onto the scene. I used to invoice, by hand, approximately one thousand members, and then send second notices to those who didn't pay. One certainly gets to know the membership that way, and it is incredible how we volunteers managed to function. We did have a lot of fun sitting around the office gossiping while we did our "jobs," which took several days to complete. The same jobs would take two hours with computer equipment today.

Over the next few years Council House became my second home. My two children spent their early years with me there, playing on the floor next to me while I did my volunteer work.

NCJW was founded in 1897. It was committed to study and service, primarily in Canada, and specifically in local communities. It was not involved in fundraising, except for its own programs. In the early days the members it attracted were the socially prominent Jews who had progressed beyond the ghetto mentality. Women always wore hats, and until 1968, I always wore one at Council social functions. Branch study groups made up most of the membership, and the subjects ranged from learning Russian to appreciating French art.

During the Second World War, Council House was at 44 St. George Street, and many soldiers came there for recreation.

NCJW was a leader in the field of service to seniors and in the development of pre-school programming for the disadvantaged. Block parents, Kids on the Block (puppets illustrating disabilities in children), and Creative Living for Seniors were all NCJW pilot projects.

While it was part of the overall Jewish community, NCJW stood somewhat separate, since it focused on the local community, rather than on Israel. However, many of its members belonged to other organizations as well — and the mandate of these organizations was to help Israel. These NCJW members directed most of their fundraising efforts overseas, which caused some difficulty because NCJW was always struggling to raise enough money for its own programs. Too many members would say they didn't join NCJW to fundraise — they did that elsewhere.

✦ During those early years, I was unfocused, but Betty Stone and I took to each other. She was my surrogate mother, teaching me how to dress properly and trying to channel my boundless energy and ambition in positive directions. She was also an expert in government grant applications, and she taught me all about them, providing me with some expertise in this relatively new field.

Betty was barely over five feet tall, with short, jet-black hair, which became blonde ten years later. She loved bargain shopping and haggling over prices whenever she could. I couldn't understand why she got such a kick out of it. She thought I was dumb not to try to get the best deal I could, no matter what the circumstances. But the girls and I had a lot of laughs listening to Betty's tales of her shopping adventures and if it made her happy, it was okay with me.

Betty was a shrewd and intelligent woman. I believe she saw in me a vicarious life for her to direct, teach, nurture, and manipulate. In so doing she would achieve the status and financial remuneration she longed for and which she felt she could not achieve on her own. I understood and accepted it, knowing she would provide me with a shoulder, good advice, absolute loyalty, and the background research and information on issues I would then advocate for, on behalf of the organization. In this way, I would acquire experience and polish.

Betty obtained information on the grants of other organizations. On more than one occasion she showed me copies of the grant applications of these organizations, along with the analysis and recommendations of the bureaucrat who had reviewed them. We also had a list of those that were refused with the comments on them as to why. In this way she knew which backup documentation was most helpful in getting government approval.

Betty said that it was inappropriate for a staff person to be the signatory on a grant application on behalf of a volunteer organization, so I signed the applications. Only years later did I learn that grants should be signed by professional staff, not volunteers.

She gave me excellent advice about softening my mannerisms and being patient. She felt I had the talents to achieve whatever I wanted, but that I had to wait until the right moment and try to network in a positive way. But I was so insecure I didn't believe her. I wanted to grab everything fast before it got away. As a result, I was arrogant and aggressive.

Despite this, I rose up the ladder, because my determination and ability to deliver outweighed, at least most of the time, my volatile personality. Two good examples occurred in 1968-69 when I chaired the two largest successes that NCJW, Toronto, had had until then. For both these efforts I received nothing but flak from the older leadership.

We ran a charitable gambling evening at Casa Loma, called Casino Royale — a new kind of program for the times. Our committee was young and enthusiastic, and we sold tickets to more people than Casa Loma could hold. Furthermore, everyone showed up. It was like being in a sardine can. The streets were full of cars, the traffic was in chaos, people had to line up to get in.

But it was a great event. All the branch members worked together running "Casino Royale" with their personal volunteers (their husbands), and many of us had solicited door prize and gambling prize donations in lieu of paying out money for winning at the tables. All the decorating was done by the girls. More than anything else, the event laid the foundation for the teamwork and spirit many of us shared for the next twenty years.

In spite of the financial success of Casino Royale, which benefited our service projects, some of the "old ladies" — past presidents and others — were so upset that our once staid organization had run such an unladylike event, with pushing and yelling and total chaos, that they called for my head. But thanks to the loyalty of the branch membership, nothing could really be done to me.

✧ The next year, 1969, my husband and I separated. After ten years of marriage, five of which I had spent trying to bury myself in volunteer work as a distraction, we both agreed it was time to go our separate ways. By now he was financially successful and agreed to maintain the children and me in our home for five years. I was twenty-seven, and for the first time in my life, I was going to go it alone. Or at least try.

He was, and is, a kind and intelligent man. We had ten years and two wonderful children of our own together, after the short-lived adoption of our first baby. The birth mother had twenty days to change her mind — and she did. I can still remember the social worker telling us that we had to give the baby back, and how I cried. After thirty years, it's still painful to think about.

Even though our life together was a time of warmth and caring, respect and consideration, something I had never known before, it wasn't enough. I wanted excitement, high living, and the luxuries I'd never had. I wanted to try everything, see everything, and still have a nest to come home to. I was driven, but had no direction. He knew where he wanted to go. Unfortunately for both of us when we got married in 1959, I wasn't able to be the kind of wife he needed.

I was given the chairmanship of the NCJW's annual Angels Ball, as a reward for my achievements. It was held in April 1969, as a thank you to all those who had donated their clothing over the year for us to sell at the Thrift Shop. Credits for the donated clothes were accumulated, and any NCJW member who collected one hundred dollars' worth of clothing was eligible to buy a dinner ticket. It was a prestigious event, and we all accumulated our used clothing and gave it to the Thrift Shop in the hope of being able to attend the ball.

Some of the old ladies wondered, out loud, if it was appropriate for someone separated from her husband to chair the ball. It sounds antiquated today, but the changes of the sixties hit Canada later than the U.S. and the Jewish community even later. Once again, others backed up my appointment, and it stood.

I buried myself in the plans for the event, which was primarily social and very posh. Being on my own wasn't as great as I'd imagined. In fact, it was scary, especially at night when I heard sounds creaking throughout the house. I started sleeping with a knife under my pillow. But the ball kept me going, along with the members of the volunteer committee, many of whom stayed with me for the next twenty years on various other projects.

The ball gave me my first taste of the limelight of prestige and my first contact with the non-Jewish elite. Ontario's lieutenant-governor, the late Ross MacDonald, was our honoured guest. He was, at that time, about seventy-five years old. I was so awestruck that I could barely contain myself. The protocol, the tradition, the incredible excitement of it was beyond words.

Ross MacDonald had an aide-de-camp who wore a divine uniform and spoke grandly. He advised me that His Honour was the Queen's representative, and therefore was to be treated according to protocol. When entering or leaving a room or elevator, I was to follow behind. I could not expect him to open the door for me, nor could I sit down before he did. I should limit my conversation to pleasantries, preferably in response to His Honour, with no foul language — and . . . *no controversy*!

I, the granddaughter of a ritual butcher from Ostrower, Poland, I, the daughter of a union organizer with a grade three education, dining with, talking with, dancing with, the Queen's representative. This was the life for me.

Of course, in my excitement, I forgot the rules. I kept walking out of the elevator ahead of him and waiting for him to open the doors for me, which he did. I wondered how he could still be standing upright after he'd drunk seventy-five dollars' worth of scotch. He was a widower, and I casually asked him if he wanted to meet anyone new who happened to be Jewish. His aide-de-camp nearly croaked. Big deal. Ross MacDonald was a charming, fun-loving, kind, and tolerant gentleman. He kept in touch with me for a long time, sending me notes and even calling once or twice. A real class act.

From that day forward, I was fascinated by royalty and my dream was to one day meet the Queen. I almost made it.

CHAPTER FOUR

Movers and Shakers

In 1972, I remarried. My new husband, Jerry Starr, was a successful sportswear manufacturer with one son, David. In 1975 our son Stuart was born, and three years later, we had another son Randy. Along with my oldest two, Evan and Brooke, we now had five wonderful children.

Jerry encouraged me to go back to my volunteer career. He could see I was getting restless and didn't want me bothering him with questions about his business and his colleagues. He wanted our home life separate from any outside involvements and took very little interest in my activities, which suited me just fine.

In 1979 the Toronto section of NCJW was approached by a group of hearing-impaired people who wanted to develop some programming and organization within the Jewish community, from which they had largely been excluded. It was our first awareness of the plight of the disabled in housing and in jobs. We did some research and found that for years the disabled were the invisible Jews within our community. Facilities were generally inaccessible to them. We became motivated by their courage and dignity, and so a Task Force on the Jewish Disabled, including the developmentally handicapped, was created within NCJW.

Spearheading the hearing-impaired program were Nita Goldband and Lesley Miller, backed up by Georgina Grossman, director of volunteers. They were the brains; they were skilled, articulate, and well educated and had the raw talent to develop and implement an innovative project such as this one. My job was to sell it, initially to the community and then to the funding sources.

Betty Stone introduced me to Jim Peterson, member of Parliament for Willowdale, to begin the process of getting a federal grant for the task force. I thought Jim was adorable — most of the girls were impressed with him. He was the first real politician I knew, and I believed in his integrity and courage.

The task force's goal was to include the disabled in the planning and implementation of their own programs. This non-paternalistic, non-maternalistic approach allowed for shared responsibility and was not very common in those years. The disabled were isolated from the mainstream of communal life and we wanted to help them help themselves to begin the integration process.

In 1981, several of the new executive of NCJW, Toronto, of which I was about to become president, went to Ottawa for the national convention. Jim Peterson took us around the capital (I'm ashamed to say it was the first trip there for most of us), culminating in a visit to the House of Commons during Question Period.

Talk about juvenile behaviour and chaos. These elected representatives, most of whom were men, kept shooting paper airplanes at each other, making faces, and hissing with lots of hand gestures.

We were seated in the VIP section right across from the Liberals, and all of a sudden, there he was, Pierre Elliott Trudeau, prime minister of Canada! We were enthralled at being so close to someone who seemed larger than life. When he looked up at us, we all started waving, but I was so excited I actually stood up on the seat, waving and smiling at him like a complete loony.

Years later, at a dinner for Margaret Thatcher, when I was a power myself, we met personally. He looked at me for only a few moments before he smiled with those incredible eyes and said, "Haven't we met somewhere before?" Of course he remembered. He wondered if in my present position I still waved and jumped up and down with excitement when I met famous people. We then had a most delightful conversation. He made me feel as though I was the only person in the room. Charisma! Pierre Trudeau had it.

◆ For the next ten years, from 1979 to 1989, Lesley, Nita, and I would be the nucleus of the team. One of NCJW's programs for immigrant mothers and their children provided a two-hour babysitting service, twice a week, for siblings, to allow the mothers to participate in English as a Second Language (ESL) classes. The NCJW volunteers could put their own kids into the program while they did their "work" — a great incentive that helped us recruit volunteers for Council House.

Each new NCJW service project brought in more volunteers who had the interest or talent to enhance it. Educational programming was being developed under the guidance of Eleanor Cooper, Donna Zener, and Phyllis Moss; Nita Goldband and Lesley Miller created the plan for community service. My role was to deliver the money and political support for both programs.

Volunteer director Georgina Grossman was the staffer who provided us, the volunteers, with most of the nurturing and backup to help us achieve the organization's goals.

And then, in 1980, we took on a major challenge — the creation of a Conference on the Jewish Disabled in partnership with Canadian Jewish Congress (CJC), the umbrella organization for the Jewish community in Canada.

The politics of this exercise were mind boggling. Congress had long been male dominated, and the women who were in leadership roles at CJC were usually the wives of wealthy men who made substantial donations. At the same time, however, NCJW had long been on the periphery: we were primarily a study and service organization with limited fundraising ability and most of our resources served the local community, not Israel. To complicate matters further, there were some longstanding grudges between the Jewish establishment and NCJW national members pre-dating my involvement.

In spite of the complexities, we in the Toronto section lined up financial support from all three levels of government for this pilot project. The Establishment, in the form of the Canadian and Toronto Jewish Congresses, joined us, despite some misgivings. The reality was that they couldn't get the money and we could, while we couldn't get the experts in the various fields on our own but they could.

Pretty soon the "out of the woodwork" gang arrived (especially NCJW recycled ones) — people who didn't help at the beginning but who wanted to be part of things once they saw that the operation would be a success.

The politics were deadly and cut-throat — a typical state of affairs in all ethnic communities and in charities of all kinds. The politics are never openly acknowledged because charity is supposed to bring out the best, not the worst, in people. But power struggles are power struggles, whether they exist in politics, business, or good works.

Nita and Lesley, along with Georgina Grossman, set up first-rate programming and speakers for the conference, leaving the politics to me. There was bickering about who would get top billing, about which executive members would get to speak or sit at head tables, and about who would get credit in the program books. It was a golden opportunity for me to show what talent I had for tact, subtlety, and non-confrontation. I failed.

My only concern was the success of the conference, and anyone who tried to introduce what we thought was mediocrity was cut down. The NCJW volunteers and staff did eighty-five percent of the work and raised all the money, as well as delivering the political support — but without the stature of the CJC as our partners, who knows if it would have been as successful.

As usual, most of the backstabs were coming from a few of our national members whose lives seemed destined to be dominated by jealousy and bitterness. We should have risen above them and treated them with the consideration they never showed us, but we didn't.

◆ During the development of this conference, we began to delve more deeply into the politics of grants.

Betty Stone found out who the key provincial staff people were for getting grants. She introduced me to Marek Brodski and Jay Jackson, bureaucrats from the Ministry of Citizenship and Culture, where most of the grants to volunteer organizations came from. For the next ten years they were the project officers for almost every grant NCJW got from the province during both Tory and Liberal governments — almost $2,500,000.

Marek and Jay worked hand in hand with us over the years. Thanks to their advice and assistance, we learned how to research and recognize grants appropriate not only for NCJW, but also for all the other organizations I would subsequently become involved in, especially the Jewish Community Centre.

In 1982 our Task Force on the Disabled wanted to create a twenty-minute training video on the plight of the disabled to be used in workshops and education seminars around the province, indeed, throughout the world. We obviously didn't have the money, but the Tory government in Queen's Park did. My job was to try to create a program description that fit the criteria for available funds while still maintaining the integrity of our goals.

There was a Wintario Grant under the provincial Ministry of Culture and Communications to enhance the citizenship participation of Ontario residents in a multicultural society. Cultural and social integration, development of leadership skills, and organizational effectiveness were the goals. How could I translate these criteria into a video, newsletter, and programming for the disabled?

Citizenship participation usually referred to new immigrants. I called Jim Peterson for advice. He arranged for me to go down and see his brother, David, Liberal leader of the Opposition and his chief aide, Hershell Ezrin. They of course couldn't help us politically, since the Tory government had been in power so long (thirty-seven years) and the bureaucracy were therefore all Tory — but we did have a productive conversation. The seeds of future relationships were sown.

I then contacted Marek and Jay, the culture bureaucrats. We went over my strategy for getting these grants (newsletter, video, training sessions) and they were somewhat skeptical. Then I went to see Bruce McCaffrey, the Tory minister of Culture and Recreation (formerly Citizenship and Culture). He referred to these funds as "pattiproof," since some of my creative interpretations of eligibility were already known. And those creative interpretations were in the area of matching funds. Most provincial grants required the recipient to match the funding provided, which on first glance seemed fair. But charitable organizations didn't have the same resources for generating revenue as private corporations.

We did, however, have the womanpower to research and implement a worthwhile program, where the private sector would have to pay for staffing. So it seemed to me to be a fair balance. We would provide the volunteers as our share, and the government would provide dollars as theirs. We obtained any other contributions we could to offset operating costs. Pretty soon we were matching most of our share of grants in this way.

Bruce McCaffrey thought we wouldn't be eligible under the existing criteria, but he encouraged us to try anyway.

Our submission was a simple one. After hours of intense brainstorming, we came up with the catch phrase *The disabled are citizens too*, entitled to the same opportunities as everyone else. They also had the right to form their own associations and participate in communal activities like anyone else. It worked, and our application was approved. Both Bruce McCaffrey and David Peterson came to Council House to make the presentation.

The NCJW video *Two Way Street* was created, along with backup booklets, training kits, seminar materials, and a newsletter which the task force developed and produced themselves. The video travelled through Canada and the United States, and even went to Israel. A volunteer team presented a seminar along with it. The ripple effect of that film continues to this day.

Lesley, Nita, and I travelled to Atlanta and Boston and Montreal at our own expense (to be reimbursed when the funds were available) to present the video to community groups as a vehicle to help them work with their own disabled.

Regardless of what has happened since, nothing can ever diminish the spark we ignited back in 1979. The presence of the disabled in our social, educational, and religious lives, especially within the Jewish community, is a reflection of the caring and commitment NCJW volunteers provided before it was fashionable to do so.

✦ As mentioned, it was quite common then for a volunteer charitable organization to match funds with volunteer hours or donated labour and material in lieu of cash. To do otherwise would have been unusual. A price was put on the time and efforts of the volunteers and shown as matching funds, *with no red flag to indicate that it was "in kind."* In this way, organizations could limit the amount of dollars they had to actually spend from their coffers. The ministries of all three levels of government were fully aware of this procedure.

Since none of us, the volunteers, ever received any money, governments and politicians looked the other way when it came to our use of "in kind" matching funds.

Indeed, the proper fulfillment of grant criteria is often in the eye of the beholder. With some creative thinking, helpful bureaucrats, political contacts, and a worthwhile project to be funded, nothing is impossible.

The federal Ministry of Employment and Immigration had several make-work projects that we were able to tap into by virtue of our willingness to hire and train visible minorities. Included in these grants were operational funds, which is how we were able to continue many of our service projects. Without operational funding, the building has no heat and hydro, and no staff to type and file reports.

Volunteers are part of a team that must include staff, and that means salaries. It doesn't look that exciting on paper, so we try to couch those costs in creative wording and budgeting, but one without the other does not go. Volunteers are the lifeblood of the community. They contribute millions of hours a year to thousands of worthwhile and needed programs, but without funding for their backup staff, many of them could not function, and vital services to people would be lost. It is revealing to imagine how many of our tax dollars would be needed to maintain even the present level of community programs without volunteers' hours.

Interpreting criteria to fit a program, or adapting parts of a program to fit the criteria, are necessary components in successful fundraising. The recipient at the end of the road must be the focus — the successful project or the enhanced community awareness on the issue is the way to get there. If you have to be flexible, then so be it.

In 1983 I had a visit from a contingent of feminists from Ottawa who had been unsuccessful in getting funding for a women's shelter. They had been told to come and see me, since I was perceived to be an expert in the field. They were militant about keeping unrestricted abortion front and centre on their printed material and as a result were experiencing a backlash from some federal politicians, as well as from other potential funding sources. I talked to them for three hours about their priority, which had to be the shelter.

"Leave the abortion issue out of it! You're not compromising your principles — you're simply not mentioning them in this context," I told them. "The greater issue must be the critical need for the shelter." I took them through the criteria and showed them how to become eligible for funding provided they did not raise the red flag of abortion.

One of the women was enraged at me for suggesting that they "sell out" their principles for government money. I hoped someone would become enraged on behalf of the women who would have no shelter if they didn't lighten up. But they couldn't agree among themselves. So there was no funding.

Two years later the Cabinet minister who had sent them to me in the first place told me they eventually modified their position and the shelter was going ahead. The most militant member of the group was still part of it. Good for her. The salvation that hostel provides far outweighs the compromise required to provide it.

◆ As the skills of our volunteers increased, so did our access to government movers and shakers. In 1981, I was elected to the boards of the Jewish Community Centre and the Canadian Jewish Congress. In 1983 I was appointed co-chairman of Special Gifts for the United Way of Metropolitan Toronto. I was also appointed to the Mayor's Committee on Race Relations in the City of North York.

By 1984, the demands on the backup administration of NCJW's Toronto organization were growing as highly educated professional women began to become involved. They wanted proper records and minutes that reflected what actually happened at meetings, as well as volunteer profiles for access to additional committee members and a proper computer system to back this all up. (By listing an individual's skills along with their volunteer experience and preferences in a proper filing system, we could immediately identify those members most interested in running the educational and service programs we were developing. A phone call would eliminate the need and expense of mailouts to the general membership (1200 members) seeking volunteers. It would also enable NCJW to provide better service to its volunteers, by offering them the kind of challenges they wanted in the community service field.)

To that end, a major grant of more than $250,000 was applied for and received in order to train staff and volunteers in a computer skills program. I could never figure out how computers worked and stayed away, but our staff and some hard-to-employ trainees (approved by the government) participated. This was part of a make-work project that would help these women get jobs as well as upgrade our own staff.

Meanwhile, the face of volunteerism and the expectations of volunteers were changing. By the 1980s charitable organizations were having to rethink their priorities and start addressing the political issues of the day. No longer could we rely on the same sources of womanpower, nor could we make the same value judgements. Our new volunteers were working women and professionals who wanted more than luncheons and teas. They wanted shared responsibility with staff and they needed to have direct input into social programs — especially their development and implementation. Despite Betty Stone's reluctance, NCJW's executive felt that our staff would have to adjust as well, and accept that twenty years of doing it the same way didn't make it right.

CHAPTER FIVE

Out of the Cocoon

In June 1984 I sat in Tridel Corporation's Dufferin Street offices, directed there by my NCJW colleagues to discuss Tridel's proposed housing facility on Prince Charles Drive in North York. We were interested in acquiring six to eight units to provide independent living for the disabled, with an attendant care component. Tridel was the largest condominium developer in North America.

A tall, thin gentleman with an understated elegance and a presence that has never been matched by anyone else I have met introduced himself as Angelo DelZotto. He invited me to join him, Tony Moro, vice-president of development, and Martin Applebaum, one of their lawyers, for lunch. Life would never be the same for any of us again.

In February 1984, NCJW's Task Force on the Disabled had brought the issue of independent living for the disabled to a meeting. Their research showed that many disabled could live on their own with only a few hours of assistance a day. Those with limited physical disabilities could live independently if their home and facilities were accessible.

Many disabled people had spent their lives living in institutions, often, for lack of any alternative, among senile elderly people. They wanted a chance to have a new life. With a few hours of care a day (bath, exercise), they could live on their own. However, most integrated housing was not accessible, and if it was, it was not subsidized. Many disabled could and did work, but given their limitations, their salaries were not enough for them to pay full rent. "Why not?" we asked. "Surely we can come up with something better?"

Once again, spearheaded by Lesley and Nita, the task force did some thorough research and came up with the seeds of a plan. But first we needed to get the right background data. We asked the Co-operative Housing Federation of Toronto to send a representative to one of our meetings to give us information on the non-profit housing industry. What a hoot they turned out to be!

The Co-operative Housing Federation is an association that develops co-op housing projects throughout the city, though they are part of a larger group that operates across Canada. They administer their projects and have the right to live in them as well. Private non-profits, on the other hand, are administered by a sponsoring group that is incorporated and sometimes has a charitable number, like ethnic associations, credit unions, or community service agencies.

All co-ops receive subsidies from the government. The decision as to who gets to live in them is made by a board of directors made up of the residents. There are fewer regulations for co-ops than for private non-profit housing, so the co-op board has a lot more leeway in selecting who is allowed in.

In Ontario, especially in the Metro Toronto area, many of the co-op residents were staff of the Co-operative Housing Federation. And a large number were members of the Ontario New Democratic Party. Some were employees of the Ministry of Housing.

The decision about allocations (the approval of funding for construction and land costs) is made by the provincial minister of Housing, but often as a result of recommendations made by ministry staff, who themselves are prospective residents in these projects. The potential conflict of interest is clear but has been ignored over the years. In fact, it's been getting worse under the present NDP government. Witness the brouhaha about former mayoralty candidate Jack Layton and his wife Olivia Chow living in a subsidized co-op, though they had a combined income in excess of $120,000.

So co-op housing is a big business with a lot of vested interests fighting for the allocations.

Large profits can be made on these projects by the developer or builder. Since the housing is subsidized, there is always a long waiting list, and prime residential land is not required to market the units. The government provides the up-front money, and private entrepreneurs with land that isn't worth much on the open market can package a co-op non-profit housing proposal, which, if approved, can make them a fortune. The present NDP government is making this into an art form, considering how many millions they blew on allocations in 1991-92, despite the terrible economic picture and the negative recommendations of experienced civil servants.

At our 1984 meeting, after a couple of hours of gobbledygook, we found out that the Co-operative Housing Federation gets 2 percent in fees, though not openly, for coordinating a housing project. They also like to suggest the management company, which earns large fees to manage the building. The co-op federation staff often live in these projects on subsidized rents — they show limited salaries, partly by not mentioning the rent subsidy as part of their income (though Revenue Canada would probably deem it a taxable benefit, if they knew about it).

An average non-profit housing project with land and construction costs totalled about $12 to $15 million in 1984. That meant $250,000-plus in fees to the consultants/co-op/management group. "For what?" we wondered out loud. We could learn to do anything they did, and as volunteers, the Toronto Section of the NCJW would get the money.

We were in a frenzy of excitement over the next few weeks. Where was it written that we, the volunteers of NCJW, Toronto Section, could not become consultants on behalf of our organization, develop our own project, offer housing to those who needed it, and provide a tremendous source of revenue for our ongoing service projects? We got every bit of information on non-profit housing that we could find. We went to visit the heads of existing housing projects, talked to Canada Mortgage and Housing Corporation (CMHC) staff, the Metropolitan Toronto Housing Company, the mayor of the City of Toronto, and the chairman of Metropolitan Toronto.

Our disabled colleagues became excited as they began to see a glimmer of hope in their quest for independent living. One member of our task force was Mike Feldman, who was the president of the Metro Toronto Housing Company. This was another version of private nonprofit housing, with a focus on seniors.

Mike knew a lot. We asked him to help us channel our energies in the right direction, and he did. I discussed many of our strategies with him, and his assistance was invaluable. Mike knew that Tridel Corporation was about to build a new housing facility and he suggested that we ask them if six to eight units could be made fully accessible for our disabled. We would seek the funding from various provincial and federal government sources, and it would be a pilot project that we would administer within their building. The residents would have to be selected according to strict criteria. Religion was not one of them, which meant that it would not be a totally Jewish project. But so what? Our mandate had never been restricted to the Jewish community alone, and NCJW's executive was gung ho. By now, Mike knew we were serious and he offered to call Tridel to arrange an appointment for us, which he did. I felt that a small group should go first to meet with them, but the girls insisted that I go first. They would follow.

So on that June day, Angelo, Tony, their lawyer Martin, and I went to an Italian restaurant on Steeles Avenue just west of Dufferin Street, and ate rapini, polenta, penne, and risotto. For two hours we talked about many things, the least of which was the housing project.

Angelo expressed his hurt and outrage at the circumstances

surrounding the work of the Waisberg Commission, which had been looking into criminal activities within the development industry some twenty years earlier.

His family was still suffering from the fallout of this investigation. His father, Jack, in particular, was intense about seeing their family name vindicated in some way for the rumours and innuendoes levelled against them, which had never been backed up with any charges or evidence. He talked about the horror of inquiries, which allow one person, empowered by the government of the day, to conduct a witch hunt in whatever way he chooses, with no protection under the law for anyone. Standards of evidence and proof of allegations are not required at an inquiry, as they are in a regular trial.

The chairman, usually a judge, along with any witnesses who appear, can give opinions, often unsubstantiated and undocumented, and remain fully protected from charges of slander or libel. The whole undertaking is reminiscent of the McCarthy hearings in the U.S. in the 1950s. The repercussions are felt for years afterwards by those "named," and they have absolutely no recourse to vindicate themselves.

Angelo also talked about honour, loyalty, and friendship. When I asked why he hadn't reacted more openly to those who had hurt him (the way I always did) his answer was: "Patience... always keep your enemies close, so when the moment is right, you'll be there."

He spoke candidly and with humour about his early days as a labourer, working for his father, building small homes in North York with his friend Rudy Bratty. They had originally immigrated from Fruili, in northern Italy, and he gave me a brief synopsis of the various regions of the country and the characteristics of the native sons.

He talked about his love for his wife and children, his parents and brothers. He even joked about his teenage years when he lived in a Jewish neighbourhood and had to "adjust" his name in order to get a date. He had been a great hockey player in his youth and had hoped to continue playing when he went to university, but he was needed in his father's business and had to leave school. However, his two younger brothers were able to go on to university while he remained the driving force behind Tridel ("tri" representing the three brothers and "del" their name).

He told stories about trouble on construction sites, union support or harassment (depending on who was in charge at any given moment), the work of bricklayers, plumbers, and electricians, and the final "rooftopping" parties that happen near the end of any construction project. Finally, when lunch was almost over, Angelo leaned over and asked if I had any concerns or questions about him. Before I could answer, Martin Applebaum jumped in, very officious, assuring me that no commitments were being made, that this was just a preliminary conversation. He seemed to be edgy about the fact that Angelo had ignored both him and Tony Moro during our conversation and was being quite candid with me.

I told Angelo that the girls were very anxious to provide at least six or eight housing units for the task force. I had limited knowledge of rezoning applications and the difficulties with local residents and politicians. However, the girls all had contacts (husbands, fathers, brothers, who were lawyers or developers), who could give us advice and direction. Angelo stared at me for a moment and then said that no one could give us better advice than our own instincts.

I knew that Tridel had already received overtures from a local church group and a credit union who wanted to be the sponsors of the building. I also knew that the NCJW executive and board would have major concerns about integrating our group into a church-run housing project. So I asked if he thought NCJW, Toronto, could do the entire project ourselves.

There was silence for what seemed like an hour. Martin and Tony looked green. Then Angelo said, "I think it's possible. It depends on the ability of your organization and its members and to a large extent, you." I looked into his eyes, which were focused on mine. My heart began to pound.

"I know you have the natural instincts of a leader, but also those of a fighter," he went on. "These are not necessarily compatible. You are very eloquent when you want to be and, I am told, somewhat inspirational on occasion. You also have a lot of enemies."

He noticed how my body tensed at that comment and before I could answer, he said, "Yes, I've had a lot of research done on you. I wouldn't have met with you at all if I hadn't.... Your group is recognized as excellent community volunteers. If there is friendship and loyalty between you, no challenge is too great, no accomplishment out of your reach. It's the level of commitment that matters. There will be a lot of confrontation and hassle because of existing political problems with the site. You girls will have to get involved in ways unlike anything you have ever done. I know you, personally, can handle it. In fact, I think you're going to enjoy it. But what about your colleagues? Do they care enough about the disabled to stand up for them when the crunch comes? Will they be able to handle the snide innuendoes about the 'Mafia connection' if NCJW goes ahead?"

What was unnerving was that he was reading my mind.

"Once you are committed, people are counting on you, their very quality of life will depend on your courage," he continued. "I will stand behind you and NCJW and commit this project and our corporation to you only if your colleagues are behind it and you, one hundred percent. Otherwise, leave them and come with me. You have the talent and creativity to stickhandle through not only this project, but others. Even though your political instincts are good, your timing leaves a lot to be desired. I find you fascinating, but you're a bit rough around the edges. You have a lot to learn. But that's good. We can teach you."

I suppressed my desire to jump up, clap my hands, climb onto the back of the white horse, and ride off into the sunset.

"Think about it, talk to the girls, and let me know," he said.

I went home, somewhat stunned. After putting the kids to bed, I spent the next few hours in deep self-contemplation.

I was torn between my own ambition and the fear of stepping outside the protected parameters of my life.

Some weeks earlier, Jim Peterson had spoken to me about his family business, C.M. Peterson & Co., which he had been managing since he lost the 1983 federal election. He was preparing to run again federally and had to find a replacement to run the firm.

"Would you be interested in taking over?" he asked during lunch at the Peel County Feed Company in Rexdale. "Salary range to be negotiated."

"What do I know about electronics?" I said.

"Executive leadership skills are the prerequisite for now," he laughed. "You can learn the rest later."

Saying no then had been easy. The idea hadn't turned me on. But this was different. I was turned on. Angelo was putting a carrot in front of my nose unlike any other.

I wanted to be a mover and shaker, to be important, to be one of the boys, to be wanted, but every insecurity I had ever felt in my life kept coming back. If I stepped out of the cocoon of my volunteerism, then I'd be vulnerable. I could be fired, I could be ordered around, humiliated, forced to do tasks I didn't like.

And what if I liked the action so much I became dissatisfied at home? I'd been through one divorce with all the problems that created for my children. Would it happen again? What if I became hardened, cynical, and devoid of emotion? What if I failed?

After a sleepless night, I met with my closest volunteer friends and colleagues within NCJW, Nita Goldband and Lesley Miller, and shared my feelings with them, both personally and from the organization's point of view. Lesley, in particular, picked up right away on my fascination with Angelo and his world. Both she and Nita intended, one day, to become professionals themselves, but not yet. They, like me, had young children and a lot more to learn. They felt that with more experience, not only in this field but in all the others we had participated in over the years of our community commitments, we could embark on successful careers down the road.

"It's too soon," they said. "We need a couple more years under our belts."

They urged me to collect a few more political IOUs, to be part of more committees and boards in the larger community before I closed certain doors. They believed that without me, neither NCJW's Task Force on the Disabled nor the Jewish Community Centre's task force could raise the necessary money and political support to continue and expand.

There would be no hope for the housing project, given the internal and external politicking that would be required if I didn't lead it. Conflict of interest would prevent me from participating in a leadership role on behalf of NCJW if I turned professional at that point.

And so it was decided. As long as the executive and board were enthusiastic and supportive, I would continue in my present role as grants officer and "political operative" for NCJW, Toronto. (I was also the past president and chairman of the board.) This would allow me to continue in my executive positions for the Jewish Community Centre and the Canadian Jewish Congress.

Lesley, Nita, and I, with Georgina's help, immediately set up meetings with a diverse group of our executive. We went through all the options of the housing project. There were about twenty girls involved in the preliminary discussions. Everyone agreed it had to be totally our housing project or nothing. We discussed the "Italian" connection and acknowledged the flack we would probably get from the establishment of our community.

"Where was the Jewish community when the Jewish disabled had nowhere to live but in a seniors' facility, with no recreation or religious programming?" asked one of our executive.

"Where were they back in 1979-80 when we, NCJW, Toronto, were advocating on behalf of accessible facilities in synagogues and parochial schools?" asked another. "To hell with them. Let's go for it!" was the unanimous decision.

♦ We didn't know the details of the problems, but everyone had heard rumours about the proposed Prince Charles site being in conflict with the local ratepayers group. Everyone had a friend or relative of their parents living around there, and we had a lot of laughs hearing some of the stories circulating. This was the Bathurst-Lawrence area of Toronto, in the heart of the Jewish community. Names like Howard Moscoe, the local alderman; David Rotenberg, the local Tory MPP; Roland de Corneille, the Liberal MP; and John Sewell, former mayor of Toronto, kept popping up. But we really didn't know exactly what was going on and we agreed that for us to undertake this project, we had to have a good knowledge base.

To that end, we needed to meet with Tridel, along with other executive members, to explore the project fully with their staff and then get a consensus before seeking board/membership go ahead. Georgina Grossman, director of volunteers, would be our staff liaison, since Betty Stone was on a European holiday for the summer. Georgina had the trust of our leadership and the ability to sense potential problems before we could see them ourselves.

I called Martin Applebaum at Tridel. He was less disconcerting to me than Angelo, who I wasn't ready to deal with yet.

And so it began. About fifteen of our executive trekked over to the Tridel offices to start the process. Martin coordinated the initial meetings, which included trips to all of Tridel's nonprofit housing projects around the city, as well as their spectacular condominiums. We met their senior executives, including Elvio and Leo DelZotto. (Elvio was a prominent senior partner in the large law firm of DelZotto, Zorzi, a Liberal candidate in the 1967 provincial election, a patron of the arts, a member of several high-profile organizations and committees, and an ardent advocate of women's issues.) The brothers gave us a tour of their corporate headquarters and a mini-lesson in the steel industry (Aluma, a Tridel subsidiary) and construction in general.

One of the buildings they took us to see was a seniors' facility on Eglinton Avenue in the heart of Forest Hill. One of Tridel's architects had come up with the concept of a roof garden, where each resident would have their own vegetable and flower patch. There were also pergolas and safe benches, and tables and chairs overflowing with plants and flowers.

Those gardens impressed us. In talking to the residents, we learned how important this little bit of "country" in a highrise meant. It also provided a place for privacy, recreation, and relaxation away from the street noises. The concept of a roof garden with recreational amenities had tremendous potential for battered women and children at risk, who would no longer have to leave the security of their building for air and exercise for themselves and their children. It was also an alternative for those not able to go far from home — seniors in particular.

At the end of our bus tour of Tridel's non-profit and senior housing facilities, we were taken to the company's luxury condominium at 2000 Islington Avenue for lunch. What a fabulous place! The penthouse, where we ate, was two storeys high, with a winding staircase leading up to a spacious patio overlooking the city. The amenities included an exercise room, pool, and tennis courts. The landscaping was plush, with beautiful flowers and shrubs.

It was here that everyone met all three DelZotto brothers, as well as N. Jane Pepino, Q.C., who had been retained by Tridel to handle this project. A slim, attractive woman, she had a streak of white hair down the back of her head. We all thought she had coloured her hair in that way as a deliberate conversation piece. But no, it was natural.

Jane, with her wonderful wit, high principles, and brilliant legal mind, would become a special part of my life for the next five years. She was also one of the most respected experts in municipal law in the province. All the girls were very impressed with her, having admired her as a leading feminist and the first woman appointed to the Metropolitan Toronto Police Commission (now the Metropolitan Toronto Police Services Board). She was going to be working with us directly in leading the project through the necessary minefields of rezoning and housing allocations, of which we knew nothing.

The girls were enthusiastic, and they were impressed with the maintenance and overall upkeep of the facilities we had seen. Most people saw assisted housing as slum dwellings, so we were doubly surprised at how beautifully these buildings were being maintained.

We were given access to the financial statements of these projects (I was the only one who actually read them), with the understanding that if we went ahead, our own lawyer and accountant would also have the opportunity to review the documentation. Tridel's staff explained that non-profit housing did not have to mean low quality. They encouraged us to return to any one of their facilities on our own to talk to the residents privately to assure ourselves that the excellent maintenance and varied programs we had seen were really so, and not just a one-day wonder set up for our benefit.

A committee led by Nita and Lesley did just that and reported that everything was as we had originally seen it. This was the beginning of our complete trust in the integrity of Tridel and their ability to fulfill any commitments they made to our organization. Nothing that has happened since ever changed that belief, at least not for those who were active and involved with our projects.

We then discussed a lawyer. I suggested Ron Miller of Robins, Appleby, Kotler — Lesley's husband. The senior partner of that firm was Ron Appleby, president of the Toronto Jewish Congress. Another senior associate was Ralph Lean: Tory fundraiser, later head of the Canadian National Exhibition (CNE), fundraiser for Mayor Art Eggleton, chairman of Tory MPP David Rotenberg's re-election campaign, and best friend of Monte Kwinter. (Kwinter later ran for the provincial Liberals, and eventually became a Cabinet minister.)

Nita was concerned about using Ronnie Miller and spoke to volunteer coordinator Georgina Grossman and me privately. Georgina also had some concerns, so we did a quick poll of our group of fifteen. Everyone else felt quite comfortable using Ronnie, as we believed he would act in our best interests and not charge us a fortune. I also trusted him.

We then discussed getting a new accountant for this project. Marsha Slavens suggested I consult her husband, Eric, who was the managing partner of Laventhol & Horwath and a chartered accountant.

Little did she know that her husband and I were already consulting, albeit on Tory politics. He was one of the fundraisers and campaign chairmen for Barbara McDougall, federal Tory Cabinet minister. Eric didn't like Marsha knowing too much about his political affairs, so I had never said anything to her, though some of my other colleagues were aware of our political relationship. The Tories were still in power at Queen's Park in those years, and during the period from 1979 to 1984, all our grants had to be approved by them. Even with the best of presentations and the most just of causes, political access was critical. Eric had it.

By this time, I had been elected to some very senior positions within the Jewish community. I was an officer of the Canadian Jewish Congress, an executive member of the Toronto Jewish Congress, an officer of the Jewish Community Centre, and a member of the executive of Ben Gurion University in Israel. Eric aspired to be the top leader in the Jewish community, so including me in his network of potential supporters was important, to a degree that I was not aware of until 1989.

The money man, according to Eric, was one Ralph Fisher, to whom all contributions were given, through Eric, of course. So most of our political dinner purchases in those early years went to the Tories, and Eric was my contact.

Eric suggested that we stick with our existing NCJW accountant, who was very good, while he would act as our consultant, at no charge of course. Once again, he "preferred" if I spoke to him directly at his office or at some prearranged spot, and did not involve his wife unless it was absolutely necessary.

He had earlier recommended a study by his firm on the administrative operation of NCJW, Toronto, which he felt would show the limitations of our existing staff, specifically Betty Stone. One of their recommendations was, in fact, that NCJW, Toronto

Section, make some personnel changes if we planned to continue expanding our programs at the rate we were then growing. However, we chose not to, then. Two years later, it was Marsha Slavens, accompanied by Nita Goldband and me, who actually advised Betty Stone that the executive was offering her a change in job responsibilities as an alternative to early retirement.

✦ At first, in July of 1984, it seemed all would be clear sailing. We were ready to make our proposal to the board of directors of NCJW, Toronto, which included several national members, for the undertaking of sole sponsorship of a private, non-profit housing project, known as the Prince Charles. We prepared an outline of the project, including its ramifications, its potential benefits both financially and as a community service, and the political implications for all of us. Ron Miller looked it over, and so did several other husbands of our members, who were either lawyers or accountants.

This proposal was duly documented, discussed, outlined, voted on by the executive, voted on by telephone poll to the board of directors, and finally sent out by referendum to the membership with a return portion requiring the casting of a vote. We had a rotating group of volunteers manning Council House for two weeks, all day, every day, to respond to any questions or concerns any of our members might have had.

There was no opposition.

So we began the process of creating a non-profit housing facility for seniors, the disabled, and families, including, for the first time, an attendant care program to provide independent living for disabled people requiring limited care.

The strategy was initially developed by NCJW volunteers and staff, Jane Pepino, and some key Tridel executives. In 1984-85 non-profit housing allocations were awarded by Ottawa, under the aegis of the Canada Mortgage and Housing Corporation. Only a limited number were given out each year. In order to be eligible, a housing project required an incorporated sponsoring group, whose primary focus was housing. The sponsoring group had to be eligible for a charitable number, *separate and distinct* from any associations.

Clear and simple. NCJW, Toronto Section, incorporated in 1897, and with its own charitable number, *could not*, under the existing regulations, be the sponsor of the Prince Charles housing project. So said our lawyers, who then proceeded to draw up and execute the necessary documentation for a separate foundation.

In order to make sure it was common knowledge that this was Council's project, we chose to name it the NCJW, Toronto Section, Charitable Foundation, so that the association was clear. This was done by board ratification in the fall of 1984 and at a general meeting of our membership as well. There was *no opposition* from our membership, only support. I was elected chairman of the foundation, Lesley Miller the secretary, and Nita Goldband, vice-chairman. We would receive no remuneration or benefits of any kind, and any out-of-pocket expenses would be reimbursed only when the project was established and funds available.

Eleanor Cooper, then section president, expressed her concerns about Lesley Miller's husband being our lawyer and Nita Goldband's husband being a developer (she was slated to be the next section president). No one else had any concerns, at least not that they were willing to express openly, and so we went ahead.

In outlining the recommended strategy to our board during that very exciting time, it was clearly reported that political activity would be part of it, including political dinners. Over the years, several of our executives attended these dinners, often accompanied by their husbands, and were reimbursed for them.

◆ In 1984, when we became involved, the Prince Charles site had already been zoned residential with limited density. North York had not yet started its development boom. NCJW's proposal of eight storeys, with an accompanying density increase over the existing buildings, which were four storeys high, caused concern among the local ratepayers — a concern that was fuelled by the politics of the time.

In order to get any site rezoned, one needs the support of local politicians — in this case, Howard Moscoe, of the NDP. Luckily, he supported this project, especially after NCJW became involved, and his support never wavered.

Provincial support was also critical, because the Ministry of Housing could have a major impact on the allocations, and the Cabinet could have an important effect on the zoning process. At that time any decision on rezoning had to come before North York's council first. Anyone who didn't agree with the council decision could then file an appeal with the Ontario Municipal Board (OMB). However, there was also a law, since repealed, that allowed the provincial Cabinet to overturn any OMB rezoning decision. This gave unlimited power to the government of the day, in this case Tory. So we needed to get the province's support to preclude any intervention by the sitting member of the area, the Conservative MPP David Rotenberg.

But the local ratepayers' association was something else. They were fighting among themselves, with their leader, Larry Wynn, objecting to our project. He kept trying to muster support from neighbouring residents to object to the rezoning of the site. He talked about traffic problems, noise, and how the proposed building would cut off the light for neighbouring houses. There had been a couple of local meetings with Tridel before we became involved. Hostility and mistrust between the politicians, the ratepayers, and the developer had already accumulated by the time we came on the scene.

To that end, we tried to meet with the local residents. With all costs paid by Tridel, our volunteers printed and distributed eight thousand pieces of mail to each household and apartment dweller in the surrounding area, explaining our plans and asking them to call and arrange a meeting with us, at their convenience. We even called a meeting, to which only eight people showed up, all friends of Larry Wynn. Obviously the "concerns" of the community were minuscule. Wynn's actual words to me were,

"We don't want our neighbourhood full of cripples in wheelchairs. There'll be more traffic and speeding in our neighbourhood."

"Wheelchairs don't travel that fast, you schmuck!" I shrieked at him. "You're disgusting. Get lost!" I shouldn't have done it. It was inappropriate and unladylike. But my colleagues and I were now incensed at this obvious bias against the disabled. More important, we were more determined than ever to get this rezoning and approval process through.

Ironically, Wynn's attitude did more to get the Prince Charles going than anything else. Our general members were beginning to stir. The discrimination we were encountering motivated everyone to work together.

◆ In 1989, the *Toronto Star* carried a front-page story given to them by Larry Wynn, who was interviewed by Derek Ferguson about my alleged "conflict of interest" concerning two parking spaces at the Prince Charles site for the disabled residents' wheelchair-accessible van.

It was a twenty-four-hour press wonder and showed how desperate the media were for inflammatory information about me, no matter how inaccurate. I guess Wynn wanted to get his revenge. The *Star* never bothered to print a clarification when Derek got the actual facts, since, as he told me, it was "old news" by then.

Because rezoning decisions started at North York City Council, it was important for us to be in touch with council members. At that time, I didn't know anyone very well on council, but Eleanor Cooper was very close friends with Mayor Mel Lastman and Alderman Milton Berger. Jane Pepino, during one of our numerous stuffing of envelopes and mail-out sessions, outlined the necessary tactics to the girls. We had to inundate North York council with letters of support, in addition to making personal visits or phone calls to lobby each alderman.

"How do we get appointments to see these people?" I asked. Eleanor offered to arrange for the two of us to see the mayor and

Milton Berger first. After that, we'd see what we could do. The other girls were squeamish about such overt lobbying, so they decided that they would coordinate all the mailings (we sent more than one thousand, two hundred letters), while Eleanor and I met with the politicians. Tridel would pick up all costs and our volunteers would do all the work, including the actual deliveries. We were all mobilized. We had volunteers show up at Council House that we hadn't seen in years. Even Jane, in spite of her usual classic control and professionalism, was showing excitement.

Our first meeting was with Mel Lastman, the mayor of North York. Eleanor was excellent, advocating our cause and outlining our plans for the building. I was responsible for discussing the financial aspects, including the funding sources and strategy for getting Ottawa's approval. We didn't know that until then, Mayor Lastman had opposed the project.

He was so impressed with Eleanor's presentation that he promised he wouldn't work against us. I didn't understand what that meant at the time, but in later years I learned that a powerful politician can zap a project — not by voting against it, but by working behind the scenes against it.

I was disappointed. I had hoped the mayor would be so impressed by our plans that he would change his position. I had not yet learned about favours owing, *quid pro quo*, political manoeuvring, and that the mayor's not working against a project was as good as his supporting it. When we reported back to the girls, I asked Jane if she felt I was too aggressive for this kind of role.

She burst out laughing, along with a couple of Tridel people who were meeting at Council House, and didn't answer. How naive I was.

Next, I got a call from Alderman Elinor Caplan, who would later be elected to the provincial Legislature and become a Cabinet minister. Her support of our project was so strong that she joined NCJW as a life member. She promised to keep an ear to the ground as to the attitudes of her colleagues and to keep us posted.

Next was Milton Berger. We had already delivered several letters and made a number of phone calls of support to his office. He is a wonderful man, a Holocaust survivor, who was in Auschwitz during the war. He told Elinor to tell her friend (me) that heavy pressure didn't work on him. Letters and phone calls only irritated him. He had read our documentation, he felt it was very good, but he hadn't yet made up his mind. He suggested that she tell me to ease up, especially when we went to see the other aldermen. Being too pushy wouldn't help. I was sitting in his office with Elinor at the time, but he was talking to her as if I wasn't there.

Now I really did feel insecure. Up to this point I had been successful at fundraising, grant getting, and program development in my various volunteer positions throughout the community. I had just finished a stint as co-chairman, with Eric Jackman, of the Special Gifts Division of the United Way. There I had been surrounded by people of a totally different background (WASP, Rosedale), but under Eric's tutelage and sensitive nudging, I had polished myself to some degree. He had expressed great pleasure with our two-year association and felt that in the area of community need, more aggressiveness was called for. In 1983 he took me to a dinner where I met Prime Minister Brian Mulroney. Eric and his wife Sara kept in touch throughout the horrors that were to come for me.

Only later, in discussion with Jane about this situation, did I realize that we Jews are more sensitive to the words "aggressive, pushy, and arrogant" than anyone else in the world. These terms have always been used to describe us in the most negative way and we go overboard to avoid them. So Milton Berger was only being helpful and sensitive when he gave me these criticisms. Years later, when we served together on the board of the O'Keefe Centre, he explained that he hadn't wanted my talents lost in being the stereotypical Jewish mother.

◆ Parallel to all this political activity, Nita and Lesley, along with a volunteer team coordinated by Georgina Grossman, were developing the actual program concepts for the Prince

Charles: the attendant care component, the lifeskills programming for the residents, and the kind of amenities we wanted in the building — specifically, provisions for exercise.

Marsha Slavens, Connie Kachuk, and Phyllis Moss coordinated the resident requirements for tenants. This had to be done in conjunction with and with the approval of the Ministry of Housing staff, both provincially and federally. After 1985, the regulations changed to make it easier, but the Prince Charles, as the last project under the old criteria, had to fit into several different categories. Core needy, dependent children, age restrictions, levels of disabilities — all had to mesh into our proposal within the guidelines of three levels of government.

With no prior experience, volunteers Donna Zener, Rochelle Reingold, Eveline Berger, and others put in hundreds of hours of research. They visited other housing projects, met with support staff in care facilities for the disabled and the aged, met with residents all over the city trying to assess priorities, and finally came up with an outstanding housing project, unmatched to this day.

Eleanor Cooper and I continued to lobby each North York alderman regularly, and finally a date was set for our rezoning application hearing: September 17, 1984.

More than two hundred of our members showed up that Monday night. I was scheduled to speak on behalf of the organization. Gary Sandler and Helen Wolfe, two disabled members of our task force, were there as well. Both of them had the kind of courage and commitment that served as an inspiration to all of us. Gary had contracted multiple sclerosis and was confined to a wheelchair. He was getting progressively weaker, but his good humour and team spirit never diminished. He had been a developer himself, and had two children. He missed his active life and was trying hard to keep his spirits up.

Helen was born with spina bifida, and her dynamism was incredible. She had a job, was very articulate, and drove her own specially outfitted car. When she first went to Tridel's offices along with Gary Sandler to meet the DelZotto brothers and look

TEMPTING FATE

over the plans for the building's accessibility, they were very moved by her courage and accomplishments.

At the meeting, Angelo DelZotto stated that no stone was to be left unturned to ensure that the Prince Charles housing project would be accessible and absolutely first class. "I want this project to resemble our luxury condos with exercise room, sauna, whirlpool, beautiful landscaping," he said. "Nothing is to be left out."

Angelo's wife later told me that after meeting Helen, Angelo came home and cried, because Helen had told him that when she was born, her mother had been encouraged to let her die on the delivery table.

Tridel's understanding and commitment to the disabled was reinforced by their working relationship with task force members such as Helen and Gary. At the North York council meeting on September 17, there was hooting and heckling by the opposing ratepayers, led by Larry Wynn, and the local MPP, David Rotenberg, who showed up to speak against our project. He clearly stated that he might exercise his veto power in the provincial Cabinet should the Prince Charles rezoning be approved by North York and then upheld by the Ontario Municipal Board. Several of the girls walked right up to him and told him what a creep he was and how they would remember him at election time.

Finally, the vote. We won, eighteen to three! There was a lot of hugging going on. Gary actually cried. But the battle was just beginning.

We needed to get the one hundred and fifty housing allocations from the CMHC in Ottawa, the attendant care approvals for seventeen of our disabled residents from the provincial Ministry of Community and Social Services (COMSOC), and partial realty tax exemptions from the City of Toronto.

The next day, with a roomful of volunteers at Council House, we celebrated with a couple of bottles of kosher wine (Jane Pepino took a taste and then took a pass) and began to develop our strategy. The deadline to have all approvals in place was April

30, 1985, some six months away. There were rumours of a provincial election being called at the same time.

The plan was simple. Inundate politicians across Canada with letters and phone calls of support. Eleanor Cooper and Georgina Grossman would organize that. Jane Pepino and I would spearhead the personal lobbying of the politicians; Lesley and Nita would coordinate the committee that developed the "meat and potatoes" of the project — namely the operational components of both the attendant care and independent living programs. The rest of the team of volunteers would start networking with other organizations who were involved in special needs housing.

And so that is what we did.

In January 1985, Nita Goldband, Lesley Miller, and I, accompanied by Tridel's lawyer, Martin Applebaum, flew to Ottawa (at Tridel's expense) to meet with the Minister of State, the Honourable Barbara McDougall. Eric Slavens had helped arrange the meeting. Its purpose was to outline our innovative plans for the Prince Charles housing project. We would then answer any questions and ask for her support in getting the necessary allocations.

Ms. McDougall's knowledge and concern about social housing issues were very impressive. She had done her homework and was very clear and decisive as to where she wanted to take her portfolio. She was also gracious and fun. She committed her support to our organization and never wavered.

On the cold January day that we returned from Ottawa, the NCJW executive embarked on our campaign in earnest. The entire membership across Canada started writing letters to their members of Parliament expressing their support of the Prince Charles and asking them to contact the CMHC on our behalf. It was very successful.

When we met with the Toronto staff of the CMHC, they asked us to "call the women off." It seems the staff in both their Toronto and Ottawa offices were being driven crazy by phone calls and letters.

Our volunteers were doing all the research, need and demand surveys, housing statistics, comparison figures for different levels of social assistance, disability provisions in housing, and all manner of documentation required, on their own. They simply followed the guidelines distributed by Ottawa on how to develop a non-profit housing project.

Whatever was asked of us, we delivered. Any and all expenses we charged to Tridel, no questions asked. The bureaucrats recognized the effort being expended by a group of volunteers. Their attitude, which had started out as rather patronizing, changed to one of respect. By the time the deadline came, most of them were rooting for us and doing whatever they could to help.

We were trying to get the attendant care project approved by the provincial minister of Community and Social Services, Frank Drea, in order to reinforce the need for the housing allocations, which came from Ottawa. Nita Goldband and I finally managed to get an appointment with him and his deputy, who was disabled himself.

We both gave the best presentations of our lives. Frank actually got choked up. He went out to his private office and returned five minutes later to tell us that the Prince Charles project would be approved for seventeen disabled attendant care units. Although their budget allocations had already been spent, he would exercise his ministerial discretion to make it happen right away.

When we left his office, we ran to the pay phones in the hall to call Council House, our lawyers, Jane Pepino, and Gary Sandler. I called Angelo. His only comment was "I knew you could do it. I'm very proud of all of you." We were on our way.

With the attendant care approval in hand, we increased the pressure on Ottawa to provide the housing allocations. Finally, Jane arranged an appointment with the then provincial minister of Housing, Dennis Timbrell, to preclude a veto by David Rotenberg. What a forthright, incredibly astute and sensitive politician Dennis Timbrell was. David Peterson told me after the 1987 election that if Timbrell had been leading the Opposition instead of Larry Grossman, he (Peterson) might not have won. Timbrell gave us his support and promised to do whatever he could to prevent a veto, though he had concerns.

✧ A provincial election was called for May 1985. Several of our group volunteered to work in the campaign offices of various candidates, trying to hedge our bets concerning the outcome.

We were racing against the clock to get federal approval for our housing project by April 30, which depended on all rezoning being finalized and in place. Jane Pepino and I contacted every sitting member of the provincial Legislature to get support and to try to prevent a veto.

In the meantime, Larry Wynn's group had appealed North York council's decision to approve the project, so the Ontario Municipal Board scheduled a hearing for early May.

Monte Kwinter, a Liberal who was running against David Rotenberg in our riding, which included Council House, offered his help. I had never met him before, but Tridel had bought two tables at his fundraising dinner at Mr. Grumps and suggested we take the tickets and attend.

Several of our volunteers and their spouses went, as well as two of our staff and their spouses. Jim Peterson introduced us to all the politicians. We moved around the room lobbying like mad, even though nobody there was in power.

Monte and I hit it off right away, and later in the evening, he offered to speak to Ralph Lean, his very close friend, about our project. Ralph was going to chair David Rotenberg's election campaign, and Rotenberg was becoming increasingly uncomfortable with the hostility of several hundred members of a prominent Jewish women's organization, many of whom lived in his riding. He was looking for a way to save face.

I was asked to volunteer in Rotenberg's campaign office, front and centre, along with any others who would help, to show that he had the support of NCJW, Toronto. I was also asked to personally raise $5,000 for his campaign, none of it from NCJW. My hope was that if the OMB upheld our rezoning, he wouldn't ask the Cabinet to veto it.

With the help of some of my NCJW colleagues, we delivered the volunteers. I delivered the money. At the OMB hearing, the judges wanted documentation that the allocations would be forthcoming from Ottawa as a justification for granting the project the increased density. If the allocations were not given, they did not want Tridel to build a condo with the extra units. But without the rezoning in place, Ottawa was reluctant to approve the allocations. So we were in a Catch 22 — or maybe more like a Bette Davis movie.

At the OMB hearings, Jane Pepino made a brilliant presentation on our behalf. Halfway through, a courier came rushing into the courtroom carrying the official approval from Ottawa for the project. The OMB had upheld our rezoning! There was chaos! We had won! The Prince Charles was going to be a reality.

Our volunteers and staff then got down to the real work of bringing this dream to reality. The Prince Charles housing project stands today as testimony to their devotion and commitment.

✦ The next few months were frenzied. Most of the real work was now being done by my colleagues while I tested my political wings.

David Peterson and the Liberals scored a tremendous upset in the 1985 elections. David Rotenberg was defeated and Monte Kwinter was elected in his riding. The Tories, who had been in power for forty years, did not receive a workable majority under Frank Miller. They would have to form a coalition with either the Liberals or the NDP unless the two Opposition parties supported each other to oust the Tories.

As a result of brilliant manoeuvring by Hershell Ezrin, David Peterson's right hand, the NDP backed the Liberals. After forty years, the Progressive Conservatives were out of power in Ontario and a Liberal, David Peterson, was now the premier.

I was there with my two youngest children that sunny day in June 1985 when he was sworn in. Some of the Cabinet ministers who, over the next four years, would become such a part of my life were there as well, but I barely knew them: Monte Kwinter, Elinor Caplan, Ian Scott, Lily Munro, Alvin Curling, Bernard Grandmaître, Greg Sorbara, John Sweeney, Hugh O'Neil, John Eakins, and Ken Keyes.

CHAPTER SIX

"Keep Your Options Open"

During that same year, 1985, with the Prince Charles project now under construction, I continued my volunteer commitments. In March 1985, NCJW, Toronto, co-sponsored a Symposium on Violence against Women in the Jewish Community with four other volunteer organizations, held in Toronto. Both Chaviva Hosek, then president of the National Action Committee on the Status of Women (NAC), and Jane Pepino, Tory feminist lawyer, played key roles.

Jane Pepino's full name was Nicholas Jane Pepino, something we always teased her about, given her feminist background. She had graduated from Osgoode Law School and had attended the University of Texas before that. From 1973 to 1982 she was a partner with Alan Blott, specializing in municipal law. She was the first woman member of the Metro Toronto Police Commission and was a key member of the Canadian Council of Christians and Jews. She also spearheaded the creation of a federal Task Force on Violence against Women and Children. In 1982 she joined the law firm of Aird & Berlis, where she quickly became a partner, with a specialty in municipal law.

I already knew Jane, but it was my first meeting with Chaviva, who was a combination of steely intellect and charming femininity. There was nothing threatening in her manner despite her tremendous clout. Born in Czechoslovakia, she came to Canada as a young girl and received degrees from McGill University in Montreal and a Ph.D. from Harvard. She went on to become an associate professor of English at the University of Toronto, always maintaining a deep involvement in women's issues. She was the president of NAC, an umbrella organization for many women's organizations across Canada. At the time, NAC focused on getting information on relevant issues out to the member organizations but they were not empowered to speak for anyone but themselves. Chaviva's leadership skills helped raise the profile of NAC and opened doors for women's concerns at all levels of government. The women's organizations commanded the respect of many more people then than they do today.

Chaviva espoused networking and mutual support in all fields, and I tried to follow her standards in my subsequent dealings in women's issues. Everyone was in awe of her, including some executives of Tridel, who helped sponsor the symposium.

This symposium was a first, and it created a lot of hostility among the religious, male leadership within the Jewish community. Unfortunately, denigration of women and wife abuse were more common than we had realized, and the Jewish feminists had already begun to attack the premise that males in Judaism were superior to women. (One prayer uttered by men in the morning says, in essence, "Thank you, God, for not making me born a woman." This seems to suggest that women are second class and deserve whatever treatment their husbands, fathers, or brothers mete out, including physical abuse.)

Some of the old traditions and regulations around divorce and widowhood and the non-rights of women once dictated by the Beth Din (the orthodox tribunal of Rabbis) are beginning to disappear, but in 1985 our symposium caused quite a stir. I had a few personal calls from the presidents of major community organizations (male) suggesting that the subject matter was ill advised.

"We (NCJW, Toronto) are only one of five organizations," I protested. "Why not call some of the others?"

"My wife is a member of Pioneer Women, an Israeli-based

organization, and she'll kill me," was one response. "It's a *shundah* (Yiddish for "shame") for the non-Jewish community to know of our failings," said another. "We have to keep our dirty laundry amongst ourselves," said yet another.

Eleanor Cooper, president of NCJW, Toronto, with her expertise on senior abuse as a result of working with the elderly, was the ideal chairman of the symposium. I was responsible for the funding and political involvement, and others chaired various committees. Thanks to the teamwork of all five organizations, the symposium was a tremendous success in both visibility and attendance. But the changes in men's attitudes were still minimal.

It was after this symposium that some officers of NCJW, Toronto, again began discussing retiring Betty Stone. We were becoming increasingly concerned by her inability to accept new administrative techniques to streamline the office and increase efficiency. But I was very reluctant.

"She's like a mother to me," I said. "Let's try to figure out an alternative, some kind of part-time job. Maybe we can hire a good assistant for her. I'll try to raise enough money." Eleanor told me I was simply delaying the inevitable. The other girls agreed with her. I should have listened, but I didn't.

Given the organization's ongoing community service commitments, internal strife at this time would be very destructive. We decided to look into how the other women's organizations handled their personnel problems. A three-member personnel committee was formed. I was not one of them, but Marsha Slavens was.

✦ In November 1985, I chaired Mel Lastman's campaign for re-election as mayor of North York. It was my first experience at the higher levels of a political campaign. Even though the polls indicated that Mel, who had been mayor for ten years, was a shoo-in, he was a little concerned. One can never predict when the public will decide enough is enough or that it's time for a change, he said. He decided to conduct an all-out campaign.

Mel Lastman was, and still is, the most colourful and successful mayor the City of North York has ever known. He's also a very astute businessman, who has run the city's finances very efficiently. Born and raised in the Kensington Market district of Toronto, which, back in the 1930s, was primarily Jewish, Mel had to struggle on his own to achieve success. He founded the "Bad Boy" chain of stores, known for flamboyant advertising and outrageous slogans — all created by the "Bad Boy" himself, Mel Lastman. In 1972 he ran for mayor and has never looked back.

He's quite short, and has curly hair, thanks to a perm and a hair transplant. He even makes self-deprecating jokes about that, which has only increased public affection for him.

Our success in the political stickhandling of the Prince Charles housing project convinced Mel that he wanted me as part of his team, and for six weeks I travelled with him on the campaign trail. I got to know his wife and children well. Marilyn Lastman is one of the most underrated women in Ontario. She is articulate, charming, intelligent, and extremely loyal and supportive, as are her two sons, Dale and Blayne. Too often people dismiss her because of what they see as flamboyance and frivolity. It's a mistake to underestimate her cunning and "smarts." She has been a positive force for North York.

The other serious candidate in that election, Barbara Greene (now a Tory MP), was a very intelligent woman, who, as the local alderman at that time, had a considerable following. She caused a lot of initial concern by insisting that there were secret plans afoot to redevelop North York, and particularly Yonge Street, into a mini-metropolis, with office towers and high-rise condos. (During the 1985 campaign, North York was still a "small town," its downtown consisting mostly of six-storey buildings clustered along Yonge Street.) But the mayor and his key associates kept dismissing her allegations of future deals with developers and mega-expansions as ridiculous. Since I didn't have enough political experience at this level to do my own research, I simply relied on the information provided by the political experts.

Well, Barbara Greene turned out to be right on, and I was

wrong. Within six months of Mel Lastman's overwhelming re-election victory, the entire Yonge Street corridor in North York sprouted new building developments, in an expansion that exceeded even Ms. Greene's predictions. This was not necessarily bad, since it generated a vast amount of tax revenue, as well as retail business. Mayor Lastman's business acumen is well known, so it is difficult to find fault with the end result from a commercial point of view. But I should have learned a lesson about listening to and then following the advice and direction of experts. As I was the visible one, it was my credibility at risk, not theirs. Unfortunately, as happened too often in my life, I didn't learn.

A month later, in December 1985, I was elected to the North York Committee of Adjustment, sometimes referred to as the miniplanning committee, or the poor man's version of rezoning. I was to remain a member of that committee until June 1989.

We dealt with minor variances in existing by-laws affecting building and property. For example, if you wanted to add a garage to your property, or a porch, or you wanted to put a deck off your kitchen, you'd most likely have to come before the Committee of Adjustment for approval. If we didn't give it, you couldn't do it. If you had already done it and we refused to grant the variance, you'd have to tear it down, unless you went to the Ontario Municipal Board to overrule us, and that would cost a few hundred dollars.

We tried not to force people to tear down work already done because of the cost involved and the fact that most of the variances were minor. We tried to stick with an expansion of no more than 10 percent, but if you were a developer and you had zoning approval for a twenty-storey building, what would another two or three storeys matter, right?

Wrong — at least from my point of view. The intent of the by-law was not to use the Committee of Adjustment to circumvent the Planning Act and therefore the Planning Board. This, unfortunately, brought me into direct conflict with some local politicians and their developer friends. Once again, instead of handling these differences tactfully and behind closed doors, I would defy them at the open meetings and work diligently to get a majority of my colleagues on the committee to agree with me and turn down these "minor variances."

Pretty soon it became a challenge for developers to try to stop, or at least modify, some of the increases in density and coverage that were brought in under our committee. If they wanted to go to the Ontario Municipal Board, they could, but I felt that the residents of local districts had to have a voice somewhere. Of course, there were many projects I did support, along with my colleagues, in opposition to the wishes of local ratepayers. Too often these ratepayers' groups were politically motivated, seeking power for themselves or their members.

My four colleagues on the committee for the four years of my term were a delight, despite our occasional differences. They were gentlemen in the truest sense of the word, and I have missed them and the fun we had together.

✧ By 1985 my visibility within the community had grown, along with my network of politicians, and the late Irving Chapley, alderman in North York, suggested it was time to expand my world beyond the Jewish community.

Irving was the moving force behind the creation of group homes in North York. For this he received a tremendous amount of personal abuse. He had suffered a stroke and walked with a cane. He was a warm, funny, and sensitive man, and was also one of the few politicians I knew who reciprocated on social outings. He and his wife Norma took Jerry and me to several ball games at Exhibition Place and treated us to mega corned beef and smoked meat sandwiches, which Jerry in particular loved. I knew nothing about baseball or any sport for that matter, but would enjoy sitting around the Metro box (a free perk for municipal politicians) gabbing with the guys and observing which development lawyers and lobbyists were "in" and which were "out" on any given day. Till the day he died in 1992, Irv stayed close to me, encouraging me to keep hanging in and always providing kind words of support and a political shoulder to lean on.

"Keep Your Options Open"

NCJW, Toronto Section, supported Irv's stance on group homes, and in fact some of us helped sensitize his people to the needs of the developmentally handicapped. His courage and strength were incredible, and fortunately for all of us, he was consistently returned to office. There are now more than one hundred group homes in North York, and no hint of a problem with any of them.

Irving began to organize support for my appointment to the board of the O'Keefe Centre — the performing arts centre in downtown Toronto — as a first step into the outside political world. The O'Keefe Centre is under the umbrella of Metro Council, the body of councillors elected from the City of Toronto and the surrounding municipalities that make up the metropolitan area. The O'Keefe's board was made up of four politicians and three citizens, who stayed in office for three-year terms. Perks included free parking, first choice of seats, access to the private lounge, and meeting some of the stars.

I was excited about the potential appointment; it represented an opportunity for me to be part of a world I had observed only from a distance. It also gave me a chance to learn about an operation that was important to cultural life in Toronto. As part of that team, I would gain experience and know-how about the tourism and entertainment industry, which would include union relationships and the day-to-day operation of a multi-million-dollar facility.

Nominations for city appointments were done by a sub-committee of politicians and then brought before the whole of City Council for ratification. If there was no consensus, elections were held.

One Friday evening, before the Metro Council nominating committee was to meet regarding the appointments, I got a call from Toronto Mayor Art Eggleton, whom I knew only casually. He asked me to withdraw my name from consideration for that year because the position had already been "promised" to someone else. He was sure I would be appointed the following year, given that the current chairman of the board, Senator Jerry Grafstein, had been there ten years and would be stepping down.

TEMPTING FATE

Senator Grafstein was an extremely powerful man, who had been a key Liberal player during the Trudeau years. He, along with Senator Keith Davey and Martin Goldfarb, a media guru and pollster, were the recipients of most of the public relations work contracted out by the Liberal government. Grafstein's wife Carole was a well-known volunteer, deeply involved in the social scene in Toronto.

During our conversation, Art also said that being cooperative would give me the opportunity to show the "boys" that I "knew the rules" about *quid pro quo* and was a team player.

I wanted to be part of the team, so I withdrew.

One year later, I had built up more political contacts and a lot more credibility as a result of the projects in which I had become involved. So in late 1986, Irv Chapley once again coordinated what he believed would be my appointment to the O'Keefe board.

But a funny thing happened on the way to the O'Keefe Centre. Senator Grafstein decided he didn't want to step down. That meant that the vice-chairman, whose appointment was also up for renewal, would have to be sacrificed if the commitment to me was to be honoured — unless, of course, I did the "right" thing and withdrew again.

There was no way.

I received a call from Mayor Eggleton. At the request of his good friend Senator Jerry Grafstein (so he said), he was asking me to reconsider this appointment, again notwithstanding the previous commitment. Our conversation is unprintable.

My friends and allies in the political world warned me that I would be coming up against the old Establishment if I locked horns with Grafstein. If I insisted on being nominated, then a three-way election would have to be held. The senator would not be happy about that because in any election, someone always loses. What if it wasn't me?

In any case, the chief kingmaker in political circles, Paul Godfrey, former North York alderman, former Metro chairman, and present *Toronto Sun* newspaper president, got involved.

"Keep Your Options Open"

Paul was one of the most successful politicians in the province, maybe even the country. Despite the fact that he had been out of office for a couple of years, I believe he had the ability then, as he does now, to make or break anyone and to orchestrate any and all political scenarios. He was a key fundraiser for the important municipal politicians; any recommendations from Paul were worth their weight in gold.

We had known each other for years, but until now, our paths had rarely crossed. Given my increasing visibility and political access, he suggested that we get reacquainted. We had fun getting to know each other again, especially after he agreed to be one of the chairmen of the upcoming B'nai Brith dinner in my honour. I loved listening to his anecdotes and comments about certain politicians and the strategies he had used to deal with them. He was a warm and gracious host, always considerate, always there if you called him, and his advice was the best.

His greatest talent was that of persuasion, and his strategy was to always have the deal made before the meeting, or the vote, so that any dissension would be resolved in an amicable way and the wheels of government could turn smoothly. I have never met anyone better at it than he. I tried to be flexible on issues when Paul asked and over the next three years responded more quickly to his suggestions and requests for assistance than those of most others.

On one occasion, he asked me to help him lobby the provincial government for the expansion of the Keele Valley dump site, even though the firm that would get the contract for the dumping of the waste was from Detroit. I did pursue it with some bureaucrats from the Ministry of the Environment, but when Gordon Ashworth, the executive director of Premier David Peterson's office, found out, he told me to back off and stay away from anything to do with garbage. Paul was very understanding when I explained what had happened, though he did suggest it wasn't necessary for me to discuss so much with Ashworth, especially if I wanted to become one of the real power brokers.

But in relation to the O'Keefe appointments, Paul made sure, with his incredible contacts and skillful deal making, that Grafstein would at least be one of the winners in the upcoming three-way election. In this way, face could be saved for Grafstein and I wouldn't have an enemy, or so it would seem. And so it came about. Three of us were nominated for the two available seats on the board and Grafstein and I were elected. A very nice man wasn't.

There was a lot of resentment towards me in some quarters because I had refused to back off. However, there was also support, and at the first opportunity, Grafstein was unseated as chairman.

Later, when Premier David Peterson decided that I was going to be the next chairman of Ontario Place Corporation, both Hershell Ezrin and Gordon Ashworth told me the senator's animosity was so intense that he had spoken to them about it. Grafstein even tried to suggest that my appointment to Ontario Place, which is provincial, should be declared a conflict with the O'Keefe Centre one, which is municipal. He had no luck there either.

✧ I loved being on the board of the O'Keefe. Fellow board member, Councillor Derwyn Shea, went out of his way to be helpful those first few months. He had a wonderful sense of humour and an upbeat outlook on life. I learned so much from the two senior staffers, Charlie Cutts and Martin Onrot, who showed me the inner workings of the ballet and opera, cultural activities I had never been part of before.

I was elected chairman of the labour-management committee, which dealt with some of the demands of IATSE, the union that controlled the staff at the O'Keefe.

I learned about the booking of shows and talent — what to look for, what sells, how to gauge the trend in the public's fancy, how to promote, what to look for in talent, and so much else. My colleagues and I were responsible for approving the proposed budget and "season" of talent recommended by staff. It was exciting to go through all the proposed shows and come to a

"Keep Your Options Open"

consensus. It was less exciting when some of our bookings turned out to be bombs.

Eventually, Toronto Councillor Tom Jakobek, another board member, and I hit it off too, after a shaky start. He was abrasive and so was I. We both thought we knew everything and argued over every single item on the agenda. But with time, his skills as an administrator and his talent in political manoeuvring impressed me, and as the "older mother" I suggested we throw in the towel and start again. It worked out well, for eventually we would work together for three years, on behalf of the Peterson government's interests on the waterfront.

The O'Keefe board were quite a diverse group, and that very diversity became a plus, since we all seemed to complement each others' abilities. We spent two years debating about and then coming to a consensus on which talent to book, improving the quality of the food, ticket sales, and public relations.

✦ In April 1986 I co-chaired the North American convention of YM/YWHAs and community centres on behalf of the Jewish Community Centre of Toronto. Several thousand dollars in government grants were received. I was also presented with the Woman of Valour Award from the State of Israel.

But politics, not volunteerism, was absorbing more and more of my time. Hershell had introduced me to Gordon Ashworth a few months earlier because he wanted me to start learning more about the inner workings of politics.

One evening in early April 1986, I hosted a dinner party at the House of Chan on Eglinton Avenue, of which my husband is a partner, in honour of Jane Pepino's recent community service award. Though she was a well-known Tory, most of the politicians there were Liberal. Their attendance was a mark of their respect for her and her accomplishments, especially in the feminist movement. It also said something about my growing political power.

I remember looking over the forty people in the back room of Chan during coffee and thinking that a page of my life had turned. I was going to have an impact on the events of this province, and perhaps one day the country. I did not ever want to run for office, but I intended to play a role in the activities of whoever did. Hershell and Gordon had both asked me to arrange a meeting with them soon. They didn't say why. I didn't care. I was on my way.

During these months my relationship with Tridel was growing, both as a member of the NCJW team and personally.

True to his word, Angelo started taking me along with him to meetings and lunches with some of his friends and associates. He also instructed his vice-president of development, Mario Giampietri, to include me in some of his meetings, where I could learn more about rezonings and municipal politics. Pretty soon my presence was accepted with no raised eyebrows.

Ostensibly, this was to teach me all about the construction business in order to facilitate the development of the Prince Charles and keep my colleagues informed. It was also personal training to increase my expertise and contacts.

At the same time, I was assisting Elvio DelZotto with some federal fundraising, including a couple of campaigns on behalf of then leader of the Liberal party, John Turner.

From NCJW's perspective, Tridel continued to pay all our expenses relating to the project, make generous contributions to our other programs, and provide us with a wheelchair-accessible bus for the residents of the building. More important, however, was their absolute commitment to the integrity of this project, the quality of its construction, and their willingness to change, even during construction itself, some of the walls and fittings to improve accessibility.

I began offering suggestions as to which political events and individuals Tridel and other developers should be supporting. In those days, corporations could make contributions from each of their subsidiaries and associated companies.

The various boards and committees on which I now sat brought me into contact with other developers, legal firms, and large corporations. Before long, they began discussing some of their political contributions and activities with me.

In time many would call me to get my opinions and recommendations before they made any decisions. It was pretty heady stuff, and I liked the feeling of power. More than liked. I loved it.

⟡ By now Gordon and I had developed a friendship and were having regular lunch meetings, each one paying the bill every other time. The Liberals were in power for the first time in forty-two years and they wanted to stay there. They wanted to access major money, and they also wanted to change the face of Ontario, bring in new social service programs, create a mosaic of ethnic participation in all government services and, most important, get rid of the old-time bureaucrats and their corrupt practices. They wanted their fundraising done openly but effectively. Would I be part of it?

My first response should have been, "What's in it for me?" It wasn't. "Of course," I answered. Hershell suggested I start following Gordon's direction. Gordon had been a key player in Pierre Trudeau's election team and government and was, according to all the experts, the best political operative in the business. Hershell would continue to deal with policy matters.

They wanted the support of the Italian community, and to do this, they needed the DelZotto family, who were highly respected. For years Angelo had been a Tory, but Elvio was a well-known Liberal. He had run unsuccessfuly for the provincial Legislature in 1967 when Bob Nixon was the leader but was no longer interested in getting involved provincially.

"What do you think it would take to get the DelZottos behind the Peterson government?"

"Gee, I don't know," I said (I did know). "But I'll ask and let you know."

Before I left, Hershell took me aside. "Keep your ties with everyone," he said. "Real power is in the eye of the beholder. Don't become a one-show stopper. Keep your options open.

Don't cut your Tory connections either. . . . Right now you can access anyone. Keep it that way.

"Be careful of the Italians. We're trying to find out who's really the Mob and who's not. Try to build some bridges, Patti. You're too intimidating. In this business, you can't have any enemies. Soften up, kid. Be patient. It will all come, don't worry. We'll keep in touch directly. When I write notes to you in green, it means I'm happy with you. Blue means business, with some concern. Red, watch out!"

I still have them.

CHAPTER SEVEN

A 7:00 a.m. Phone Call

"We need the support of the Italian community. The DelZotto family is critical to getting that support. We think they got a bad rap fifteen years ago when the Waisberg Commission was so negative in its findings. We want them with us. What will it take?"

We were in Hershell Ezrin's office, right next to that of Bob Carman, who was the chief bureaucrat, officially called the secretary of the Cabinet. Everyone was whispering because all the offices leading up to the premier's connect, and the walls had ears.

Along the upper mezzanine where the Legislature sits are several offices next to each other, with numbers on their doors. They belong to the premier, his staff, the secretary to the secretary of the Cabinet, then the secretary himself (Carman), then the principal secretary to the premier (Ezrin) and his secretary. From the outside, they look separate, but there is an internal passageway of connecting doors between them that allows one to go from office to office without ever being seen by anyone in the halls, specifically the press. Gordon Ashworth's office was on the third floor, but from there you could go down the back stairs and into the premier's offices unnoticed.

I knew, though I hadn't told anyone, how much those unproven allegations of criminal activity within the construction industry had hurt the DelZotto family. And how frustrating it was that no process existed for vindication. Their well-earned reputation as the foremost condo developers in Canada helped, as did their various involvements in charitable causes. But still they felt their name had been tainted, and their father especially wanted it cleared for the sake of his grandchildren.

Before I could answer, Gordon piped up, "There's an opening coming up on the Ontario Police Commission," he said.

My initial reaction was one of disbelief. "What kind of position is that?"

"Look," he said, "what could make a more definitive statement than having a DelZotto, once alleged to be involved in criminal activity, sitting on a commission that regulates policing in this province? Wouldn't that reinforce the confidence of this government in the DelZottos' integrity and show the public the family was given a raw deal in the past?"

"You'd have to get backup documentation on what happened fifteen years ago," Hershell interjected, "especially all the statements of support that were submitted on their behalf at that time. I think Gordon's got a point. I've always been offended by witch hunts and McCarthy-like hearings. If we can get our hands on some credible rebuttal that was documented at the time, it's worth a shot. I think you should raise it with the DelZottos."

Why did I get the feeling their suggestion wasn't as spontaneous as it seemed?

Shortly thereafter, I brought the matter up for discussion with all three DelZotto brothers. In a subsequent discussion, their father, Jack, was present too. He expressed eloquently how much his family's good name meant, not so much for him, but for his grandchildren. He saw the subtleties that Gordon and Hershell had alluded to, but asked me only one question: "Can we trust these people?"

"Absolutely," I said. "I know Clarence and Marie Peterson, the premier's parents, primarily through Jim, the eldest brother. They're fine people. Besides, words that come from Hershell Ezrin's lips might as well be coming from David Peterson himself."

And I believed it.

Angelo, however, was against this, or any other kind of political appointment for their family. "We don't need or want any visibility

A 7:00 a.m. Phone Call

in these matters again. Old enemies will crawl out of the woodwork. We don't want any appointments. We will support this government if they represent our interests. Otherwise, no!"

I left the meeting assuming the matter was closed. So I was surprised when I got a call the next day asking if I would drop into the Tridel offices as soon as it was convenient. There I met with Angelo and his brother Elvio again.

Elvio handed me a thick envelope. "I've decided to allow my name to be submitted to the Ontario Police Commission for an appointment to its board," he said. I looked at Angelo, who said nothing.

"Here is a package of documents relevant to the Waisberg Commission and the subsequent attempts we made to have our name cleared through the courts. We've included statements of support from the Solicitor General of Canada, the Attorney General of Ontario, as well as various prominent business and political leaders.

"The same package was prepared for the former Tory government (Bill Davis was premier, Roy McMurtry was attorney general), who said they wanted to right the wrong. They also wanted our financial support, which we gave them. They never got around to the other."

I passed the documents on to Gordon. Arrangements were made for copies to be sent to Attorney General Ian Scott. I personally delivered sets to David Peterson and to Monte Kwinter, minister of Consumer and Commercial Relations, who was going to organize Cabinet support. I also met with Jim Peterson, the premier's brother and a federal member of Parliament, and his wife, Heather, who was the premier's patronage chief, at their home on Hillholm Road in Toronto.

We talked through all the potential difficulties such an appointment might present — both personal and political. I shared with them my discussions with both Gordon and Hershell about the ramifications if the government tried to shaft the DelZottos as the previous one had. But I wasn't worried. So far, I'd participated in about $175,000 of political fundraising for this government because I believed in their promises for change. I knew they would be honourable.

The documentation supporting the DelZotto family was absolutely clear, even to the most unsophisticated reader. It was obvious that unproven allegations and innuendoes, by one or two people, should never have been given the weight they had been by given by Mr. Justice Waisberg. It wasn't hard to understand why the family's wounds were deep.

I was taking a personal risk by trying to persuade my friends and associates to put their trust, and dollars, into the hands of a government that was functioning in an accord with the NDP, who were perceived to be anti-business. Quite rightly, as it turned out.

I needed to hear directly from Jim that he was in support of Elvio's appointment and would make sure we all wouldn't be made fools. Both Jim and Heather gave me their commitment of support and promised to "keep on top of everything." I believed them.

Arrangements were made for me to speak personally to the attorney general, Ian Scott. At the time, I was a member of the board of the Metropolitan Toronto Housing Authority (MTHA), which provided the housing of last resort for the indigent and homeless in Toronto. I had been to only two meetings and was still learning about its operation when the Elvio DelZotto appointment was undertaken.

Regent Park, the largest subsidized housing project under the authority of MTHA, was located not far from the mansions of Rosedale where the WASP establishment lived.

Regent Park was a simmering powderkeg of drug dealing, assaults, wife and child abuse, and robberies. It also housed many people who were law abiding, responsible, and caring — who were struggling to give a better life to their children. Both Rosedale and Regent Park were in the downtown core of Toronto, and both were represented by Ian Scott.

I had first met Ian at the groundbreaking ceremony for the Prince Charles housing project in September 1985. I loved the way he spoke and found him engagingly biting and witty in his comments about life in general. He was so charming that more than once I had to remind myself not to take his flirtations seriously.

When we arranged to meet about the appointment of Elvio DelZotto to the Ontario Police Commission, I was told that the reasons for our meetings were being documented on his appointment calendar as pertaining to MTHA and Regent Park. Though we did discuss some of Ian's concerns there, and I did follow up on his suggestions with the MTHA Board, the DelZotto appointment was our primary agenda item. It was Ian Scott who told me that, technically, the submission would have to be made through Ken Keyes, solicitor general, whom I did not know. Ian said he would take care of it, which he did, by writing the following letter on the letterhead of the attorney general of Ontario, which he copied to me:

The Honourable Ken Keyes   May 9, 1986.
Ministry of Correctional Services
Whitney Block
Suite 5320
Toronto, Ontario
M7A 1A2

Dear Ken:

I am pleased to enclose a letter from the National Council of Jewish Women of Canada in support of the nomination of Mr. Elvio DelZotto to the Ontario Police Commission. I trust that you will give this nomination every consideration when a position becomes vacant.

        Thank you for your consideration.
        Yours very truly,

IAN SCOTT
Attorney General
c.c. Patricia Starr

Ian seemed very supportive, in fact, almost enthusiastic, about having someone like Elvio on that commission. He was very familiar with the support documentation given to him, which I wondered about at the time. If he knew all about it, what did they need me for?

For a long time I was led to believe that the appointment was moving forward. Even though it had to be handled very quietly, this government, I was assured, had found nothing in their own investigations of the DelZotto family to change their support.

These words, in different variations, were spoken to me directly by David Peterson and several of his key aides and Cabinet ministers, including Monte Kwinter (who was supposedly in charge of the Cabinet support) and Jim and Heather Peterson.

During this time, the Elinor Caplan affair blew up. Caplan was the local councillor in North York back in 1984 when NCJW was trying to get its housing project passed. She was also a member of NCJW. After her election in May 1985 to the provincial Legislature, she was made a Cabinet minister, chairing the Management Board and becoming minister of Government Services. She was very powerful, and deservedly so. Elinor was viewed by many as one of the most astute and balanced members of the provincial Cabinet.

Unfortunately, her husband's business affairs involving lobbyist Ivan Fleischman erupted in scandal. June 1986 saw a lot of screaming headlines, and Elinor was being pressured to resign her Cabinet position until the matter was cleared up.

I received a frantic phone call from Hershell Ezrin.

"Can you get letters of support for Elinor? Petitions, notes, phone calls, anything. We want her to stay in Cabinet, or at least be able to come back when this garbage is over."

NCJW's membership responded with a petition of support, which was sent to the premier's office. The Italian community collected further signatures on a petition, along with many individual letters and phone calls.

The Caplan affair seemed to solidify the support for Elvio's appointment even more, because now the powers of the day saw,

A 7:00 a.m. Phone Call

first hand, what a witch hunt and its attendant publicity can do. I had never seen Hershell so angry. Elinor stepped down from her Cabinet position on June 16, 1986. Eventually the matter died down and she was returned to Cabinet.

◆ Things were going along smoothly on the DelZotto appointment, with the only fly in the ointment, according to Gordon, being Vince Borg, the premier's former driver and longtime personal aide, who was "uncomfortable" with the idea.

I had met Vince in 1982 at the Liberal convention where David Peterson was elected as leader. I was holding a large Peterson sign on the convention floor and waving it around a little, when he told me to climb up on a chair and really wave it.

"Get lost, kid," I said. "I'm not climbing up on any chair like a yoyo."

"Listen, lady, you get up on that fucking chair and wave that fucking sign. This is the ballot that counts. You're here to elect David Peterson leader. When I tell you to do something, *do it!*" I did it.

(In 1989, when the TV screens were full of the Starr Affair, the CBC aired old footage of David's convention victory. There, standing on a chair, waving a Peterson sign with a sour look on her face, was one Patricia Starr. Despite the anguish I was feeling, I burst out laughing when I saw it.)

I hardly ever saw Vince when I was at Queen's Park, but if we did bump into each other, neither of us was very friendly to the other. Gordon told me not to try to talk to Vince personally about the appointment. In fact, he said to stay clear of him.

Some time later I sat with Ian Scott at a political fundraiser. As Rosedale was in Ian's riding, some very prominent Establishment people were there. We were both enjoying the wine and Ian was at his biting best, talking about a few of the "social elite" in attendance. He saw them as self-serving, shallow hypocrites and seemed quite upset. To change the subject, I brought up Elvio's appointment again.

Ian stared at me quizzically for what seemed like a very long time, and then launched into a monologue.

"You are everything many people in this room dislike. Ambitious, aggressive, shrewd, and Jewish. You're also a friend of the Italians. Don't be so open about your feelings. Remember that man sitting in my receptionist's office last time you were there? You made a joke about his blue socks and brown shoes? He was a former senior OPP (Ontario Provincial Police) officer. You never know who you're sitting next to, or who is your enemy.

"The DelZottos are not the godlike figures you think, but neither did they deserve what happened to them. Some of our information is hard to believe. Many prominent developers were concerned about where the Waisberg Inquiry might lead, and they weren't all Italian. Premier John Robarts (premier of Ontario from 1961 to 1971) had close ties to some of them."

Ian expressed concern about the possibility that for some reason a decision was made to finger the DelZottos and in so doing to get the heat off the others. "It couldn't have been done without inside help," he continued. "A lot of money had to change hands. Even the OPP man you saw could have been one of the inside men. He's now retired. This is one of the reasons we've tried to keep everything so quiet. Elvio's appointment would make them all vulnerable to exposure. Knowing his tenacity, he would probably track them all down. I want to get to the bottom of it. I need to know if there are any other inside connections to the OPP. You've got to keep quiet till we get it sorted out. This is not a tea party."

I was afraid to tell Angelo or Elvio what he had told me, and only discussed it with Gordon and Hershell.

✧ In the meantime, I coordinated the Heritage Dinner, individual events, and straight contributions of about $150,000 for the provincial Liberals. Corporations would be asked for $5,000, and at that time, each of their subsidiaries was eligible to contribute $5,000 as well. Legal and accounting firms could contribute substantial amounts and allocate them to individual associates, often issuing receipts.

In this way, the contributions would be spread out among

several individuals and companies in order to avoid the appearance of too much influence in too few hands. There was an inner circle of fundraisers created under Don Smith, president of the Liberal Party of Ontario (OLP) and CEO of Ellis-Don Construction Ltd., one of the largest construction companies in North America. He was a charming and delightful man, whose wife Joan became a Cabinet minister in the Peterson government in 1987.

Included in this group of twelve were some very prominent business leaders and lawyers, and our discussions included ways of "getting around, legally," restrictions on political contributions. Our fundraising meetings were usually held once a month at the University Club or in the premier's Cabinet office for lunch. We were all assigned a number so no one outside the group would know our names and who was bringing in the large contributions. I was assigned two numbers, 11 and 17. I don't know why.

We would go through the "A" list of contributors and divide them up. Most of us knew each others' friends and business associates and rather than solicit them more than once, we would just split them up. I'm sure any flies on the wall had burning ears as we did our regular "You take that one, I'll take this one" or "He's got business before the government, turn the screws on" or "He's so cheap, anything you get is better than nothing" routines.

All the major contributors, corporate or individual, were male. I was the only woman in our group, though Kathryn Robinson, the woman who would eventually succeed Don Smith as the Ontario Liberal party president, would sometimes sit in. During all the years I knew her, she never spoke to me directly. Gordon told me that "I made her nervous."

The Premier's Heritage Dinner raised $4,000 a table. We would approach companies and associations to buy a table of ten, to which receipts were often allocated individually. From 1985 to 1989, I personally sold ten tables each year to that dinner. NCJW's Capital Fund bought one, which the girls went to every year. The other nine tables were sold to others.

There were also individual fundraising dinners for various MPPs, which averaged $2,000 per table of ten. Any political fundraising NCJW participated in was for events such as these dinners or cocktail parties. All other donations raised by me went directly to Gordon Ashworth, Hershell Ezrin, or Don Smith.

From 1985 through 1989, the Ontario Liberal Party's computer print-out showed more than $600,000 raised from number 11/17. Of that amount, approximately $24,000 came from NCJW's capital fund. For that reason, namely the relatively minuscule sum, I didn't run away but stayed to fight in February 1989 when the wildly inflated stories of NCJW's political contributions were being circulated. It was a terrible decision, one that I would live to regret.

✦ In 1986, at the same time the DelZotto appointment was under consideration, my other volunteer activities had increased. Since 1981 I had been an executive member of the Jewish Community Centre (JCC), where I met Martin Mendelow, architect and developer, who was its president. I was also an officer of the Canadian Jewish Congress (CJC), Ontario Region, which was the umbrella organization of the Jewish community. In both agencies, I held the positions of assistant treasurer and grants officer. I dealt with the allocation of millions of dollars in charitable contributions to programs within the community and worked with staff in seeking out government funding. I then advocated on behalf of the programs and groups deserving support.

As in my other grant application work, criteria interpretation (finding the category one's project could fit into within the government guidelines) was extremely critical. It often entailed creative program descriptions and the expansion of goals in order to be eligible.

Political lobbying was another critical component of my work. Despite the worthy causes and challenging programs being developed by volunteer organizations, we didn't have the resources of private corporations. It was a constant struggle just to keep going.

Government funding was critical to the survival of our social service programs. Getting the support of the decision makers — politicians and bureaucrats — required phone calls, meetings, socializing, and, when appropriate, financial support.

NCJW's Council House, the Jewish Community Centre, and the Canadian Jewish Congress's building were next to each other on Bathurst Street. For eight years I walked back and forth to my various volunteer positions, the common thread being grants — municipal, provincial, and federal. During my terms of office, almost $2,500,000 in grants was raised for NCJW, $258,000 for the JCC, and close to $100,000 for CJC.

As a signing officer for these agencies, hundreds of cheques and support documents would be put in front of me each month for my signature. I also signed cheques for the operation of the Prince Charles housing project with an annual budget in excess of $1 million.

✦ In the early fall of 1986, Gordon Ashworth told me that the appointment of Elvio DelZotto to the Ontario Police Commission was going to go through. I then got a call from Monte Kwinter saying "he" had gotten it done. The matter was scheduled for the following Wednesday's Cabinet meeting, at which time it would get formalized approval, known as an order-in-council. I was excited for the family.

"You shouldn't say anything yet," Gordon said, "but if you do, let me know how Mr. DelZotto (Jack, the father) reacts."

One of my sons had an open house at school, and that prevented me from contacting Angelo right away. I decided I'd better put it off until the next morning.

But I never got the chance. My phone rang at 7:00 a.m.

"Trouble. Pick me up and drive me down to the office," Gordon said. (Gordon had never learned to drive.) My heart sank. I knew it, I just knew it. Something had gone wrong.

"What do you know about the DelZottos' Florida operations?" Gordon demanded as we drove down to Queen's Park on that beautiful autumn morning.

"Nothing."

"Cut the crap, Patti. You must know something."

"No, I don't," I insisted. When we reached the Legislature, the security guard waved at us as I parked in my unmarked reserved spot.

When we got into Gordon's office, he told me that late the night before, the premier's office — Vince Borg, he said — got a call from a reporter in Florida. This reporter had "heard" some weeks earlier that one of the DelZottos was being appointed to the Police Commission. His source had been someone from the OPP. The allegation was that the OPP were enraged and were looking for any kind of incriminating information on Tridel's U.S. operations, since they couldn't get anything on its Canadian one. Supposedly this reporter had "found something" and was going to "break the story" as soon as the appointment was official.

Naturally the OPP made their objections known to the premier's office, to the extent of saying there would be major problems for the premier if the appointment went ahead.

It was decided to back off from the political minefield the appointment might become.

I slumped into the armchair, the colour draining from my face and my insides turning to mush. I wanted to cry — with frustration, rage, and a deep sadness for Jack DelZotto.

"This is what politics is all about," Gordon said. "We tried everything we could, but there was too much opposition.

"After the Elinor Caplan Affair, this government can't sustain another dirty fight. Besides, David doesn't have the heart for it. What if there really is something to this reporter's story? My priority must be to protect the premier."

"You sound just like *'they'* must have sounded fifteen years ago," I said. "I don't believe this. Who made the decision to give up? Who is this reporter? What are these allegations? All of a sudden, after all this time, and all the investigations, a phone call ends it? What happened to all those speeches about courage and principles? I know David's a wimp. But you too? And Hershell? Who's really behind this?"

A 7:00 a.m. Phone Call

By now, I was as angry as I had ever been. And I didn't know who was really responsible for the situation. I was pacing around Gordon's office, staring out his window overlooking University Avenue and noticing, despite my agitation, the fact that the flowers in front of the Legislature were still blooming.

"And what am I supposed to tell the DelZottos?" I said, turning to face him. "I believed you! I persuaded other people to believe you! I know you, Gordon. This isn't like you. You're bullshitting me. Tell me the truth."

"That's all I can tell you right now," he answered. "David told me last night. He doesn't want any trouble with the OPP."

"What's he afraid of?" I asked.

He didn't answer.

"So — we're good enough to raise money for you guys but not good enough to stand behind in a crunch. Well, forget it! I'm going down to let David have it personally!"

"Don't bother. He's gone out of town," Gordon replied, with a slight sneer on his face.

"I'm not surprised," I replied. "What a chicken! He should have had the guts to call Elvio personally."

With that, I stormed out of Gordon's office, almost smashing the glass as I slammed the door. Feelings of betrayal rushed over me. I believed I had been had, but by whom I wasn't yet sure. I flew down the back stairs into the premier's office. It was about 8:30 a.m., so there was only one receptionist on duty. I went into his private office directly to see if he was there, and lo and behold, who should be sitting behind the premier's desk but Vince Borg.

"You are a first-class schmuck!" I snarled at him. " Your only claim to fame is that you're half Italian. Unfortunately, it's the wrong half. Somehow, I know you're behind this. I'm sure all the Mangi-cakes (whitebreads, Wasps) are dying to hear from you! Let them raise money for you. I sure as hell won't!"

"Expecting your period are you, dearie?" he said. "Why don't you find some new friends? Those guys are trouble. If you like Italians so much, I'll introduce you to some good ones you should be getting to know."

"If the DelZottos aren't good enough for your premier, then neither am I," I said as I walked out.

The drive up to Tridel's offices was very sad for me. Even though it was a clear, cool day, to me everything was gray and depressing. True, as instructed, I had never told them that the appointment was in the bag, but neither had I ever discouraged them from being optimistic. They had put their trust in my judgment and my ability to make the right political decisions on their behalf. And I had failed.

In my arrogance I had ignored the comments that others had made over the years about David Peterson's weakness under pressure. I thought I knew better. I was wrong. Now I'd have to face them. The hardest part would be telling Mr. Jack DelZotto.

When I got there, Angelo knew right away from the look on my face that something had happened. For the first time, I told both Angelo and Elvio everything that had been said, not only by Gordon that morning, but by Ian several weeks earlier.

Angelo said nothing, but Elvio was furious. "Again! It's happened again!" he said. "We never should have trusted any of them. They're all the same!"

Just then Elvio's secretary, Marissa, interrupted to say the premier was on the phone wanting to speak to Elvio. "Tell him we're not available," Angelo said. "We need some time to think about all of this. I don't want any words spoken in anger that cannot be forgotten."

Elvio then left for another meeting and I got up to leave.

"Where are you going?" Angelo asked me, quite sharply.

"Back to Council House, where I belong," I replied. "I'm finished with backroom politics. I haven't got what it takes. I believed everything they told me. I can't face your father. I'm going to concentrate on the opening of the Prince Charles (set for early November 1986) and the renovations in Council House."

"Sit down," he snapped as he closed his office door. "Is this all you've learned in two years? Now, more than ever, you have to stay close to these people. You can't continue to take everything personally. You have taken us farther politically than we've ever been before. Now we just have to hold our cards a little closer. In the meantime, our community's Famee Fulane housing project is starting to happen. Without you, it won't move through the process smoothly enough for the guys."

He was referring to Marco Muzzo, Joe Zentil, Primo DeLuca, and Rudy Bratty, who were all from Angelo's birthplace, Fruili, in northern Italy. They were the driving force behind this seniors' facility and had contributed thousands of dollars in labour and materials to its construction. But they did not want any publicity, especially about themselves, so it was important that this project be kept clear of any political hassles.

"If NCJW wants another housing project," Angelo continued, "it will ultimately need provincial approval, and that means your input. We aren't burning any bridges, at least not yet."

"Was it my fault?" I half sobbed. "Could I have done it better? I thought I left no stone unturned. I spoke to everyone. I had all the support documentation. I can't figure out what happened. If I did something wrong, how can I learn if I don't know what it was?"

"You didn't do anything wrong. It's possible they really did want it to happen — especially Ashworth," he said. " Maybe they really tried."

He sat down behind his desk and put his head in his hands. After a few minutes his back straightened, and he looked up at me and said, "Even though Elvio never gives up on anything, I think it's time to stop. After fifteen years, it's enough. At least some of the pieces of the puzzle have now fallen into place. Be back here at twelve noon. Did you forget we have a lunch meeting at LeParc with Fred and Marco?"

He paused, got out of his chair, and walked over to look me straight in the eyes.

"By the way, I presume you handled all of these matters in an appropriate manner," he said.

He could tell by the look on my face what must have happened.

"Bella, bella, when will you ever learn? Don't let *them* know what you're thinking. Don't give them ammunition to use against you. Remember what I keep telling you. Stay close to the enemy — then you're there when the moment is right. If you burn your bridges, you're isolated. The sweetest revenge is a lovely smile and pleasant words. Now we have to plan our next moves. The first thing you'll have to do is mend the fences."

I must have grimaced. "Don't look at me like that," he said. You'll have to apologize for your outbursts. Yes, you will. Then we will be unavailable for a few weeks. No fundraising, no committees, nothing. Let's see how long it takes. In the meantime, let's make sure the Prince Charles opening goes well. It's now the flagship of Tridel's non-profit housing division. I want you to come up with a strategy on how to deal with the politicians after today."

✦ And so it was. My colleagues and I worked on the opening of the Prince Charles, scheduled for November 6. Every politician from all three levels of government who mattered was invited, and most were there.

NCJW volunteers organized the entire day's program, invited all the residents, and with great joy and pride brought to fruition a dream we had all worked so hard for during the past two years.

For a year our volunteer committee had visited the construction site every two weeks. My colleagues' input, and the cooperation of the construction crew, made this truly a shared project. We watched the bricks being laid, the wiring and plastering, and even had input on the colour of the tiles. Tridel gave each of us our own hard hats, which we proudly wore on all our visits.

Everything about the project, including its day-to-day operation, was within the scope of our volunteer committees. The successful completion of the project was a magnificent tribute to the skills and commitment of NCJW's volunteers. How proud everyone was, and how exhilarated.

One of the greatest joys of all was that Gary Sandler, who had fought through the rezoning and allocation process with us, was now a resident. He spoke at the opening ceremonies. Several prominent members of the Italian and Jewish communities were there, as well as the three DelZotto brothers and their father Jack. A number of provincial and federal Cabinet ministers spoke. David Peterson sent his regrets.

Hershell and Gordon were both there.

I had kept in touch with both of them by phone, always pleasant, but aloof — a new role for me. Nothing more was said about what had happened on the DelZotto appointment, except for my apology to Vince, by phone, for my attack.

"We want you to come down and talk to us," Hershell said on that gorgeous, sunny day when the Prince Charles opened. I did, the following week.

The conversation was a rehash of earlier ones. But now the success of our housing project, my increasing involvement in North York's politics, and the two recent awards I'd received for volunteerism from the State of Israel and the province had increased my credibility. Despite what had happened, I was still on the move, with or without them.

They had presumed that they could continue to channel my energies for their own benefit. But they also knew I was close to some prominent Tories, especially Jane Pepino, who was often touted as the only woman in Ontario qualified to become premier. Jane was an ardent feminist who combined the shrewdness needed for success with a caring for people. That made her high on everyone's "A" list.

I'm sure the Peterson group were concerned that my efforts, expended on their behalf in the past, might be transferred to their opposition. How right they were.

"The premier wants to meet with all three DelZotto brothers for lunch," Gordon said. "Will you see if they'll be receptive?"

"Do I look like someone's private secretary?" I answered. "Let David make his own arrangements."

"Come on, Patti, we know you're dying to be at that lunch," Gordon said, smiling. "It seems the Italian community has been giving David a bit of a cold shoulder lately and he's not happy about it. You know he likes everything to be calm and pleasant."

"I have a proposition for you guys to think about," Hershell said. "The chairmanship of the Royal Ontario Museum is coming up for reappointment. Stop sneering, please. Guess who the present chairman is? None other than Eddie Goodman. Don't you think it would be ironic if, given what happened fifteen years ago, Eddie Goodman was replaced by Elvio DelZotto?"

Goodman had been a key political player in the Robarts government during the Waisberg Commission Inquiry. He was still a powerful man.

"Gee, won't you have to get the OPP's permission first?" I asked as sweetly as I could. My friends would have been quite angry at my sarcasm if they had heard me, but I couldn't resist the temptation. Then I relented.

"Okay, give me some dates and I'll speak to the brothers. But David will have to ask Elvio personally if he wants him to even consider it. No more messengers."

A week later, the three DelZotto brothers, Hershell Ezrin, Gordon Ashworth, and I joined David Peterson for lunch in the Cabinet boardroom. We had shrimp, salad, and rice.

David was as charming and witty as only he can be, but everyone else was subdued. The conversation was mostly about development issues, including rent controls, condo conversions, and land development outside Metro. Almost all the land was controlled by Marco Muzzo. We also discussed Toronto's waterfront.

Before long, David and Elvio were going at it hot and heavy, almost to the point of what, in polite circles, would be called conflict. Finally, the offer of the chair of the ROM was put to Elvio. He politely declined. Angelo barely spoke. Leo, being very personable, tried to keep the conversation going, but it didn't last much longer.

As we left, Angelo thanked the premier for his hospitality and assured him of his continuing support. He also told him that he was not interested in any political appointments for his family beyond their artistic involvements, which he perceived as non-political. David then asked Elvio to prepare a written commentary on the issues that had been raised during lunch in terms of how the government could become a viable partner with developers to enhance the industry and create more jobs. Elvio agreed, and within two weeks forwarded it to Queen's Park.

✧ A week later, I was back in the premier's office. Hershell, Gordon, and Heather Peterson were also there. Without asking my opinion on the matter, David told me that he was considering putting me in charge of Ontario Place, the appointment coming up the following May (1987). He talked about his long-range plans for the development of the waterfront, his hopes for the 1996 Olympics, and his concerns about special interests across the road, at Exhibition Place.

He also expressed great anger at what was seen as a deterioration of Ontario's waterfront showplace and rumours of corruption and porkbarrelling.

To chair the board of Ontario Place, with the kind of hands-on management he wanted, would be a tremendous personal challenge. I wanted it! In my excitement I missed the subtlety of his strategy. Knowing me as he did, it was a safe bet that I would do nothing to "blow it." In this way, he figured, I'd be controllable for the next six months. He was right.

Shortly thereafter, in December 1986, B'nai Brith of Canada announced that I would be their honoree at a tribute dinner to be held on March 24, 1987. They felt it was time to single out a woman who had carved her own niche beyond the financial contributions of her family. They also wanted to recognize the accomplishments of a woman community leader who had gone beyond the stereotype of "lady bountiful."

Given my contacts, the political access and visibility this dinner would provide B'nai Brith's many humanitarian services would be a bonus. For me, it would be the pinnacle of my volunteer career. I was thrilled to be chosen.

The keynote speakers were David Peterson and federal Cabinet minister Barbara McDougall. Jane Pepino and Jim Peterson were the dinner co-chairs. Paul Godfrey was co-chairman of the B'nai Brith Foundation division.

As most tribute dinners within the Jewish community are also fundraisers, the tables of ten cost $2,000 each. By the first week in March, all forty-five tables were sold out. Tridel bought five tables and gave the tickets to NCJW, Toronto, for the girls to attend at no cost.

The week before the dinner was March break, and the Pepearson family, as they were affectionately called (Jane Pepino, her husband Jamie Pearson, and their three children), joined our family for a week in Manzanillo, Mexico, where I worked on my dinner speech. By now Jane had become one of my dearest friends. We shared many hours of conversations on issues ranging from the serious to the trivial. We both enjoyed and appreciated men, though our tastes were very different. Her feminism didn't require that she become anti-male as it did for so many others. As a result, she was highly respected by both the men in power and the women's groups who were trying to find non-militant, non-threatening ways of improving opportunities for women. As a development lawyer, Jane was absolutely brilliant when it came to strategizing the rezoning process for her various clients, of which Tridel was only one.

One very hot morning, we decided to go shopping in Manzanillo while our husbands took all the kids scuba diving. Once in the main part of town, we got lost wandering around. Pretty soon we got nervous, as some of the local men appeared to be following us. I wanted to start running when Jane, ever prepared, pulled out a big, black folder and flipped it open. Eureka! A big gold police badge. Apparently she'd received it as a member of the Metro Police Commission. She held it out in front of her like a shield, and everyone backed off. Instantly. Under this odd aegis, we scurried back to our cab. We laughed a lot, but for a few minutes we were both really scared.

◆ The night of my dinner was an incredible evening. My husband Jerry, who was a sportswear manufacturer, had his designer create the most spectacular ivory silk *peau de soie* suit for me, all beaded, for the occasion. He and the children were so proud that night and I was so happy.

When David arrived, he looked at me and said, "My God, that outfit is fit for a Queen." From that day on, that suit became known as the "Queen suit."

The whole evening was videotaped and during the Starr Affair, the CBC aired excerpts. The comments of various speakers were very flattering. David's remarks, as well as those of Ian Scott, referred to my determination when it came to reaching my goals and never letting anything stand in my way. They also referred to me as "our Patti."

◆ One week after the dinner, on Tuesday, March 31, 1987, I got another 7:00 a.m. phone call. It was Hershell.

"We're in trouble with Chaviva. The nomination meeting is only a week away. Our numbers show she's going to lose. We need help. Will you talk to the guys?" (meaning the DelZottos).

David Peterson had been wooing Chaviva Hosek to run for the Liberals in the next election, and when she'd finally agreed, there was lots of press hoopla. Then it was announced she would run in the riding of Oakwood, located in the St. Clair-Dufferin area of Toronto, in the heart of the Italian community. The Liberal party workers in that area greatly resented her and the premier for parachuting her into their riding. They felt, and rightly so, that this was their turf. They had worked hard to organize it, and one of their "own" was entitled to the nomination. The fact that Chaviva was a woman, and Jewish, didn't help.

Until that morning phone call, none of us had been contacted for help. We had understood that her nomination campaign was being run by Vince Borg. So, with only one week to go, the request was unexpected.

"What's the matter? Can't the former driver deliver?" I asked.

"Patti, I don't have time for pettiness," Hershell snapped. "We're running out of time and David needs to show his ability to control the party politics. He also wants Chaviva in his Cabinet. Can you get the guys to help?"

"Hershell," I said, "the nomination meeting is only eight days away. It's impossible. Okay, I'll see what I can do."

TEMPTING FATE

Ten minutes later Chaviva called. "Hershell said you would help. I want to thank you," she said.

Ten minutes after that, David called. There was a lot of static, so I assumed he was in his car. "We need help, Patti. We're going to blow it if something isn't done right away." He actually sounded humble.

"I'm unavailable for a while, so Hershell is acting for me," he went on. "Arrange a meeting with whoever is necessary and Hershell will attend on my behalf. My credibility is on the line."

I met with Angelo and Elvio DelZotto later that day. They had already gotten some background on the nomination fight going on in Oakwood. The riding had been represented in the past by an Italian, and the other serious contender for the nomination this time round was an Italian, Ottavio Ariganello, who was closely connected to some prominent and well-liked Italian leaders like Joe Volpe and Tony Ianno.

Even though Elvio had some misgivings because of the political fallout, the DelZottos were prepared to support Chaviva against some of their own — because of their great respect for her, not because David had asked. They knew that old rivalries and grudges would be awakened, but Angelo, who had heard Chaviva speak at the Violence Symposium of 1985, and had read some of her publications, was adamant in his support of her.

He called in his right-hand man, Mario Giampietri. If anyone could pull it out of the hat in eight days, Mario could.

✧ On Friday, April 3, 1987, a breakfast meeting was held at 8:00 a.m. at the Inn on the Park. In attendance, besides me, were Angelo and Elvio DelZotto, Hershell Ezrin, Mario Giampietri, and Councillor Betty Disero, who was critical to any political success in Oakwood. Betty had served as a school trustee prior to her election to City Council. She was well known and liked within her riding and the Italian community in general. Given her background, many ethnic women related to her. More important, she had political smarts. She had a lot of credibility, as she was a tough but very straight-up politician who could deliver when it counted.

Missing from this group, but just as critical to success, was Joe Foti, a former City of Toronto employee, friend of the Liberal party, and absolute kingmaker in local Italian politics. Joe was up in the air, literally, en route home from Australia.

Hershell was, as always, brilliant in his presentation. He spoke of the ongoing desire of the Peterson government to bring in the best and brightest to serve. Individuals like Chaviva Hosek, with their education and integrity, were critical to lifting the level of our elected representatives. The premier had considered it quite a coup to get her to join his team. He had gone out on a limb, and now his credibility was on the line. Hershell took the responsibility, personally, for using bad judgment in relying on "amateurs" — people who talked about what they could do rather than actually delivering — for the nomination. He asked for our help.

Angelo, who rarely speaks in public, did. He explained his tremendous feelings of respect and admiration for Chaviva and why she was worthy of support. Her precise commentaries on the unequal opportunities for women in the workplace and the extra pressures on them sensitized him to the problems of working women trying to balance home and careers. As well, she had made him aware of the plight of battered and abused women in such an effective and moving way that he had never forgotten it. He believed she'd make a brilliant Cabinet minister, especially in portfolios like Education or Finance, where she was so qualified.

"She'll be an inspiration for other young women," he said. "After all, I have two daughters of my own." With that, he turned to Mario and told him to do whatever was necessary to get the job done.

When Hershell left, Angelo asked Mario what he would do about getting Joe Foti on side, given the politics of the riding. It was agreed that Foti had to be picked up at the airport and hustled out before the other factions could get to him. He'd have to be persuaded to support Chaviva before he committed to another candidate.

I wasn't there, but I'm told it was like a Keystone Cops movie, with Mario and Betty hustling Joe through the airport with a coat over his head, into his car, and back to the Foti home before the other interested parties who were waiting for him knew he had arrived and was gone. Personal phone calls from the premier and his top aides helped Joe agree to commit his support to getting Chaviva the nomination. The election would be another matter.

The next morning, a Sunday, Chaviva, Betty, Elvio, Mario, and I were at Joe Foti's home. Over the next several hours, more than one hundred and fifty Italian gentlemen, many from outside Metro, came to "pay their respects" and meet Chaviva. Standing on either side of her were Elvio and Joe Foti. Mario was working the room and getting commitments of support.

Betty and I were relegated to serving the proscuitto, cheese, bread, and wine to those present, and we loved it. It was absolutely fascinating. Everyone came in the back door, a traditional way of showing warmth and friendship. Only strangers come to one's home via the front door. Many of the men bowed when they shook hands with Elvio and most of the conversations were in quietly spoken Italian. Chaviva, who would ultimately become fluent in Italian, said a few words. The respect shown to the DelZotto family was impressive.

The volunteer team, mobilized by Mario, included office workers, door knockers, sign crews, and drivers. The premier's office assigned a bright, young political operative, John Webster, to work with us as their liaison. He was part of Elinor Caplan's staff.

Once Chaviva was nominated, they would stay on to help with the election. Betty organized all the riding membership on her computer and Joe Foti made the phone calls. Joe Riccuiti, another well-respected Italian Canadian, was brought in to help coordinate. For four days everyone worked night and day. It was necessary to identify those who would be eligible to vote in the nomination process, and where possible, to try to persuade them

A 7:00 a.m. Phone Call

to support Chaviva. If they were already committed to someone else, we tried to change their minds.

Joe Foti's house was the command centre. Drivers, cars, vans, were rounded up in order to make sure that every single person who said they would vote for Chaviva was driven to the meeting, scheduled for April 8, 1987, at the Holy Blossom Temple on Bathurst Street. The phones rang day and night.

This all-out effort also forged friendships and loyalties that never wavered during the horrors to come. At least almost never. In the annals of grassroots politics, it was a classic.

My job, of course, was to seek contributions, primarily for the election to come. We never considered losing the nomination fight. Many large developers and corporate executives I knew personally were solicited. They all responded positively. A candidate like Chaviva made it easy. Several of my NCJW colleagues volunteered to make phone calls on her behalf.

Everyone assumed that when Chaviva won, given her academic brilliance and her executive position with Gordon Capital, she would be made minister of Education, or Finance, or something fitting her credentials. For all of us, it was truly a labour of admiration and respect.

✦ Nomination night was ugly, very ugly. Lots of innuendoes against the DelZottos were whispered and most of the arguments were spoken in Italian. Naturally there were cracks made about Jews. You could have cut the tension in that hall with a knife.

However, when Elvio arrived a noticeable deference was shown. He said very little, just stood at the back of the hall. At six foot three, he was hard to miss.

And then I saw them. People marching in front of the temple carrying placards that read, "(JEW) HOSEK SUPPORTS ABORTIONS, JEWS KILL THE UNBORN, OAKWOOD FOR ITALIANS." And they were chanting obscenities and anti-Semitic slogans. All of a sudden, I was fourteen years old again. "I'm going to kill those anti-Semitic animals, Mario," I shrieked. And with that, I flew down the steps of the temple towards Bathurst Street where they were marching. Mario and Joe Riccuiti came flying after me, with Elvio yelling, "Patti, don't, don't!" I didn't hear anything. All I saw were those signs and all I heard were their taunts, and in front of a Jewish temple.

Joe and Mario grabbed me and had to drag me back and throw me in Mario's car. Without realizing it, I had fought them off so hard that Mario's cheek was scratched and Joe Riccuiti's shirt and tie were askew. For a few seconds I didn't know where I was.

Lucky for me the reporters who witnessed that scene never reported it. I was shaking and crying and pounding poor Mario's arm with rage and frustration. How dare they? How could those narrow-minded bigots get away with parading up and down with their inflammatory signs? Who gave men the right to tell women what they could or could not do with their bodies? Did any of those people ever provide foster care to abused and neglected children? Did they care what happened after these children were born? No! After a while I calmed down. Mario and Joe took longer.

However, the incident soon became one of the vignettes of Chaviva's nomination, with both Mario and Joe telling variations of the story over the years.

Chaviva won the nomination.

✧ Mario took charge of Chaviva's campaign, along with Joe Foti, Joe Riccuiti, Toni Varone, Paul Pelligrini, John Colloleo, and some other loyal and competent Liberal political operatives. That same team would be brought together again during the federal election of 1988 to help Jim Peterson in Willowdale.

A well-organized campaign is impressive to see. Volunteers walk up both sides of a street, knocking on doors and asking first for support and then for permission to put a sign on the lawn. The candidate follows behind to speak personally to anyone who wishes.

In this riding, people basically wanted to see Joe Foti, Mario, and Joe Riccuiti. Chaviva would often be waved at, but most of the residents were satisfied to support her if those guys did. By now everyone knew that she was a friend of the DelZotto family, and that helped.

When I went out campaigning, I was usually relegated to following Mario or Joe around with the printed flyers or taking down complaints. A sign crew followed behind the march, and as soon as someone was willing to have a sign, bang, it was put in immediately. A whole street could be blanketed with election signs within fifteen minutes. Sometimes Chaviva and I would walk down the middle of the road while the guys worked both sides of the street.

It was during these walks that Chaviva began instilling in me a commitment to women's issues, and in fact, to women in general. Until I met her, Jane Pepino was the only kind of feminist I respected. My experience with women had often been negative and marred by a lot of petty jealousies and backbiting. In Chaviva, however, I saw the epitome of what a woman could be, and I started to think about getting involved in the feminist movement.

Chaviva was part of a women's support system that seemed to be predicated on respect and trust rather than jealousy and suspicion. Many times, especially during pressured political situations, I wished I could shoot the breeze and brainstorm different strategies from a woman's perspective. But in my world at that time, ladies didn't get into the action the way I loved to; it was "unseemly." So it was only the men to whom I was able to relate when it came to the business of politics. Why couldn't more women develop the same kind of networking that men relied on, and that in fact Chaviva and Jane seemed to be a part of? I wanted to pursue the possibility.

Sometimes Jane Pepino would join us, not to actually campaign for Chaviva, since she was a staunch Tory, but to show her personal support for Chaviva, whom she respected. It was a whole new chapter for me.

They, on the other hand, were impressed with my ability to

"get it done," whatever "it" happened to be. Chaviva and Jane once had a conversation about me as though I wasn't even there.

"How do we turn the words ruthless political fixer into a nice, ladylike description?" they asked each other.

"Facilitator — that's it! From now on, you're a facilitator," they laughed. The truth was, perception far exceeded the reality, but that's the way they saw things.

At first I questioned their admiration for me, but eventually I came to feel more confident in who I was and who they were. I could stickhandle any project through political opposition, and this allowed them to keep above the fray. It was an effective combination that worked for us, since I loved the action and they loved the high ground.

Chaviva won the election by 2,500 votes.

And how did David Peterson show his appreciation to the DelZotto brothers? By appointing Chaviva Hosek to his Cabinet as minister of Housing, effectively cutting off Tridel's ability to lobby or expand their development interests in the province. Perceived conflict of interest and fear of the taint of political favouritism proved to be solid barriers.

CHAPTER EIGHT

Chairman of the Board

With the nomination of Chaviva Hosek, my political fortunes took another upswing. I was seen as a power broker, though once again, perception exceeded reality. It was the rest of the team that had delivered the nomination and election, not me.

I was becoming uneasy about my growing reputation for always being able to pull the rabbit from the hat. It meant constant pressure to keep on delivering, whatever that might mean. But I was being invited everywhere, lavished with attention, and treated as a VIP. It was unlike anything I had ever known before. I loved it, and pushed any misgivings out of my thoughts.

Thanks in large measure to Jane Pepino, some federal and municipal doors were opening for me. Her networking on my behalf added to my credibility. I had developed the ability to juggle several different projects at once, as well as raise lots of money. But so what? Where was I going? I was still floundering, looking for direction. I was jumping from project to project.

"Jane, you always talk about career paths," I said to her one day in April 1987. We were at my favourite place for lunch, Il Posto in Yorkville, one of the trendiest blocks in Toronto. I was there at least twice a week.

"I don't know where I'm going. I don't have nearly the power people think I do. I'm always being asked for favours, for introductions and the like. I keep driving myself to deliver on everything."

TEMPTING FATE

It was Jane's birthday and we had decided to celebrate with a two-hour lunch. We sat at my usual corner table and put away a whole bottle of wine. I remember that day so vividly because Mila Mulroney also came in for lunch, accompanied by her RCMP security. She spoke to Jane, of course, and she impressed me with her graciousness.

"Even though it's true that power is an aphrodisiac, I'm getting uneasy. So many of the power people I deal with now are so shallow. Full of complimentary words to one's face, but who knows what they say behind closed doors. But I'm afraid if I stop, everything will disappear. Sometimes I feel like I'm living a dream, with everything simply an illusion that will soon evaporate. I'm forty-five years old. I need security. Help me channel my energies and abilities towards a goal that will provide it."

Jane, as usual, was ready with a response that was right to the point, no holds barred. "You're trying to walk too many thin lines," she said. "Your volunteer life, with awards, board memberships, and unlimited corporate and political access, is starting to conflict with your backroom political manoeuvres, especially where the Grits are concerned. I've told you this before. You're hiding behind your volunteerism. You're playing both sides of the street. It's going to backfire. It's time to get out."

"But NCJW needs me," I said. "We're talking about another housing project. Fundraising is getting harder and we're relying more and more on grants to fund the operations. Ten years ago our operating budget was less than $75,000 a year. Today it's $500,000. We sponsor so many community service programs. Besides, I've spent my entire adult life as a volunteer there, almost twenty-five years."

"You're deluding yourself, Patti," she said. "You and I both know that no one is indispensable. They'll get along just fine without you. Why don't you come up with some splashy fundraiser that will give them a kickstart on their own and then you can retire gracefully?"

"Well," I said, "when the sales tax rebate for the Prince Charles is approved, the girls and I decided to ask Tridel to let us keep half of it. Maybe after that."

"Are you talking about the rebates the builders get for sales tax paid on 'bricks and mortar'?" she asked. (Non-profit groups with a registration number are exempt from that tax. Since the builders usually pay it at the time of construction, getting a refund isn't uncommon.) "Tridel will never go for it," she went on. "Didn't you sign your rights away when NCJW completed the development contract?"

"No, we didn't. Martin Applebaum and I got into a little difference of opinion at the meeting with our lawyers Robins, Appleby, Kotler, and I refused to sign it. However, since Tridel was so generous to NCJW and kept putting extras into the Prince Charles, the girls felt it was only right to relent and apply for the rebate anyhow. We'd then turn it over to them, naturally anticipating a very generous donation to our services. NCJW's accountant gave us a statement reinforcing the position that Tridel was entitled to the rebate because of the construction costs already paid on our behalf."

"Well, good luck," Jane answered. "I've never heard of the sponsoring group getting the rebates. It always goes to the builder by prearranged agreement." Jane then took the opportunity to bring up another point. "I've told you several times that I'm extremely uncomfortable with the political activities you girls are getting into. I raised it with one of my colleagues and he isn't so sure you're covering your rear end. Are you sure you're okay with it?"

"Of course," I answered. "Remember, Lesley Miller's husband Ron is our principal lawyer, and Marsha Slavens is an officer of NCJW's board. You know that Eric Slavens and I work together in the community. He's the treasurer of the Canadian Jewish Congress (Ontario) and I'm the assistant treasurer. We've discussed all this a million times. If there was something wrong, they would have said something, especially since their wives are very active members of our group."

"I hope so," she said.

I ignored the skeptical look on her face. I wish I hadn't.

TEMPTING FATE

✧ Back in 1979, as NCJW's community service projects were starting to expand, we began to realize how important political access would be for our organization. So we began attending political dinners as a group. In 1982, our executive reinforced the decision to continue participating politically whenever we felt it was appropriate and to the extent that we could afford it. In 1985, the monumental lobbying that went on to get the Prince Charles housing project approved underscored for us the importance of political activity as a means to our ends.

This activity was discussed with our lawyers, our accountant, and Eric Slavens, who was the managing partner of Laventhol & Horwath, a prominent firm of chartered accountants. They were the first to use the term "gray area" in reference to us. Section 87-1(8) of the Income Tax Act, Charities Division, says, "Whether a particular activity is fundamentally charitable or fundamentally political depends on the facts of the particular situation; it is a matter of degree that must be judged on a case-by-case basis." Their opinion was that at worst, Revenue Canada could rule that our activities did not fall under their guidelines and we would have to stop. Until such time, we could carry on as we were, as long as we did so in an open and forthright manner.

And so we continued with our political activities, never using, for political purposes, funds that we had raised in the name of NCJW's services and for which a charitable receipt was issued.

In February 1987, Council House was upside down with renovations. The provincial government, through the Ministry of Culture and Communications, had approved our 1986 grant application for $1,500,000, which would allow us to get the building outfitted with automatic doors, an elevator accessible to the disabled, ramps, accessible washrooms, additional classrooms for the literacy and ESL classes, and air conditioning. We were all busy cleaning out files and cupboards when we found a circular from Revenue Canada that had recently been mailed to all charitable organizations. In the office with me were some of my NCJW colleagues and our bookkeeper.

It said, "A charity (or its supporters), that wishes to sponsor political activities which go beyond the limits permitted by the Income Tax Act, may set up a separate tax-exempt organization or TRUST to pursue those activities which would otherwise interfere with the charity's status under the Act."

It went on to say that "a registered charity may pursue its charitable purposes by undertaking limited political activities that, when ancillary and incidental to a charity's established charitable purposes and activities, are permitted within expenditure limits."

In my opinion this meant that certain political activity, especially on behalf of our housing project(s), clearly fit into this regulation as long as we didn't use money that had been receipted as a charitable donation. All that was required was the creation of a separate non-profit trust (our Capital Fund). We could then invest the capital without having to distribute 80 percent of it in a given year and use the earned interest to offset NCJW's administration costs. We would also use these monies to buy tickets for political events. The gray area would then become white.

I called Eric Slavens immediately and told him what we'd just read.

"If my interpretation is right," I said, "then we're really going to put the heat on Tridel to give us part of the sales tax rebate. What do you think?"

He said it sounded good and he'd get back to us. He suggested we ask our NCJW accountant to call Ottawa without mentioning any names. We then called our lawyers, and their response was the same.

Our accountant spoke to five different bureaucrats in Ottawa at Nita Goldband's direction (NCJW president) and made notes on what they said, which was essentially what we had already been told.

I especially remember Eric's comments. "Well, Patti," he said, "it looks like you've found a loophole. Maybe you and I should take your act on the road." At the time it seemed funny. The girls with me also thought it was funny.

"I still want you to set this up properly," he went on. "I'm sure you girls will have to incorporate another entity. Speak to Ron. It has to be done through the Ministry of Consumer and Commercial Relations." Hooray, Monte Kwinter, we all mouthed.

My colleagues and I were now seeing the possibility of long-range financial security for NCJW's programs. Another housing project would add a further $200,000 in consulting fees to our coffers. It was our intention to invest whatever capital we could accumulate and use the interest to offset Council House's operating expenses. From this would also come the money for our political dinners.

It also meant, especially for Nita, Lesley, and me, an opportunity to begin easing out of our full-time volunteer commitments to NCJW. We could hand over the reins to new leadership, along with a secure financial base — one we had not inherited ten years earlier.

✧ In June 1987 NCJW received the $250,000 sales tax rebate on the building materials used in the construction of the Prince Charles. The overall cost of the project was $12 million. I went over to Tridel's offices to ask Angelo to let us keep half the money. After a discussion with him, it was agreed that NCJW's Capital Fund would keep all of it, in lieu of any further payments from Tridel relevant to consulting fees or costs on the Prince Charles and the upcoming Ridley project at Avenue Road and Wilson.

When I came back to Council House, everyone was ecstatic. After a lengthy discussion with several executive members, we agreed that the officers of this Capital Fund were to be Marsha Slavens; Lesley Miller; Nita Goldband; Eveline Berger (treasurer, NCJW, Toronto); and me. I would be the sole signing officer of the Fund, for several reasons. Ron Miller, Lesley's husband, was our lawyer. Since some of the interest from this fund was going to pay for NCJW's political activity, having his wife as a signing officer might constitute a conflict of interest for him. Eric Slavens, Marsha's husband, was a Tory, and the campaign chairman for Barbara McDougall. He was concerned that Marsha's signature on cheques for Liberal events might come back to haunt him. Sam Goldband, Nita's husband, was a developer. He owned Midtown Properties, which had been part of the Cadillac Properties buyout deal, coordinated by Eddie Cogan, a well-known developer. I was in the process of trying to get rezoning approval on one of their other projects, for which I had insisted that they make a donation to NCJW in lieu of a consulting fee (they did). Sam and I agreed that Nita's signature on any cheques for political events might be deemed a conflict. Eveline Berger was hoping to become the next president of NCJW, Toronto. We all agreed she should wait until her election was in the bag before becoming a signing officer on this account to avoid any unforeseen problems.

The document authorizing me as the sole signing officer was signed by Lesley, Nita, and Eveline, all officers of NCJW, Toronto Section, with Marsha Slavens included in the original document of incorporation. This information was then reported to the board of NCJW, Toronto, along with our plans for continued political activity. More than forty board members were listed as being in attendance, including some national NCJW members. Support was strong.

✦ Halfway through our bottle of wine at Il Posto, Jane and I got into the subject of Ontario Place.

My appointment as chairman of its board was already known within government circles, but it wouldn't be made public until after the visit of one of the Japanese royal family, scheduled for May 1987. I had promised Premier David Peterson I wouldn't say anything much until then. It was killing me to keep my mouth shut.

"Here's where your future career path might begin," she said, referring to Ontario Place. "The waterfront has tremendous potential for creative development if all three levels of government can get together on a long-range plan. Since you already sit on boards appointed by each, you might be able to act as a catalyst to get the wheels in motion, and then be in line for a senior position for the implementation."

She agreed with my decision not to take any per diem for the time I might spend at Ontario Place beyond that of the board meetings held once a month. It could then never be suggested that money was the motivator for my hands-on involvement. In my tax bracket, over 50 percent of my earnings went to Revenue Canada anyway.

We also made a pact that we would never charge each other for time spent working on each other's projects. Any lobbying or consulting Jane needed for a client, I would do gratis. Any legal advice or access that she could provide me with would also be done gratis. In this way, we'd never have a conflict problem between us and our advice to each other would always be free of monetary considerations.

✦ In early May of 1987, my husband Jerry and I, along with Wilma and Monte Kwinter, attended a reception at Ontario Place in honour of the brother of the Emperor of Japan.

It was strategic that few people knew of my upcoming appointment as this gave me the opportunity to observe the operation of Ontario Place incognito.

I fell in love with the place, an island of splendid architecture and serenity, away from the bustle of the city. The way the buildings sat over the water on steel pilings, the futuristic look of the Cinesphere from a distance, the feeling that lingered even when the Forum was empty, the happy sounds from the waterplay area for children, the cool breezes blowing off Lake Ontario as you walked along the winding paths — it was a world away from it all.

Ontario Place had been established in 1972 by the late John Robarts, premier of Ontario, as a Crown corporation, to replace the government building on the Canadian National Exhibition grounds across the road. It consists of three artificial islands holding five pod structures, including a Children's Village, restaurants, the Cinesphere, and the Forum. A three-hundred-plus-slip marina is also located there. By the time I was appointed chairman, Ontario Place was a waterpark complex renowned across North America. As with all Crown corporations, it is administered by an appointed board of directors which sets direction and policy.

Board members are paid a per diem of $150 per meeting, and meetings are usually held once a month. In addition, the chairman is entitled to $175 for every day (over two hours) spent at Ontario Place on the park's business. The role of staff is to advise on, assist with, and implement all policies set out by the board. The job descriptions of both board and staff are clearly defined, as are those of most boards and commissions, whether federal, provincial, or municipal.

After the reception, the Kwinters walked over every inch of Ontario Place with us. We talked excitedly of its potential and tossed around ideas of how it could be used to bring a greater focus on the waterfront.

Monte had once been chairman of the Harbour Commission and belonged to the Island Yacht Club, where his sailboat was "perched." He had coordinated the Tall Ships visit to Toronto. He reminisced, nostalgically, about his involvement with waterfront issues and how much he missed being part of the action there.

I felt so comfortable sharing this happy afternoon with our friends. When Jerry and I had first met the Kwinters back in 1984, we had hit it off right away. Wilma was fun to talk to, sincere, and down-to-earth. After Monte's election in 1985 and his subsequent appointment to the provincial Cabinet, she never changed, at least not to us. My two younger sons, who were nine and six at the time we first met, loved Wilma, especially since they thought she was related to the Flintstones.

The Kwinters were big fans of the House of Chan, a restaurant Jerry and I partly owned. Rarely did a week go by when one or both of them weren't our guests for dinner there. We believed they had become close and caring friends.

In early June, almost a week after my appointment became official, I still had not been contacted by any Ontario Place officials. Virginia Cooper was the general manager. Six other senior managers reported to her, along with a further one hundred permanent employees. Seasonal staff (Ontario Place was open four months of the year) accounted for another twelve hundred positions.

Unwilling to wait any longer, and feeling so enthusiastic, I finally called down to Ontario Place and identified myself to the general manager's secretary. She asked me to hold. A few moments later she told me the general manager was busy and would call me back. She did, the next day. Hardly the enthusiasm one would expect to be shown a new chairman! Nonetheless, we amicably set up a meeting for a few days later at her office.

When I pulled up to the gate, the guard asked my name. "Sorry, madam, I don't have you listed as a guest or a passholder," he said. "You'll have to turn around and park in the other lot and walk in through general admissions." I asked him to check again, which he did, but my name wasn't on his list.

It was just the type of situation that fed my persistent sense of insecurity. The bait was being dangled, and I bit. "Get the general manager on the phone," I ordered in a very cold voice, "and tell her the new chairman of the board has arrived."

The poor kid's face went white. He opened the gate immediately while he called up to the main office. There was no way this wasn't a deliberate slight, I fumed to myself. Perhaps someone was trying to establish their territory.

Later I was told about the joke circulated by one of the senior managers to staff that morning: "The new chairman has just flown in and she can't find a place to park her broom." Actually, I thought it was funny and repeated it to everyone.

In the reception lobby that day, I was left to sit for another twenty minutes. By now I was livid. I proceeded to walk down the hall towards the general manager's office, unannounced. Her secretary looked me up and down and asked for my name. When I gave it, she got up with contemptuous slowness and knocked on Virginia's door.

A very apologetic Virginia appeared. "Someone must have

forgotten to arrange for your admittance," she said. She couldn't understand it, but she'd look into it right away. I decided to give her the benefit of the doubt.

She then introduced me to the rest of the senior managers, some of whom were friendly and enthusiastic, some of whom were not.

For the next three months, every petty irritant that could be thrown in my face, was. Virginia was supportive, but I kept hearing the old comments from some of the others. "Are all Jewish people aggressive?" "Do all you Liberals drive Cadillacs?" "Do all you people have money?"

I was unprepared for this negative reception. It might have been caused by personal animosity, political interests, or just a natural contempt for a Liberal do-gooder, as I was sometimes called behind my back. But I also began to wonder if the real cause was fear, and if they had something to hide.

I handled it the only way I knew. And it was the wrong way. Confrontation. The more they goaded me, the more vigorously I reacted.

I shouldn't have been surprised that new blood would be unwelcome at Ontario Place, especially after eighteen years. During the times I had met with David and his people prior to my appointment to discuss Ontario Place and the waterfront, they told me they had concerns. There had already been one scandal resulting in the arrest of a former senior manager a few years earlier.

As the Tories had been in power for so long, it didn't take much imagination to figure out how well established the network was!

I knew that the power of the bureaucracy was even stronger than that of the politicians, who are only in power at the whim of the electorate. The wheels of government continue no matter who is elected and which party is in power. And the spokes of those wheels are greased by the civil service.

After forty years of Tory rule, maybe they were afraid of the new Liberal regime. It never occurred to me, at least at that point, that vested interests along the waterfront and inside government were worried about their turf and unsure what direction Ontario Place might take.

At meetings discussing the situation, David had sat in a chair with his feet up on the coffee table, tie undone, chain smoking, and swearing like a trooper. His door was always open, and during our discussions about Ontario Place, Bob Carman, secretary of the Cabinet (Ontario's chief bureaucrat) would often wander in, along with Hershell Ezrin or Gordon Ashworth. Anytime I was there, Vince Borg wasn't.

"We've got to figure out a way to control what's going on at the rest of the waterfront," David would say. "I could declare a provincial interest, but that would make the municipals go nuts and the shit would really hit the fan. There's so much porkbarrelling going on down there. It's already costing the province close to $4,500,000 a year to subsidize Ontario Place. Who knows if it's worth keeping? Let's try to find out."

He'd laugh, almost diabolically, and tell me, "Letting you loose down there is sure to shake up the bureaucrats!" One time he gestured grandly and said, "Carte blanche, madam, you've got it. Apply some of your famous deal-making skills to the place and maybe we can turn it around. As far as I'm concerned, the existing staff can all go, especially the dynamic duo who are running the place now.

"You've got a good deputy minister of Tourism there, and Carman will try to keep things moving smoothly. As soon as you have a problem, let us know directly. I'm putting Clare Copeland, CEO of Granada Industries, in as your vice-chairman. I have a feeling you'll hit it off, once Copeland gets over the shock."

Clare was a very close friend of David's youngest brother, Tim. Nobody was ever sure what Tim actually did for a living, since he always said he was "dabbling in this and that" when asked. But he was a lot of fun and both his older brothers treated him with obvious affection.

Clare was a delightful man, very supportive and creative, though he had an old-fashioned view of a woman's role — at least that's what he said. But never once in the two years we worked together at Ontario Place did he do anything but provide constructive suggestions and show absolute loyalty to both Ontario Place and me.

David also told Gordon to arrange a meeting between Duncan Allen and me. Dunc was David's newly appointed special adviser on waterfront issues, and he would be the premier's liaison, his man in charge. This would promote the appearance of David's being hands off, of his relying on a representative to deal with the different interests down there. Duncan was given a lot of leeway. He was an experienced bureaucrat in the days when governments still encouraged creative entrepreneurs to work in partnership with them. Like so many of his colleagues, he brought expertise, experience, vision, and good humour to his task.

He was also quite irreverent when it came to politicians and their power. He was impressed by very little, and skeptical about any commitments politicians made, either publicly or privately. He often warned me not to believe everything "they" said. He had been burned during his years in government, despite promises made to him. At our first meeting we just looked at each other and burst out laughing, as we had both heard such exaggerated stories about each other. Well, maybe they weren't so exaggerated. We had been "prepared" for each other's shortcomings, as delineated by mutual friends.

All the warnings had been unnecessary. We had the right chemistry, and our mutual respect was immediately evident.

David usually called people by their last names, whether they were present or not. To my face, he most often called me Madam Starr. On this particular day, he was up — very enthusiastic and confident. Things were going well. The economy was good, his popularity was soaring, the coffers of the Liberal party were overflowing. Only Gordon, of all the people around David during those months, kept trying to remind him, and everyone else, that politics is like show business.

"You're only as good as your last hit," he'd say over and over again. He kept counselling prudence, especially when it came to long-range plans.

TEMPTING FATE

◆ In June 1987, when I had just begun my term of office at Ontario Place, Paul Godfrey and I had lunch at one of his favourite spots, the King Edward Hotel. At this point, Paul Godfrey was president of the *Toronto Sun*. He wanted to help me "take off" in my new role, and he suggested that some joint promotions with the *Toronto Sun* might be a good idea. As a first step, he had in mind to assign one of his senior writers to do some stories on Ontario Place's new direction. He also offered the *Sun's* services to promote some of our special events at no charge.

Paul felt the public needed another kick-start just to be reminded that Ontario Place was still going strong. After eighteen years, many people had forgotten what a wonderful place it was. In addition, with so many new attractions down at the waterfront, competition was hot and heavy. Ontario Place's budget didn't give us the dollars for promotion that we needed to make a mark in the existing market.

One evening, the Ontario Place Pops, under the direction of Boris Brott, was appearing at the Forum, featuring a musical program for children. David brought his three kids, Jane Pepino brought her three, and I brought my two youngest. We walked around the park unrecognized, and wound up at the Laura Secord ice cream stand, where everyone ordered something sinfully delicious. Then the bill was presented. Jane and I looked at David.

"Why you cheap...," he chortled. "Come on, pay up. Besides, I don't have any money on me." I paid the bill, and Jane and I spent the whole evening razzing him about being cheap and threatening to tell everyone. We also talked about Paul Godfrey's offer of help. David was impressed and commented how shrewd Paul was, since Paul obviously was laying the groundwork for some long-range plans.

As I soaked up the ambiance of the Forum, felt the excitement of not only our children but also the other kids there that evening (who all listened to Brott's wonderful orchestra with rapt attention), I felt totally energized. I had never believed more strongly that Ontario Place had a critical role to play in the lives of the people of my province.

The next day, I couldn't wait to get to Ontario Place to fill them in on Paul's offer.

"Guess what Paul Godfrey is offering?" I said, and repeated our conversation almost word for word, ending by triumphantly announcing the name and phone number of the person Paul said we should contact.

Deflating me with a cool sneer, one of the staff said, "We've never had much luck with the *Sun* before. How come Godfrey is being so helpful now? Maybe you've got some special talent nobody knows about yet. Besides, isn't Paul Godfrey a Tory?"

"What difference does that make?" I asked, my enthusiasm rapidly disappearing. "Ontario Place belongs to everyone. Why can't we just make the call and see if something can be worked out?"

"I know why he's helping you," the staffer went on. "You Jews always stick together."

"You're getting fired for that, you creep," I said.

"Try it," came the sarcastic reply. "You have no idea how things work around here. You can go running to your Liberal friends all you like. They won't be around for long, and neither will you."

"I'll be here longer than you," I answered.

After a discussion with the deputy minister, Ontario Place vice-chairman Clare Copeland, and my colleagues on the board, instructions were given to begin dismissal procedures. Legal action was threatened, but a settlement was reached and pretty soon it was over.

✦ In August, after I'd been in charge for about three months, I was contacted at my office at Council House by a group of mid-level Ontario Place managers, who asked for a private meeting. My initial reaction was reluctance, since the correct process would have been for them to ask the general manager to contact me on their behalf. Their actions, if made known to their superiors, could be grounds for dismissal. But if they were risking their jobs, the issue must be important. Besides, I was the last person to question the circumvention of due process. I'd done it more than once when circumstances warranted it.

We agreed to meet outside the Haida complex, near the main entrance to Ontario Place, where the large crowds would make our presence less noticeable.

At first we exchanged pleasantries, but I could feel an undercurrent of fear. They had come to tell me about improprieties that they felt were hurting Ontario Place. I stayed silent as they catalogued their concerns. They spoke of disappearing inventory, and food supplies arriving in one door and going out the other, with no adequate record keeping. They told me about senior managers who were eating and drinking at different restaurants and not paying for their meals, contrary to government regulations. Managers, according to them, were going to the ball games across the road at Exhibition Place and charging everything to Ontario Place. One invoice shown to me was for $440.40. They also reported drunken staff parties that had turned ugly, requiring the police to be called in.

I interrupted to ask why they were coming to me, considering the risks involved. Their reasons were simple. Most had started working at Ontario Place as summer help when they were kids. They loved the park, they loved the programs being offered to the public, and they wanted them to continue. They feared that the irregularities they saw would ruin Ontario Place, and they felt that now, with a new government and fresh faces, was the time to speak out. They were hearing bitter complaints from some senior managers about my appointment as chairman and about all the questions I was asking, and they felt I would be receptive to their concerns. They hoped something would be done. I promised that it would be.

At the end of our meeting, they provided me with further information that I decided to pursue with the help of a senior manager I trusted and two of my board colleagues. It turned out that one of Ontario Place's advertisers was making cars available to senior managers. Not only was this practice contrary to government policy, it might also be a major conflict of interest, since advertising rates and promotional perks were set by these same managers. A log book was being kept, recording who used the cars and where they went, but when I asked for it, it had "disappeared" without a trace. No further explanation was given.

We became aware that guidebooks full of advertising were being distributed at Ontario Place's entrances, where nearly eight hundred thousand people were admitted in a season. I learned that no revenue was paid to us for this highly visible free publicity, even though the publishers sold the advertising space and kept the money. When I asked for the rationale behind this giveaway, staff said that the guidebook included a map of Ontario Place and a listing of its restaurants and activities.

I set out to deal directly with the guidebook's publishers, after getting the strong backing of the board. When confronted, the guidebook's principals said they earned "only" approximately $90,000 a season. The board advised them that henceforth a $40,000 fee would have to be paid to Ontario Place if our facility was to be used to promote private-sector business. Even though the guidebook's publishers complained to the premier's office about Ontario Place's position and me personally, the board's decision stood.

Then came the discovery that another staff member was a shareholder in one of the companies that supplied services to Ontario Place. It wasn't exactly a secret, because the person was listed in their annual report. We later learned that this same person had acquired the distribution rights for equipment scheduled to be purchased for another of our concessions. An overseas phone call confirmed it. We thought this was inappropriate, and after meeting with the deputy minister, the person decided to retire, on terms that I thought were too generous.

Initially I had been unsure of what to do when I first heard about and then began to confirm some of these allegations. But I didn't waste any time before calling the key people at Queen's Park.

"Keep quiet, make notes, ask questions, but don't rock the boat, at least not yet," I was told.

The upcoming election was expected to cement the Liberals' hold on the province and make our plans for control of the waterfront more viable.

"We'll call for a special audit that will uncover some of this, if it's true," they promised.

◆ Over the next six weeks, I started going through the printouts of Ontario Place's financial operations. I also started reading the minutes of the board from the previous five years, looking for clues as to how decisions were made and who participated in them.

I received a lot of help from board colleagues and staff, most of whom were committed to the first-class operation of the park. I was amazed at the skillful way these young professionals ran the park. Most spent twelve hours a day there during the season. Their greatest concern was for safety. Every inch of the grounds, along with all the equipment and attraction rides, was checked by senior staff personally. They often invited me to accompany them, and we started to share ideas about how to attract more visitors to the site. "Better food," they would say each time we talked. "It's critical. We hear complaints every day."

We created a food services subcommittee to work on this problem. Eventually many new concessionaires opened up at Ontario Place, and most have done well.

The staff's vision of a "new" Ontario Place was ratified enthusiastically by the board. As they became more directly involved, their commitment to the park grew. Every morning at 6:00 a.m. we'd anxiously listen for the first weather reports of the day. The threat of rain invariably hurt our attendance, even if the forecasts were wrong, which they usually were.

We worked together to create a new mini-golf course, so popular with the youngsters. New audio-visual attractions, a free shuttle boat to take visitors from the main entrance to the west island, better shows at the Forum, and an enthusiastic spirit helped to increase attendance. Despite their uncertainty about the new government and the new board of directors, most of the staff were prepared to cooperate and help whenever possible. They were, and still are, true professionals.

Other disturbing discoveries were made during those first months. The amount paid out for staff salaries and overtime was not always easy to determine. Certain departments, such as food services, had been showing a profit in the reports circulated throughout the ministry, which is why sloppy record keeping had gone unchecked. Closer examination showed that most of the salaries paid to the seasonal staff, as well as overtime for senior managers in this department, were being charged to administration. When we allocated these salaries to the right place, it became clear that the food operations were actually losing almost $275,000 per year.

Through diligent scrutiny, our board learned that Ontario Place was paying about $300,000 a year to the solicitor general of Ontario, ostensibly for Ontario Provincial Police security on-site during the four-month season. Yet OPP District 5, which was providing this security, was paying for the service out of its own budget.

So where was our $300,000 actually going? Into the coffers of the consolidated revenue fund, that's where. Just another name for the Treasury. Ontario Place's deficit included a security expense, borne by the taxpayers, that was simply a journal entry, to justify the transfer of these funds to the Treasury, where they stayed. Essentially, the Ontario government was giving funds to Ontario Place with one hand and taking them back with the other. The Treasury thus ended up with an extra $300,000 to spend in legitimate but unbudgeted ways.

It was a rip-off, pure and simple. In 1988 the board refused to continue this charade.

Then we learned that Ontario Place had paid out approximately $240,000 during a single season for wining, dining, entertainment, promotion, sales meetings, and staff travel. One breakfast meeting at the Trillium restaurant, located on the western part of the site, had been billed, and approved, for $1,300.

This was the final straw for the board. From then on, staff expenditures were restricted and carefully monitored. We demanded careful records of all staff expense accounts and began to compare chits to billings and sales reports from the concessionaires. Things were not adding up. Despite the board's appreciation of staff's efforts, we had to pursue this course of action in order to fulfill our mandate.

Of course, before long, I became the focus of staff hostility.

"Things were running smoothly before she came on the scene," was one lament. "Why is she sticking her nose in where it doesn't belong?" was another one.

For the first three months, I walked around Ontario Place with a knot in my stomach, feeling as if I'd been thrown into the lions' den. I had grown to like and respect so many of the staff and did not enjoy the dislike some felt for me. Couldn't they understand that if the park became too much of a drain on taxpayers, it would have to be closed?

Then the threats started. And the anonymous letters to the press (which the press did not print) about my involvements with the "Italian Mob." And the accusations.

One of the staff members who ultimately left had been telling concessionaires that I had opened a slush fund at Ontario Place for David Peterson. Exactly how this was being done was never explained.

Even the smallest problems were ascribed directly to me. One day, at the conclusion of a job, some plumbers were let go. It got back to me that they were told I had given the direct order to fire them.

I needed advice, but I had to be careful who I asked. I didn't want to go running to Queen's Park again, especially since they were now concerned with an upcoming election and didn't want anyone making waves. So I talked to two old friends — Jane Pepino and Norm Gardner, a Metro councillor and a lifelong friend of my husband. They advised me to see the OPP.

"I'll call and make the arrangements," Norm said. Jane agreed, even though she knew of my concerns about the OPP because of what had happened to the DelZottos during the Waisberg Commission. Jane felt that what we had discovered at Ontario Place might only be the tip of the iceberg. If something really nasty was uncovered, I could be at risk. The stakes were getting higher, and I was beginning to get a little scared. But not enough to stop.

In August 1987, I told the OPP everything I knew and everything I feared. They were familiar with some of the rumours. They confirmed the drunken parties and that a couple of the staff had been charged. They promised to conduct an investigation, but suggested I encourage the provincial auditor to come in for a special audit, unannounced. They would wait for the results. I felt somewhat relieved.

In early September of 1987, a special audit of most, but not all, of Ontario Place's operations was announced, to begin the following week. Some of the staff resigned immediately.

All of this commotion was understandably disruptive to Virginia Cooper, whom I still regarded as a valuable asset to Ontario Place. I felt none of the problems were her doing. So I decided to make an overture to her. With the departure of some of her former colleagues, she appeared to warm up. I had assumed her attitude was the same as the others' — but maybe I was wrong. Perhaps she had been used by them. It would be hard for me, but I wanted to reach out to her.

Despite the constant support from Queen's Park, I still felt isolated, hurt, and disappointed. They had dropped me in the middle of a mess without adequate preparation. But if Ontario Place was going to be turned around, I would now have to make the first move of conciliation, and mean it.

The right moment came when the provincial treasurer's office sent a memo to staff demanding information about some incomplete reports. As punishment for our sins, they were threatening to hold up Ontario Place's operating grants, without which we couldn't pay our bills. After years of involvement in public boards and commissions, I knew that this kind of threat from bureaucrats was usually inflicted for some trivial transgression, real or imagined. More often than not, it was just muscle flexing on the part of some minor official wanting to feel important.

Virginia, along with some of the senior staff, was quite upset. As chairman of the board, I was notified of this "crisis." They were working feverishly on responses to the ministry and alternate plans for covering the park's operating expenses.

To put a Crown corporation through this was the stupidest waste of time and human resources I had ever seen. Did the government really intend to bounce Ontario Place's cheques? Our staff was being forced to do ridiculous paperwork when we had a park to run.

Nonetheless, Virginia, as a career civil servant, had to respond, and did so, succinctly and effectively. During our brainstorming for her report, staff started telling me hilarious anecdotes about some of the bureaucrats. For my contribution to the exercise I simply picked up the phone and called the treasurer, Bob Nixon. Everyone was laughing until he got on the phone.

With their mouths half open, they listened while I read Bob the ridiculous memo we had received from his ministry and Virginia's biting reply. He chuckled and started to hum quietly while I spoke. I went on to comment on the brainless bureaucrats and non-supportive government directives getting in our way while we were trying so hard to deliver a winning season. He burst out laughing and told me to respond in my usual way. "Just ignore it," he said. Judging from the looks on the faces of my staff, I had just earned some points.

For a fleeting moment, we really were a team. Staff and board, working in partnership. It was a philosophy I had always believed in and practised for twenty-five years. Even though I didn't really know how, I would try to be humble and extend the olive branch to those senior staff members still in place.

"Virginia," I said when we were alone, "I know I reacted very strongly to some of you when I first got here. I shouldn't have. I was wrong and I apologize. As chairman of the board, I should have risen above the pettiness. But we're two women out here facing an entrenched male dominance. You have expertise in areas I don't. I could learn a lot from you. Ontario Place will benefit if we keep working together."

Virginia seemed torn, but made no response.

In November 1987, the auditor's report on Ontario Place was released. It was critical of the park's management. The board concurred in its findings and authorized its recommendations. Virginia wrote a scathing rebuttal to the auditor and the deputy minister of Tourism and Recreation, and then resigned. I was very disappointed that I hadn't been able to persuade her to stay.

When the election was over, I got a call from Dennis Timbrell, former Tory MPP from Don Mills. He had run for, but narrowly lost, the leadership of the Progressive Conservative party in Ontario to Larry Grossman. Dennis wanted me to join him and a friend for lunch, which I was happy to do. His friend was John Bitove, Sr.

A self-made man of Macedonian descent, John was a staunch Tory and a close personal friend of Prime Minister Brian Mulroney. He was also interested in being part of any future waterfront development and was frank about his interest in getting to know me. The Peterson government was in power, he believed they'd be in power for a while, and he had heard rumblings about Ontario Place's new aggressiveness. He told me straight up at that first meeting that he thought I was fronting for the government, and not for Tridel, as was the rumour on the street.

I didn't respond.

We went on to talk about Tory politics, Liberal politics, and Ontario Place. When I related David Peterson's comments that he would have lost the election had Dennis been the Tory leader, they laughed, somewhat ruefully. This was the point they had stressed during the Liberal party's leadership race, but Dennis had lost anyway.

John then offered the services of the Bitove Corporation in any way Ontario Place might wish. I suggested that his team meet with OP's staff to see if there was a way we could work together to mutual advantage.

In 1988 the Bitove Corporation contracted to run Ontario Place's food services. A profit was made for the first time in a long time. John and I had many mutual friends and associates and for the next two years shared ideas and strategies about future development. I loved his style and charm. He also kept my office at Council House supplied with five-pound jars of Hershey kisses and ju-jubes, which Ontario Place staff made me declare as a "benefit received," since the value exceeded $200.

Over the next two years, John often warned me about my high profile and the perception people had of my ruthlessness. "Drawing attention to oneself is like tempting fate," he would say. He himself never accepted public appointments and suggested I rethink all of mine. "Backroom politics is the deadliest game of all," he would warn me. But I ignored his advice. I could handle it. After all, wasn't I as clever as everyone said I was?

My board colleagues and I continued to spend more time at Ontario Place. New staff were hired, and some exciting new attractions developed. I began to solicit corporate sponsorships for some of our attractions, specifically Forum concerts. Tridel Corporation was one of those who contributed $25,000 to sponsor the Toronto Symphony's presentation of the "1812 Overture."

We began charging for advertising space on the walkways over the Lakeshore between Exhibition Place and Ontario Place. Molson's contributed substantially during the Molson Indy race, which disrupted our access and parking. Staff did their share as well by voluntarily cutting back on their expenses and trying to streamline administration costs.

During the next two years, hands-on management by the board enabled us to reach our goal of a deficit reduction. By the fiscal year ending March 31, 1989, Ontario Place had reduced its joint operating and capital deficit by $2,100,000. In December 1989, as a result of the Starr Affair, another provincial audit was done and released on Ontario Place. It showed that during my two-year term as chairman of the board, I had spent $819 of the corporation's money on promotion, declared the candy I had received from John Bitove, and waived approximately $42,000 in the per diem payments I was entitled to for the hours spent at Ontario Place.

Despite pressures to do otherwise, our accomplishments during the 1987-89 seasons were also acknowledged. To this day, Ontario Place is a reminder of a time in my life that was filled with great challenges, happiness, and accomplishment.

CHAPTER NINE

In the Maelstrom

Early in the summer of 1987, while I was still getting my bearings at Ontario Place, I was also trying to fulfill my responsibilities at NCJW.

Council House was totally upside down with the ongoing renovations. Betty Stone had rejected the executive's offer of a retirement package, and since her lawyers had advised her not to leave until a settlement was reached, things were very tense. The air was thick with allegations and threats of reprisal.

The executive directed the section's president, Nita Goldband, to tell Betty to leave the premises, for good. Betty then launched a wrongful dismissal lawsuit against NCJW. Our lawyers, Robins, Appleby, Kotler, handled the matter.

So just as I was wading into turmoil at Ontario Place, the volunteer leadership of NCJW, Toronto, had to commit itself to sharing responsibility for the day-to-day operation of our programs until a new executive director could be hired.

This included me, and I was driving back and forth from Council House at the north end of Bathurst Street to Ontario Place at the southern end every day, usually a forty-minute drive. On top of all this, the Prince Charles housing project still required my presence, though we did have good backup staff there.

The monthly meetings at the Prince Charles were like an oasis. There I was simply an NCJW volunteer, dealing with issues that could be resolved quickly, and for the most part, positively. The enthusiasm of the residents and their appreciation of our efforts made the other pressures on me seem unimportant.

Life had turned into a frenzy of activity, which I loved. I was always on the phone, always getting messages. Ontario Place, O'Keefe Centre, Committee of Adjustment, MTHA, provincial politics — it seemed that I was being swept along by a raging river.

And my NCJW colleagues were supportive. They would step in when I had to leave meetings early and were rarely critical of the hubbub that surrounded me, most often from other commitments. They were far more tolerant of me than I would have been of them.

Most of us had been volunteering together for fifteen years or more. We had marched in Ottawa on behalf of the Soviet Refuseniks and sold serviettes at Loblaws during Passover, facing the anti-Semitic slurs together. We had watched the Prince Charles get built, brick by brick, and seen our ESL classes, literacy classes, and Kids On The Block Puppet troupe grow beyond our wildest dreams.

NCJW and my colleagues were "home" and I always tried to give them the best I could.

My husband was now semi-retired and enjoying the change in his lifestyle. This allowed him to spend more time with the kids, which they loved, as well as to pursue his own interests. He came to appreciate the children in a way many fathers never have the opportunity to do. Jerry is a fabulous cook, so our family had no problem with the change of roles. I couldn't have accomplished anything without his support, which remained constant through the good and bad times to come.

Amidst all this feverish activity, a provincial election was called for September 1987.

I was asked to come to Queen's Park to talk about the campaign. Again, David was sitting in his office, feet up, smoking and swearing. He took a few moments to compliment me on my activities at Ontario Place while noting that some of his "spies" were complaining about the ice water that obviously ran through my veins.

"This election has to be a phenomenal win so we can move ahead with our plans without those fucking NDPers," he said, blowing smoke rings. "First class all the way. We're going to need lots of money."

He gave me a lopsided smile, similar to the looks he gave when he was conning someone. "You and Borg better start getting along," he said. "Now that his girlfriend has gotten to like you, it's time you guys buried the hatchet. Besides, he's a nice guy and if you ever need a stud, he's it, or at least he can get one for you."

I felt like smacking him in the mouth, but he was the premier. Besides, he always talked that way.

Vince and I arranged to have lunch in the Legislature's dining room. He knew, along with all of the Cabinet, what was happening down at Ontario Place and my total commitment there. So when I told him I wouldn't coordinate any more fundraisers, he understood. But I did agree to contact people and corporations for donations. He asked how much I thought I could raise after the writ (the official calling of the election by the lieutenant-governor) was dropped and campaign contributions were limited, but I refused to commit to any specific amount.

Vince always chuckled when he referred to the regulation limiting contributions. We both knew that any limits could be circumvented by collecting cheques from subsidiaries of corporations, from employees, and from associates such as those in law firms. The donations could then be reimbursed under the "promotion" line of their financial statements. Receipts would be sent to those names allocated by the contributor. Nothing secretive or clever.

It wasn't anything I'd discovered myself; I'd learned it back in 1984 from Monte Kwinter's fundraising committee. At the time, Seymour Iseman, who was then president of the federal Liberal party in Ontario, had come to Council House along with his associate, Marty Cohen, to ask us to contribute $100 each to Kwinter's campaign. When we told him we didn't know how many of the girls could afford to do that, he told us that the organization could reimburse us under the loophole which he then pointed out. Tridel, however, had already bought two tables to that fundraiser and were giving us the tickets. We had no intention of spending any of our own money even if it could be reimbursed. Both of them left Council House that day quite angry.

The Commission on Election Finances raised no objection to this hundred-dollar-contribution procedure. Although the commission had been set up to regulate election contributions and was invested with far-reaching powers, including the ability to subpoena documents and levy fines, in reality little of this was done. The commission had been created, as were so many other government committees, as a makework project for old politicians and their friends. Few party pros cared one hoot about them and often let them know it.

During the hectic weeks before the election and in between my other jobs, I called people for political contributions. Given the popularity of the Peterson government and the scrambling of those who had been "in" with the Tory government to get "in" with the Liberals, raising the money wasn't too difficult. The first batch of cheques totalling $126,000 was delivered by me personally to Hershell Ezrin's office at the campaign headquarters on Adelaide Street.

Only his secretary Annie seemed to be impressed with the numbers. Everyone else acted as though it was commonplace, so I didn't think my efforts were anything special. On the one occasion that I gave cheques to Gordon, he reacted enthusiastically. We were walking around Ontario Place and I handed them over, not wanting to carry any political cheques around with me for fear of having them "disappear."

◆ Sometime near the end of this election campaign, I saw the first sign of dissension between Gordon Ashworth and Hershell Ezrin. I had walked into Hershell's office, and Annie was very upset. According to her, Hershell had committed substantial chunks of the PR for the election campaign and afterwards, for the government, to Martin Goldfarb. Even though

Gordon had been part of the Trudeau team that included the backroom boys Keith Davey, Jerry Grafstein, and Martin Goldfarb, he was very unhappy about the commitment given. Words had been spoken and Hershell had left the building. Annie then told me she was thinking of getting out of political work.

"Too much backstabbing," she said.

That night I phoned Gordon at home, to ask what was going on and if I could be of any help.

By now he and I had become close friends. Our spouses had hit it off, and we had lots of family get-togethers. Any political business we had to discuss was usually done during lunch meetings or in Gordon's office. He was a great strategist, and I doubt if anyone will ever match his political smarts. The son of a career soldier from British Columbia, he was raised in a strict United Church family. His principles, and those of his wife Dyanne, were very high. He was not one of those who flaunted rules or told lies easily to achieve an end. He was also somewhat strait-laced, and when we gossiped about certain politicians' transgressions or sexual peccadillos, he would often blush and look uncomfortable.

He insisted that we take turns picking up lunch or dinner tabs to ensure that our relationship was balanced and not open to criticism. "Equality," he would laugh. "You girls want it, I'm giving it to you. Why should men have to pay all the time?" We really were an odd couple. But somehow we had "connected" at that first meeting in early 1986 and our affection and loyalty for each other remained constant.

Dyanne and Gordon were having a dinner party a few days after my call and he said he'd talk to me then. During the evening, Dyanne, who was an excellent cook, was complaining about their old fridge.

"Why don't you go up to Midnorthern Appliances and get a new one?" I suggested. "The late owner (Ted Richmond) was a very special person in my life and his children are very close friends. Anytime I need something or send somebody up there, they get a wholesale price."

Too bad my tongue didn't fall out of my mouth.

Dyanne looked at Gordon. "Is there any problem?" she asked. "After all, we're not getting it for nothing."

"Technically, even wholesale prices might be questionable," he answered. "It's still a personal benefit."

Oh boy, what would he say if he knew how much shopping certain politicians' wives and girlfriends had done at Jerry's sportswear factory?

Then he smiled and told us that both he and Hershell had resigned from their official positions for the duration of the election campaign as per government regulations. Technically, they were unemployed, no longer civil servants and not subject to conflict of interest guidelines. And so arrangements were made for Dyanne to visit the showroom and order a fridge. She picked a floor model with an icemaker and was quite excited about it.

When it was delivered, Jerry went over to help her change some lighting and get it into place, since the delivery men had just dropped it inside the front door. I assumed, and I know she expected, that an invoice would be sent and then paid for by her. We had even discussed the price.

After the 1987 election and the tremendous victory for the Liberals, Vince Borg announced he was leaving government and joining Decima Research. To celebrate and wish him well, I hosted a small dinner party at the House of Chan with some mutual friends, including Gordon Ashworth, John and Beth Webster, and Mario Giampietri, vice-president of Tridel Corporation. Vince had decided to sell his country house and move back to the city. We discussed where he could get some appliances, including a Jennair, for his new house.

"Let me know when you're ready," I said, "and I'll tell you where to get it wholesale."

CHAPTER TEN

On the Waterfront

Throughout these months, unchecked development along the waterfront continued to be a major concern. During my meetings at Queen's Park, time was spent talking about what Peterson called the "greedy developers and their lackey political henchmen" and how they could be prevented from carving up the entire waterfront with ugly highrises before his vision could be brought to fruition.

Ontario Place was a showpiece, and it occupied a place of prominence on the waterfront. Perhaps it could be the vehicle to stop what was happening down there, or at least slow it down, he said. A plan would have to be devised, one which ensured that the public would never suspect that the province might be meddling in municipal affairs. Control of the waterfront in terms of zoning, land use, and public services rested with the municipal government — specifically Metro Toronto. Most of the lands had been given over to the city by the federal government around the time of Confederation (1867), but the provincial government could, in "extraordinary" circumstances, declare a "provincial interest" and override the decisions Metro might make. It was a power rarely used.

During discussions in the weeks before my appointment and afterward, the shape of a plan started forming. Duncan Allen, the premier's waterfront chief, became the sounding board.

Without him, it wouldn't work. He sharpened the strategy until it was razor sharp.

In a series of meetings and phone conversations that included key Cabinet ministers, lawyers from the attorney general's office (who represented Ontario Place in all matters), David Peterson himself on occasion, and some municipal politicians — specifically Tom Jakobek, we discussed strategy for taking control of the waterfront. Nineteen eighty-eight was agreed on as the opportune time for the strategy to be implemented.

Ontario Place would begin to take a direct interest in all activities surrounding it, becoming the major force along the waterfront. At the time of its development, transportation to Ontario Place was very poor and parking was inadequate. During the past few years, Exhibition Place, across the road, had been in conflict with Ontario Place over the issues of joint access, promotions, the Molson Indy, and a number of petty matters. We were losing a fortune in potential revenue because of limited access, especially since Lakeshore Boulevard was being closed at the whim of Exhibition Place's staff when it suited their interests.

As a first step, it was proposed that Exhibition Place and Ontario Place be merged, with the province holding the balance of power by creating a Crown corporation to run it. By taking an aggressive position and insisting on representation whenever and wherever the waterfront's interests were being discussed, Ontario Place could stall any decisions that might be harmful to the province's long-range plans, which included the 1996 Olympics.

And the groundwork had to begin soon, because we suspected that Toronto mayor Art Eggleton was working hand-in-hand with private developers to develop the waterfront. Lobbyist Ivan Fleischman, Art's longtime friend, was representing developers Huang & Danczkay, who had already built two controversial towers on the waterfront. Another of Ivan's clients was Harbour Quay Developments, also known as Ramparts, located on Queen's Quay on the waterfront. They were lobbying for expanded zoning approval.

At the rate things were going, there might be nothing left for the province to protect if we didn't act quickly. We would have to begin as soon as possible.

Exhibition Place, long a thorn in the side of the province, ran its own agenda. They wanted to build another mega trade centre, although the Metro Toronto Convention Centre was only a few blocks away. I think their real agenda was the development of the surrounding lands, specifically those north of Exhibition Place. A fortune could be made for any private developer with inside information on future plans and the clout to affect any political decisions, especially in relation to rezoning. But the province, with its own influence on the Ontario Municipal Board, could hold things up if they wanted to, and the "boys across the street" at Exhibition Place all knew it. Municipal law also allowed Ontario Place to have input on any development adjacent to its site that might be deemed to have an impact on our operation.

I received several calls and had a number of meetings with some of the "boys," who wanted to get a sense of how Ontario Place would react to their plans for future development. One in particular, Metro councillor Mario Gentile, was very aggressive about who should be the major player on the waterfront. He should. He was planning to take over the chairmanship of Exhibition Place and had his own plans for its development and that of Ontario Place. It never occurred to him that I was anything more than a "pretty face David Peterson had to amuse by a political appointment," as he would often put it. He was angry at what he saw as my lack of cooperation. Unfortunately, I didn't respond to his chauvinistic comments as coolly as I should have, and more often than not, shot back some snarky response about his own agenda. He wouldn't tell me whose interests he was representing, but I guessed it wasn't the public's, who would gain diddly squat from Exhibition Place's development plans other than an increase in their municipal taxes to pay for the whole thing.

At one point he was so angry he threatened to speak to former

Toronto mayor David Crombie about me. I wondered why he thought that would concern me. Crombie was a close friend of both John Bitove and Paul Godfrey, and I had a lot of respect for him. Besides, Dunc told me not to worry about Crombie.

Some of the other players at Exhibition Place included lawyer Ralph Lean, of the firm Robins, Appleby, Kotler, who was Mayor Eggleton's key fundraiser; Tom Greer, the mayor's assistant and Ivan Fleischman's bridge partner; and lawyer Gerald Charney, another bridge expert and partner of both Fleischman and Greer. Since they had such strong ties to the mayor, we believed any actions on the part of Exhibition Place (whose land was owned by the City of Toronto) had to have the blessing of Mayor Eggleton.

Harbourfront, a federal agency controlling more government land on the waterfront, was another key factor. Using "program development" for the public as its umbrella, much of their property had already been negotiated away to developers — with more to come, including the Ramparts development at 441 Queen's Quay mentioned earlier. Once again the lobbyist for this project was Ivan Fleischman, along with another former Eggleton aide, lawyer Cindy MacDougall.

Enter Ontario Place, according to plan. Transportation would be the issue.

In late July of 1987, I had made the first official approach to Dennis Flynn, chairman of Metropolitan Toronto, on the issue of future uses for Exhibition Place. The amalgamation of this site into Ontario Place was to be the first step. In November 1987, in keeping with our strategy, I officially contacted Eggleton to raise concerns about the Ramparts development. Preliminary approval had been given them to extend their proposed building about seven metres into the existing right of way. This would effectively eliminate the possibility of a light rapid transit line (LRT) along the waterfront route to Ontario Place that would make public access to our site cheaper and easier. This proposed development had to be stopped. But since any developments proposed for the waterfront would earn millions of dollars in profits for their owners and for those who lobbied on their behalf, developers/lobbyists would do almost anything to stop those opposing them (like me). The stakes were getting higher.

The province's hidden agenda was the extension of the LRT not only to Ontario Place, but farther west, eventually turning north up Islington Avenue and ultimately going to the airport. David envisioned parkland; arts and culture facilities, including a ballet/opera house; and an appropriate site for the 1996 Olympics, which he intended to get for Toronto.

If the waterfront was dotted with ugly highrises helter skelter, his plans would be nipped in the bud. To ensure that no one's antennae would start twitching, all correspondence between Ontario Place and others was to come from staff whenever possible. The board of directors knew from the beginning that the long-range plan was to take over Exhibition Place, provide adequate transportation to Ontario Place, and stop the random development along the waterfront.

On December 22, 1987, again according to plan, the first official letter of concern was sent from Ontario Place to Mayor Eggleton.

A few days later, at a cocktail party given by Dyanne and Gordon Ashworth at their home to celebrate the holiday season, I was confronted by Ivan Fleischman.

"You're sticking your nose into matters that don't concern you," he said. "You're just an amateur. Why don't you butt out. This is big boy stuff. What are you up to?"

This was bad. Had he seen through the smoke screen? Though he was a close friend of Gordon, I knew Gordon would never have told him anything.

It turned out that Ivan thought I was acting on behalf of Tridel or some other competitor's interests. He even asked me directly if any of David Peterson's friends had a piece of the waterfront they wanted to redevelop. If so, the "boys" would be happy to share the action with them. It had never occurred to him that some of us really did believe in a common goal for the benefit of the entire community, not just ourselves. He also didn't believe anything could be happening provincially that he or Art didn't know about. So that was good.

Dunc and I agreed that we needed a municipal partner, and our first choice was Tom Jakobek. Tom and I had sat on the O'Keefe Centre's board together, he sat on Ontario Place's food services committee, and most important, he was very bright, with real political smarts. He was also a key player in the Toronto Transit Commission (TTC), which was a critical part of our plan.

But first I spoke to Queen's Park to make sure that Tom was acceptable. He was.

✧ In January 1988, the first steps began. City Council's Land Use Committee was asked to reconsider the Rampart project, along with any others that might have an impact on long-range transportation planning for the waterfront. This elicited outrage from the principals and their lawyers. But our goal of easy public access and transportation across the waterfront lands was a good one, and many politicians came on side. The proposed Ramparts development was stopped.

An official letter was sent to Ralph Lean, still the chairman of Exhibition Place, asking for support in our efforts to improve public access to both our sites. He did not respond positively. We decided to go around him.

On February 24, 1988, at the direction of Queen's Park, I wrote an official letter to the Ministry of Tourism and Recreation on behalf of the Ontario Place board. In it we outlined our long-range plans for the development of Ontario Place, recognizing the potential of the 1996 Summer Olympics and Expo 2000.

We then officially requested that the province, in right of the Crown, establish control of a combined CNE–Ontario Place site under the jurisdiction of a special commission reporting to the premier. The point here was to be on record, long before the final showdown.

If our strategy worked and the premier was left smelling like a rose, then the chair of this powerful commission might be mine.

TEMPTING FATE

This was the carrot being dangled in front of me and I reached for it.

"Your biggest test is going to be keeping your direct involvement secret," Hershell said. "Other people will be front and centre, and get the credit for whatever happens. If you can lie back and keep quiet, then you'll be ready for bigger things."

Control of the waterfront is what David Crombie wanted and in fact had for a while. And it's also what Mayor Art Eggleton wanted, from day one. Only he thought it would come from his friends once all the waterfront lands were developed and in their hands.

For the next few months, Ontario Place, through its staff and board, continued to press the Land Use Committee to rethink its position on waterfront development and public transportation along the western lakeshore. Lawyers from the attorney general's office as well as government services started working on land ownership issues, very discreetly. They attended some of the city committee meetings on our behalf and no one questioned their presence. Tom Jakobek handled the internal politics and negotiations with the TTC, the city solicitor, and city planning staff.

Then pressure started coming from the developers' lobbyists and friends. They were calling Dunc regularly to complain about the screw-up going on down at the waterfront. He would then call me and laugh about their tunnel vision.

During one conference call with Bob Carman and Gordon, they all assumed I was "pleased" with being in the shadows and not participating in any of this action openly. I wasn't.

In May 1988 Hershell Ezrin contacted me about two matters. The ballet/opera house and Sonja Bata. David saw both as part of an expanded, dynamic waterfront. Sonja Bata, wife of Thomas Bata, the owner of the shoe manufacturing company Bata Limited, was a prominent and very accomplished woman. She had established a world-class shoe museum in her offices, but she felt they needed a proper home. Promises made to her by Harbourfront officials for a location were not coming to fruition because

A Brownie — that's me in the front row, third from the left, 1950.

Fourteen years old and pretending I was sixteen; with my mother, the late Beatrice Stern, 1956.

My first wedding, four days after my eighteenth birthday. The look says it all.

With me at the presentation in 1982 of the provincial grant for the NCJW movie *Two Way Street*, are *(to my right)* Bruce McCaffrey, minister of Culture and Recreation, and *(to my left)* Ruth Gillespie and Eleanor Cooper of NCJW, and David Peterson, then leader of the Opposition.

The bureaucrats behind the grants: with me are *(left)* Marek Brodzki, supervisor, Ministry of Culture and Recreation; Eleanor Cooper, president of NCJW, Toronto; and Jay Jackson, project officer, Ministry of Culture and Recreation.

Final approval, in 1984, of the model for the Prince Charles housing project, under the protective arms of Angelo DelZotto: Nita Goldband, Helen Wolfe, and me.

With me at the violence symposium in 1985 are *(left)* Dennis Timbrell, minister of Housing; Jane Pepino, Q.C., moderator of the symposium; and Angelo DelZotto, CEO of Tridel and one of the sponsors.

In 1985, with Frank Drea, minister of Community and Social Services, on the approval of the NCJW attendant care program and violence symposium grant.

A happy day, in 1985 — the Prince Charles groundbreaking. *Right photo*: Nita Goldband, me, and Lesley Miller with Gary Sandler, one of the first tenants and a force in seeing the project through. *Photo below*: Gary with John Sweeney *(left)*, minister of Community and Social Services; Angelo DelZotto; Dennis Timbrell, MPP; and John Oostrum, MP.

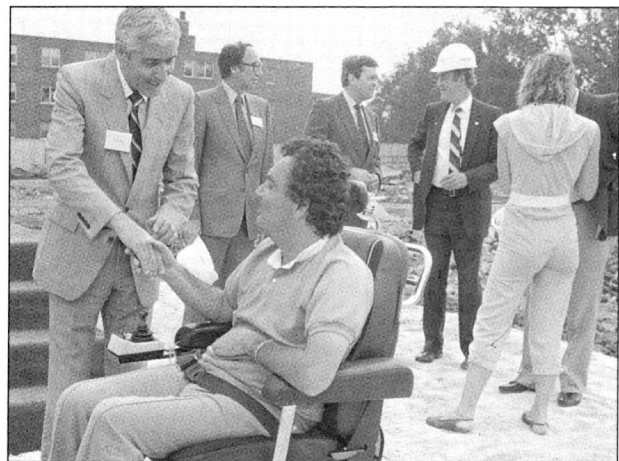

With Marty Mendelow during planning session for the 1986 convention of Y's and community centres across North America, held in Toronto.

Ian Scott embracing the "girls" — Elinor Caplan, me, Barbara McDougall, Nita Goldband — at the groundbreaking of the Prince Charles housing project.

At the B'nai Brith Tribute dinner in 1987 . . .

With Barbara McDougall

Jane Pepino and Jim Peterson

North York mayor Mel Lastman

and Toronto mayor Art Eggleton

My North York family: Planning Commissioner Don Newman *(photo right)* and my colleagues on the Committee of Adjustment, 1987.

Their smiles seemed as though they'd last forever: Ron Appleby *(left)* of Robins, Appleby, Kotler, and Eric Slavens, FCA, Laventhol & Horwath.

My guests for lunch and drinks at the 1988 air show at Ontario Place: Howard and Gloria Moscoe *(photo left)* and Ralph Lean.

Joining me for dinner at Ontario Place, 1988, were Monte Kwinter, minister of Industry, Trade, and Technology; his wife Wilma; and Timmy Peterson, youngest brother of David, the premier of Ontario.

Welcoming HRH Prince Edward to Ontario Place, with David Peterson *(left)* and Ontario's lieutenant-governor, Lincoln Alexander, and his wife Yvonne.

The odd couple, in a rare unreserved moment: Gordon Ashworth and me.

At a Liberal fundraising reception, David Peterson makes a witty comment as Peter Hernndorf and I meet.

The Molson Indy board of governors meets in Indianapolis during the 1988 Indy 500. *Front row*: Monte Kwinter *(left)*; Hugh O'Neil, minister of Tourism; Hal Moran, CEO of Molson's; Paul Godfrey; Craig Prentice, vice-president, Molson's. *Back row*: Ralph Lean, Art Eggleton.

The 1988-89 Ontario Place Corporation sponsors, representing $400,000 in new revenue. Ontario Place vice-chairman Clare Copeland is second from the left, standing, and the Hon. Hugh O'Neil, minister of Tourism, is standing to my left.

1992, moving on — I've reached the big 50, and the best is yet to come.

"something or somebody" was screwing everything up. She had contacted the premier's office to ask for help. Hershell thought this might be a potential attraction for the waterfront and would be another rationale for my involvement without raising any suspicions, since the shoe museum might be located on the Ontario Place site, or close by.

By now some of Dunc's concerns about broken promises were getting through. "Write me a letter asking me to get involved," I told Hershell. He did, and so did Mrs. Bata.

In May 1988 Thomas and Sonja Bata invited me to their estate in the Bridle Path area of Toronto for lunch to discuss the options. It was like being in a magazine picture, everything was so exquisite. Despite their charm and warmth, I felt out of place and awkward, especially when they served salt in a little silver container with a spoon. I wasn't sure how to use it, so I didn't. But we all agreed to work together to see if something could be done.

As for the ballet/opera house, it was a commitment made by the previous Tory government. The proposed site was at Bay and Wellesley in the heart of downtown Toronto, but David Peterson envisioned it on the waterfront. So did Gordon, Bob Carman, Duncan Allen, and I. But those directly involved with the ballet/opera committee didn't — specifically Hal Jackman, now lieutenant-governor of Ontario and former CEO of Royal Trust, and David Silcox, the deputy minister of Culture and Communications. They were applying major pressure on the minister, Lily Munro, and the premier to give the final go-ahead for the Bay-Wellesley site and cough up some $40 million in grant money.

I wondered what difference it made to them where the ballet/opera house was, as long as it happened. I still couldn't figure out why the O'Keefe Centre simply wasn't renovated to accommodate more ballet and opera, saving the taxpayers millions of dollars.

One day I got a call at Council House from David Silcox. As deputy minister of Culture and Communications, the ballet/opera house came under his jurisdiction. He had heard some rumours about a new site for this project and wanted to take me to lunch to discuss it. I couldn't believe how that man's antennae always picked up even the slightest movement, and I got a sick feeling. He obviously knew something. I decided I'd better talk to David Peterson before I met Silcox at The Bottom Line in Yorkville for lunch the next day.

"Don't talk about the waterfront at all," David warned me. "Silcox has spies everywhere and I'm sure he suspects something. Try acting like a dumb broad for a change. You might enjoy it, ha ha."

✦ Late in 1985 Silcox had been brought in as deputy minister to replace Bernie Ostry, who was moved over to TVOntario. The minister, Lily Munro, was Silcox's boss. Her executive assistant was David Michener.

I had met Lily late in 1985 when Les Scheininger, the chairman of the Canadian Jewish Congress, and I had gone to meet with her about a grant for the CJC, Ontario region. During the presentation of the grant, Lily addressed the members of the Jewish community who were in attendance. She had taken the time and effort to learn a few words in Hebrew and spoke them fluently. Very impressive. She and I hit it off; her early struggles in her long road to success earned my admiration, and she was also a lot of fun. She asked me to attend several cultural events as her "escort." I was also privileged through her to meet some outstanding artists.

Over the years she shared with me some of her personal difficulties, including the deterioration of her marriage. Her husband, John Munro, had been a federal Cabinet minister in Pierre Trudeau's Liberal government and had failed in his bid to win the party leadership in 1984, nearly going broke in the process. I asked for her permission to discuss her situation with Jane, to find some solutions. She looked at me quizzically at first, but I assured her that politics would never come into play with Jane in a matter of women's mutual support.

The situation was particularly difficult because John was living in her Toronto apartment, and since Lily did not want to live with him, she had herself driven home to Hamilton every night, telling no one but her closest staff and me. She had moved her nine-year-old son in with her family there, and she had to get up at 6:00 a.m. every morning for the return trip to Toronto. Sometimes the only sleep she got was in the car being driven back and forth between Hamilton and the events she had to attend. Most often she refused to stay in Toronto with friends because she wanted to spend at least some time with her young son every day.

As a result, she would occasionally appear exhausted at Cabinet meetings. Too often she did not participate actively in some of the discussions, and a number of her male colleagues started belittling her and referring to her as an airhead. Considering their own shortcomings, both intellectually and in other ways, it was a good example of antiquated chauvinism and the double standard. At one point, I suggested to both Monte Kwinter and Ian Scott that it would be nice if they could encourage their colleagues to be a little more sympathetic to her situation.

Lily lived in fear of the press discovering her personal problems and putting an end to her career. In addition, John wasn't earning enough money. Without her Cabinet position, she would be in trouble financially.

With Lily's permission, Jane spoke to one of her colleagues at Aird & Berlis who specialized in family law. He was prepared to help, confident that the matter could be kept out of the media. The next move would be up to Lily.

"I can't understand how any woman lets a man push her around," I said to Jane. "In today's political atmosphere, do you think anyone still cares if a woman is divorced?"

"These people have spent their whole careers in politics," was Jane's answer. "From the beginning of time, the perception of family harmony was critical to any successful politician's career. It's not so easy to change an attitude that's so engrained."

One Friday night some weeks later, I got a call from Lily's executive assistant. Apparently John had come to Hamilton, angry words had been exchanged, and Lily had decided she would

TEMPTING FATE

have to end the marriage. Would I make some arrangements with Jane to get the wheels in motion?

The following morning, Gus, Lily's driver, brought her to my home. Her son stayed to play with my kids while she and I went over to Jane's house. Lily wore dark glasses and looked extremely drawn.

"I can't go on," she told us, choking back tears. "I'm so tired and I'm afraid. I can't do this anymore." Jane made a couple of calls, and arrangements were made for Lily to see a divorce lawyer right away. Every effort would be made to keep it quiet.

Jane would call some Tory friends, and I would drop into the members' lounge in the Legislature the next week to speak to the Tory politicians I knew. I hoped they could be persuaded to ignore her personal problems when the separation was official.

I called Gordon Ashworth at home that Saturday afternoon to bring him up to date. I couldn't resist a shot at the lack of sensitivity being shown to Lily by David and some Cabinet members. There was no sympathy from Gordon, though, since he wasn't a fan of her or her husband. He'd already heard the rumours and couldn't care less.

A week after Lily's visit with Jane and me, I dropped into the lounge on the "other" side of the Legislature. The result of that meeting was positive: during the election of 1987 and the Starr Affair of 1989-90, Lily's personal problems were never leaked or raised by the Tories.

But the word around the arts community was that Lily's deputy minister David Silcox clearly disliked her. Prior to this lunch, Silcox and I had had words about his treatment of Lily, especially when the media articles on the highlights of her ministry were all about him. Most civil servants are required, and in fact prefer, to keep low profiles, in deference to their ministers.

In late 1987, at a reception in the ministry's offices, Bluma Appel, a well-known philanthropist and community activist, took me into a corner. She felt Silcox was making life difficult for some of her friends regarding the McMichael Canadian Art Collection in Kleinburg, just north of Toronto. Then she asked if I knew that Silcox, prior to entering government, had worked as a consultant for a group led by Hal Jackman that was pushing for the ballet/opera house Bay Street site. She also asked if I had heard any of the rumours that there were people pushing to sell the land across the street from that site to a foreign group hoping to build a hotel. I told her that I had, more than a year earlier.

I was getting some bad vibes, and I wanted to ensure that Lily was in the picture, so I called David Michener, Lily's executive assistant, over and asked Bluma to repeat her statements, which she did. The next day I filled Gordon in, who said to leave it with him and say nothing more.

◆ So that day in 1988, sitting across from Silcox, I started off by just listening. He was up front with me. He'd heard that the premier and Ashworth were favouring a waterfront location for the ballet/opera house. Bob Carman and Duncan Allen were favouring another site farther east on the lakeshore. He also heard rumblings about an increasing role for Ontario Place in future developments. He "knew" that somehow I was involved in all this and he wanted to present his case.

How the hell did he know so much? I wondered. Who was feeding him his information? I did my best to be evasive, though I'm sure my body language must have been something else.

It was at this meeting that he first spoke to me directly about the renovation grant for NCJW's Council House, which had been approved by his ministry. He started off by asking me to help him lobby the premier to keep the Bay Street site for the ballet/opera house, even though he knew I was committed to a waterfront site. He then went on to question the way NCJW's grant application had been prepared and offered to help me fix it to reduce the bureaucratic hassles.

"What the hell does NCJW's grant have to do with the waterfront?" I asked him. He told me not to be stupid. He knew that I knew about his consulting fees, which he said had ceased, now that he was in the Peterson government. He said that he had disclosed his former relationship with Jackman's group to those who had to know. He told me, without elaborating, that the Bay Street site was critical to the success of the ballet/opera house.

I was furious, banging my wine glass down so hard it spilled over my brand-new suede skirt. "Are you crazy?" I said through gritted teeth. "Do you really think I need your help? I've been doing grants the same way for years. I'm a volunteer. I don't get paid for my services in these matters, unlike you. Besides, your ministry has always approved them, including this one. If there was a better way to make applications, why didn't anyone make suggestions before approval was given?"

When I look back and remember that scene now, it's like looking at one of those Greek tragedies, where the heroine is completely unaware that she is tempting fate and foreseeing her own downfall. I also never dreamed back then that once Betty Stone received her settlement package from NCJW, she would make a complaint to the ministry about this grant, which had been applied for and approved while she was in charge but completed and signed by Nita Goldband and me after she left.

After that lunch, I drove right up to Council House to check the files on the renovation grant. Even though we were still waiting for the breakdown of donated services and materials from Mendelow and Verdiroc, everything was in order, or so I thought.

Marty Mendelow was an architect who also flew his own plane. He was first introduced to me in 1979 by his good friend, Betty Stone, who brought him to Council House to assess the possibilities of some renovations. She wanted to know if he would match NCJW's portion of a government grant with donated labour and materials. The three of us walked around the building for about an hour discussing some ideas, but it was decided to do nothing at that time.

He had invited me on a flying trip around the outskirts of Toronto, which I agreed to, despite my fear of flying. I was impressed with his commitment to the Jewish community, specifically the Jewish Community Centre, located just south of Council House on Bathurst Street. When he asked me to get involved "down the street" in anticipation of his election there as president, I agreed.

Marty wanted some new blood to join his team and had also recruited several others. Harold Green, one of the principals of Verdiroc and Greenwin, was also an officer of the Jewish Community Centre. He was part of Marty's team as well.

Over the next five years, the volunteer team that Marty recruited for the agency formed a nucleus of support when the politics got hot and heavy. When a movement was begun to get rid of him, we mounted a counter-offensive on his behalf.

When he flew us to New York for an international meeting relevant to community centres, we discussed the renovation of Council House again. He agreed to provide the matching-in-kind donations for his part of the job, as long as his associate, Harold Green, was able to do so as well. When I spoke to Harold, there seemed to be no problem.

So I rejected Silcox's offer of assistance. Perhaps he was simply hoping to become the head staff honcho of the ballet/opera house group. Gordon agreed that it was best to just ignore him. How I wish I hadn't.

And then a real bomb was dropped.

Back in March 1988, parallel to the activities going on municipally to stop the waterfront development, I had asked Ontario Place's lawyers to look into the actual ownership of all these lands in the hope that they could find some loophole that would strengthen Ontario Place's position. Rumours had been going on for years about the land rights of the City, Metro, the Province, and the federal government. They were confirmed by a call I made to Barbara McDougall. I wanted to make sure the feds didn't have any real interest in our waterfront. Jane Pepino had heard they were sick of all the petty conflicts between their agencies there: the Harbour Commission, Harbourfront, and everyone else.

Barbara immediately wanted to know what was up, since she was sure Jane and I wouldn't be calling her just to chit-chat. I decided to tell her. As usual, she was interested and supportive. As far as she knew, there was no intense interest in our waterfront, though she knew David Crombie was looking for a job. She also knew that Art Eggleton was intending to retire as mayor and was therefore looking for a job as well. She alerted me to some competition that might be going on between them. But she said she'd check around and tell me if there was anything of concern happening that she did not yet know about.

In the meantime, Toronto City Council froze all future waterfront development for at least one year.

I then received a phone call from one of our lawyers from government services, asking to meet me privately on a matter of utmost urgency. We met in the Forum at Ontario Place, sitting out in the cold wind because we wanted to be sure no one else heard his report.

"In our legal opinion, all the lands in question were, before Confederation, and still are, owned by the province — not the federal government."

I nearly fell out of my seat.

To quote the correspondence and backup documentation that followed: "Land grants that were given by the Federal crown to the City of Toronto and the Toronto Harbour Commission are, without question, invalid, since the lands fell outside the area of Toronto Harbour at the time of Confederation and were therefore provincial property." In simple English, the federal government had given away land on the waterfront that they didn't own. It still belonged to the province and was ours for the taking.

The implications were mindboggling. Exhibition Place, all the lands to the east of Ontario Place, and much of Harbourfront and its development, belonged to Queen's Park.

The lawyers for the ministry of government services, which controlled provincial lands, sent us a formalized letter with their opinions and comments as to the very "political" nature of these matters. There was the potential for a three-way struggle between the federal government, the province, and the city over the ownership. Millions of dollars in revenue were at stake. Future development, including the 1996 Olympics and Expo 2000, could be affected by who controlled the land.

Usually matters were handled through cooperation between all three levels of government. But until now everyone had believed that some of the lands in question belonged to the city by virtue of a grant from the federal government decades earlier. With this news, the balance of power had suddenly shifted. All the strategy, plans, and machinations we had developed over the past year to gain control of these lands had been unnecessary. Eggleton might have lost his trump card and Peterson might have gained it.

When I called and told Gordon, I could hear his breath being sucked in, and he was silent for several moments. "My God, this is a bombshell!" he said. The potential for power in the hands of anyone who had this information was incredible. Imagine being able to negotiate development deals knowing who really owned the land and the advantage one would have over their unsuspecting competitor.

"Have you told anyone yet?" he asked.

"Only one senior Ontario Place staff member has seen this. Why, what's the big deal? Several of the AG's lawyers must know. Now we can drop the charade."

"Don't say anything, at all, to anyone," he said. "I'm telling you, Patti, no one. This information is dynamite!"

But I did. To be perfectly honest, I was becoming uneasy with the cut-throat politics in which I was embroiled and needed the advice of a few people I trusted. I also wanted the chairmanship of this future commission and needed to make sure all my efforts wouldn't be forgotten in favour of one of the network "boys."

◆ Back in September, Hershell Ezrin's daughter had been Bat Mitzvahed. We sat with David and Shelley Peterson (who left early), Senator Keith Davey, Monte and Wilma Kwinter, and Martin and Joan Goldfarb. Both Keith and Marty barely spoke to me. I wondered if their hostility was the result of their friendship with Senator Grafstein, who was not one of my admirers. I also wondered if they could throw another monkey wrench at me. To make things more complicated, Hershell had told me privately that he was planning on leaving the government to consider future career options. So I was a little concerned about my own plans.

During lunch, Ian Scott came over to our table, in very good spirits.

"I need your attention for a very serious matter," he said. "Ben Johnson has just been picked up for pointing a toy pistol at someone driving alongside of him on the highway. Should he be charged?" Johnson was the Canadian sprinter who had won the gold medal in the hundred-metres at the '88 Summer Olympics only to be stripped of his title because traces of steroids were found in his urine samples. The scandal that erupted resulted in the government setting up a judicial inquiry on drugs in sports, chaired by Mr. Justice Charles Dubin.

A lively discussion then ensued within the group about the Dubin Inquiry and the "bloodthirsty lawyers" (Ian's words) who were trying to cash in on "poor Ben." Ian then went on to say what might have happened to the other driver if he had panicked when he saw Johnson pointing the gun at him.

"Okay," Ian joked, "let's have a vote. All those who believe Johnson should be charged, raise your hands." Eight hands went up.

I felt sick at how blithely I had participated in such a silly exercise.

I was now part of an inner circle of the most powerful people in the Province of Ontario. I had wanted it so badly, once, but now I was becoming more and more uneasy. Where was all the joy I was supposed to be experiencing? Were they simply getting off on controlling other people's lives? And I knew, though I pushed it from my consciousness, that they were controlling me too. I was nothing more than a cog in the machinery that kept power in the hands of a select few. It was the way the game was played, where only the players changed, never the rules.

For the first time, I had a premonition of impending doom. Ben Johnson was in fact charged. I asked Monte Kwinter what he thought the press would have done if they had had a tape recorder under our table that day.

"Buried all of us," he replied.

CHAPTER ELEVEN

The Housing Battle

Shortly after that luncheon, John Sewell, chair of the Metropolitan Toronto Housing Authority, and Chaviva Hosek, minister of Housing, who was his boss, dropped all pretence of cooperation and started to go at it.

I had been appointed to the board of MTHA in 1986. Alvin Curling, then the minister of Housing in the provincial government, had asked if I would serve as a balance to some of the entrenched "bleeding hearts" he felt were permeating the social housing bureaucracy of his ministry. At first I refused, citing time constraints and overwork. I didn't want to get involved in any more heartbreaking situations, where no matter how hard you tried, your ability to effect real change was limited. It was hard to forget some of the MTHA residents even when I was at home.

But anyone who knows Curling knows how absolutely convincing he can be. He persuaded me that this appointment would be a golden opportunity to learn more about social housing from the inside and to provide some new impetus for that board. As a novice Cabinet minister, he wanted to have people he could trust strategically placed within the boards and commissions of his ministry.

He laid on some guilt as well, stressing how fortunate I was to have a home and family when so many others didn't. He said he needed me there as his pipeline, especially since I had no vested interest. This appointment would be a volunteer one. My experience in non-profit housing with the Prince Charles project and my work with disadvantaged youth (NCJW support projects) and psychiatric outpatients (the mental health centre at 999 Queen Street West) had given me the right credentials.

Unfortunately, too many of the residents of MTHA fell into the above categories. And Curling was concerned that many of those involved in social housing were either looking for a job or were working for the co-op movement and wanted to make sure that the housing of last resort was MTHA, not one of their co-ops.

"Okay," I said. "One term only."

In agreeing to his request, I would become embroiled with John Sewell, former mayor of Toronto. This would turn out to be a major mistake.

Sewell prided himself on riding to and from his office at City Hall on a bicycle when he was mayor. He was a staunch supporter of gay rights, low-rise housing, and "green" living. Though his family background was Tory, most viewed him as extremely left wing. Many developers and private business interests saw him as the enemy. In their view, he was inflexible on new developments and created animosity between City Hall and the business establishment, who provided most of the jobs for the residents of the city.

In 1980, a group of Tory and Liberal backroom boys — Paul Godfrey, Ralph Lean, David Smith, Jeff Lyons — combined forces to help oust him from office. Of course they were successful only because the people of Toronto had had enough of Sewell as well.

After his electoral defeat, he was hired as a columnist for the *Globe and Mail*. Many of his barbs at developers, particularly in North York, were focused on Tridel. When NCJW became involved in the Prince Charles back in 1984, Sewell had already written some negative articles and I called him about it. I also ran into him when he covered Mel Lastman's re-election campaign.

In late 1986, Gordon took me to Il Posto for lunch to break the news that Sewell was being appointed for a two-year term as chairman of MTHA at a salary of more than $50,000 a year.

"Good," I said. "Now I can quit. I'm not going to be part of

Sewell's return to public life on the backs of those in public housing. Who's the genius behind this appointment?"

The Peterson government was still living with an "accord" with the NDP, and the Sewell appointment was engineered to keep them happy. But there had to be more to Sewell's appointment than that. I knew Curling wouldn't be happy about it, since responsibility for MTHA was part of the ministry of Housing. So this decision had to have come from someone else. I asked Gordon if it was Ian Scott. He didn't answer.

Regent Park, the largest public housing project in Toronto, now came into play. It was located in Ian's riding and was similar to the projects in Chicago that grew in occupancy beyond the ability to maintain them. When it became politically incorrect to prevent various men from moving in with the single mothers who had qualified for this assisted housing, chaos ensued. More than one family could be living in one small apartment, and the overworked supervisory staff wouldn't find out for months. Vandalism, drug pushing, and alcoholism ran rampant. The majority of the residents, who were trying to provide a decent life for themselves and their families, were becoming increasingly frustrated by the maintenance problems and management's slow response to their concerns. If that powderkeg ever blew up, Ian could be in trouble, and someone like Sewell would fan the flames of discontent for his own ends, since it was no secret he wanted to return to public life.

So the powers that be figured to bring him in, make him part of the team, and eliminate any reason for him to stir the pot. Fat chance!

Gordon said that Queen's Park, along with Ministry of Housing staff, wanted me to stay on MTHA for at least another year to keep abreast of what was going on just in case the appointment backfired. Sewell was often referred to as a loose cannon, but then so was I.

So I agreed to stay on the MTHA board. Big mistake.

During the next year I was often impressed with Sewell's abilities, especially his understanding of organizational structure and the cleverness of his written reports. For a while everything went along smoothly.

However, after the 1987 provincial election, Curling was moved to another ministry — colleges and universities — and Chaviva Hosek then became the minister of Housing. At the same time, Sewell began using what some on the MTHA board felt were inappropriate opportunities for publicity. He would invite the press to tenants' meetings and in front of them promise to "fix" whatever problems they had.

As a former mayor, he knew full well how slowly the wheels of bureaucracy work, but that didn't stop him from blaming the "uncaring" government when the complaints weren't handled immediately. This was guaranteed to get him media coverage. He also started talking about redevelopment as though it was a simple task that he, Sewell, would undertake for the people if the government would only let him.

MTHA board minutes show our concern about the "carefully orchestrated" program that Sewell was conducting in an effort to embarrass the government and diminish the credibility of MTHA's efforts. The board, on more than one occasion, told him to stop these tactics.

So his three supporters on the eleven-member board started giving interviews on his behalf. The media loved it, especially his former colleagues at the *Globe and Mail*. In September 1988 I got a call at Council House from Chaviva. She was almost in tears. Rumour had it that Sewell and his supporters on the board were planning a move to try to impeach her, though for what we didn't yet know. Despite the fact that he didn't have board support to do it, the ensuing press coverage might cause her political damage.

"Please, make sure the board is behind me and see if you can stop him," she said. "We will not be renewing his contract when his term ends in November and I'll have to try to hold out till then. He's trying to provoke me into something and I don't want to play into his hands. Patti, I'm counting on you."

◆ A day or two later I was called at Council House by two of Chaviva's staff, Sean Goetz-Gadon and Sam Borenstein, as well as some senior ministry staff, who reiterated the government's concern over Sewell's growing defiance of due process. They asked for reassurances that the MTHA board would stay behind Chaviva. I gave it.

Gordon was going off to the Orient to try and cement some high-level investments in Ontario, and Hershell was getting ready to leave his position at Queen's Park. Both of them told me *not* to stick my neck out on this matter and leave it to Chaviva. It was the first time in a long time I had heard the same advice from both of them. They didn't elaborate, other than to stress that I didn't need any problems.

But I was into my "we women have to stick together" mode. After all, Chaviva had asked — in fact, had almost begged. Her staff was almost in a panic and besides, what could Sewell do to me?

So, once Gordon was out of town, I ignored his advice and consolidated those on the board who opposed Sewell. I was unprepared for the press assault that followed. This, despite the documentation showing that Sewell did not have the majority of the board's support. There had even been complaints about his recommending consulting contracts for his former associates. I became the target for the pro-Sewell forces. And like a fool, every time an article would come out demanding that Sewell be reappointed, or taking a jab at Chaviva, I would respond.

Nasty memos started flying back and forth between Sewell and me regarding inaccurate press stories he was leaking. On one occasion he had to issue a letter of apology and retraction to the *Toronto Star* for his false accusations against me. But I wondered how many people read the Letters to the Editor section.

Into all this hoopla came Vince Borg, returning to government after his unsuccessful stint as a PR consultant with Decima Research. He was replacing Hershell Ezrin as principal secretary to the premier.

Columnist Michael Valpy of the *Globe and Mail* then picked up the cause. He was particularly incensed at the government, Chaviva, and me for what he perceived to be the unfair treatment Sewell was getting. And what was that unfair treatment? His employment contract was not going to be renewed.

The press threw anything and everything into the pot on Sewell's behalf. They were hoping to pressure the government to overturn Chaviva's decision not to renew Sewell's contract in November. They tried to discredit anyone who did not support Sewell. I was a sitting duck.

And then I got a call from Patrick Gossage, former press secretary to Prime Minister Pierre Trudeau and now a PR consultant. He was advising the Peterson government, and I'd heard that Martin Goldfarb's nose was a little out of joint because of this. Gossage, whose firm had also been retained at one time by Elvio DelZotto, had been following the press attacks and wondered if he could be of any help. Of course I said yes.

Patrick arranged for me to meet with Valpy over drinks at the Harbour Castle Hilton. Patrick would be with us. Before the actual meeting, Patrick gave me some tips on the proper way to deal with the press. This time I was determined to listen to advice.

"Don't talk too much. Listen. Look into his eyes. Never lie about anything. It's better to be evasive. The press never forgive lies told to them."

The meeting was bizarre. Despite the fact that we had never met before, Valpy clearly didn't like me. He was almost snarling as he spoke about his friend John Sewell. He wanted to know if this vendetta against poor John was being encouraged by Tridel, my "great and close" friends. I tried to tell him the facts. He didn't listen. He "knew" that I was the one behind Sewell's ouster. The way he said it made my antennae go up. I couldn't understand why I was the target. He kept saying how "they" would get me and anyone else who was responsible for this travesty against Sewell. Patrick was getting whiter and whiter and kept leaving the table to go to the men's room.

The Housing Battle

I tried to raise the question of loyalty to a government that had given Sewell a job when he was out of one. His two-year appointment was over. Why was there any obligation to extend his contract? I talked about Sewell's manipulation of the press and suggested that Valpy get copies of the MTHA board minutes to see what had really gone on.

By now, he was clearly agitated. I kept asking why he was focusing on me when I was only one of eleven board members. He just glared at me. The meeting was over.

In November 1988, Sewell's appointment was not renewed. My term on the MTHA board ended in February 1989. In 1990 Gordon Ashworth told me that during this period in 1988, unknown to him at the time, the press had been briefed by "impeccable sources" within the government that I was the one behind Sewell's ouster, not Chaviva. That would explain some of the hostility towards me.

✧ In 1988, NCJW had finalized the selection of a new site for a second housing project, called Ridley. Tridel owned the property at the northwest corner of Avenue Road and Wilson Avenue, and our project would be part of a luxury condo complex of three others they were building.

Housing ministry regulations did not permit a volunteer group to receive the consulting fees, no matter how skilled they might be. They had to be professional, or in other words, they had to have been paid. In my opinion, this was done to protect those "consultants" who are found everywhere in the NDP co-op movement from "unfair" competition by the volunteer sector.

So we had to use a professional group, and they were entitled to 2 to 3 percent of the total project costs. The Ridley costs were projected at about $15 million.

We certainly had no intention of paying that kind of fee to anyone besides ourselves, even though it was part of the funding provided by the government.

Lesley Miller and Nita Goldband had formed their own consulting company, Futurac Consultants, in anticipation of turning professional. They were going to be the official consultants for Ridley, and then turn over the consulting fee of about $250,000 to the organization. As protection, however, Futurac went through the steps of declaring their involvement in NCJW with the ministry and getting approval from them as Ridley's consultants. This included providing them with the executive's minutes of approval and Futurac's acknowledgment of their fees coming back to NCJW as a donation.

When Tridel's executive came to the NCJW board meeting to get the official go-ahead on Ridley and present the drawings, there was considerable excitement not only because of the money we would earn, but because of the approval of a new pilot program.

It was the Outreach Attendant Care program, through which our volunteers could provide services to those disabled who could still live at home and were within a certain radius of Ridley. Our special bus would be used to transport the disabled back and forth to the new building when appropriate. Additionally, a daycare centre was being provided on site for the residents, coordinated and supervised by our own volunteers and to be led initially by Joan Tobe. Our volunteer team had put this package together, directed by Lesley and Nita, but also relying heavily on the skills of Eveline Berger, Eleanor Cooper, Connie Kachuk, Phyllis Moss, Shirley Switzman, Rochelle Reingold, Donna Zener, and so many others. Once again my job was to sell it to the government for the necessary approvals. And once again the government complied, recognizing the long-range benefits.

We were really flying that day, and the girls were telling Mario Giampietri and other Tridel executives all kinds of jokes about missing the political battles we had fought for the Prince Charles.

"It's no fun, it's so easy now," they said. "Come on, Mario, we need some excitement."

Mario smiled, but only I knew it was a sickly one — for Howard Moscoe, an NDP Metro councillor had entered the picture. His riding did not include Ridley, but he had seen an opportunity, and he had to grab it.

The Housing Battle

In order to develop the new site, old four-storey buildings would have to be demolished. As is required, tenants being displaced would be given the choice of payment for moving costs or first choice in the new facilities, with the exception of the subsidized-disabled components of NCJW's building, since this was under COMSOC housing regulations. Suddenly, out of nowhere, comes Howard Moscoe with a few existing tenants whom he claims to represent, making unreasonable demands in terms of cash payments for relocating expenses.

A year earlier I had suggested to Mario Giampietri that Howard might appreciate one of the fabulous fruit baskets that Tridel, like so many others, sent out as Christmas gifts to various people in North York. And then, to our outrage, Moscoe called in the press to tell them that both he and his NDP colleague Maria Augimeri were returning their fruit baskets to Tridel. He said they had been "shocked" to receive this unsolicited gift, which might be used as an attempt to influence them in the future. After all, the NDP didn't take gifts like other politicians did. They couldn't understand why Tridel had sent the baskets to them.

I blew up and confronted them both in their offices at North York City Hall the next day. But of course the damage to Tridel had already been done.

Maria whined that it was Howard's fault; she hadn't known that he was going to call the press, but when he did, she'd had no choice but to back him up. I didn't buy it and had it out with Howard. He blamed it on Maria, saying it was her idea to call in the press.

Once again, Angelo reminded me about how one must keep their enemies close. "Howard is still a presence in North York," he said. "You and Mario were stupid to send the fruit basket to him. Mario, especially, should have known better, so it's our own fault. Now mend your fences."

◆ Some weeks later Howard and I met for breakfast at Sutton Place. He brought NDP Councillor Dale Martin along and we talked about Ontario Place, the waterfront, and the LRT

165

extension. Dale was a member of the city's Land Use Committee, and he agreed to consider supporting a freeze on Ramparts' project. He suggested I arrange to meet with the Land Use Committee's chairman, Nadine Nowlan, which I did. Howard picked up the bill.

Some months later Howard called to ask if I would get him and his wife tickets for the Joan Rivers show at the O'Keefe Centre. He also mentioned that he had never been to Centro for dinner, and he had heard I had a regular table there.

Jerry and I went with them to the show and to Centro afterwards for dinner. Past differences were not mentioned.

Until his appearance on the Ridley scene, I had no longer had any concerns about him. But his interference could be enough to delay the rezoning process necessary to build the project, which would then delay the allocation process.

The girls and I met with Tridel to discuss the situation and see if there was anything we could do to help. It was agreed that I would call Moscoe first to see what he wanted.

"Okay, Howard, what's up?" was my opening comment.

"Did Mario put you up to this?" he said, laughing. "Usually he does his own dirty work."

"After your last stab in the back, Howard, no one there is anxious to get involved with you again," I answered.

He then gave me a ten-minute lecture on the immorality of displacing these poor people without a guarantee of replacement housing along with an appropriate financial remuneration which he, Howard, could administer. But Howard already knew Tridel was offering all kinds of replacement housing in the area and moving costs as well. There was more to this than appeared on the surface.

"Howard, this is NCJW's project," I said. "Most of the future residents are our people. You won't hurt Tridel by screwing things up, you'll hurt your own community. And eventually it will go through anyhow, but for some people, it'll be too late. Find something else to ruin, Howard, but please not our project."

I decided that I had better call the girls together to discuss the situation. At the meeting at Council House later that day, it was the usual group of girls at the table: Lesley Miller, Nita Goldband, Eveline Berger, Marsha Slavens, and Gita Arnold. I remember looking around the room thinking how different we all were now. No longer the naive volunteers we had been four years earlier when the Prince Charles project was getting off the ground. In a way it was sad. As we sat around discussing how we should handle Howard, along with other politicians we knew about, there was no discomfort. It was business, nothing more. A means to an end. And I kept encouraging the group to continue its efforts. The successes, the high we were on when we saw our programs functioning so well, allowed us to push aside any misgivings.

We had learned in a conversation with Howard that his daughter was running as a North York school trustee in the upcoming municipal elections, and we decided to make contributions to her campaign, hoping this would reduce any hassles with the Ridley project.

Marsha Slavens especially wanted to be included in the list of contributors. As a known Tory, she hoped some other NDPer would notice who Moscoe took money from. However, since the money was going to his daughter, it was unlikely anyone in the party would ever see it.

Howard wanted individual cheques, not one from the Capital Fund, so after we collected ten for $100 each, the fund reimbursed us. I handed the cheques to Howard personally a few days later. The girls and I agreed not to tell Mario what we'd done. We knew how angry he would have been, since Tridel had asked us to leave any problems on the Ridley project to them.

We hoped that Howard would no longer create difficulties for the project. But he persisted, so I decided to call in every marker I had in North York to get the necessary approvals, despite him. With the help of my colleagues, I was successful, and Ridley was on its way.

But by May 1989, my life had started to come undone, and the project, now called Avenal, was taken over by the Toronto Jewish Congress (now the Jewish Federation of Greater Toronto) and completed as planned by Tridel.

Like the Prince Charles, it is a testament to the dreams of a small group of committed volunteers who saw a need within their own community and tried to fill it.

CHAPTER TWELVE

A Visit from the *Globe*

The next year, 1989, did not start off well. The bookkeeper for NCJW, Toronto, was having trouble getting the documentation on the donated labour and materials Marty Mendelow and Harold Green of Verdiroc had promised as part of our grant for the renovation of Council House. Both Nita Goldband and bookkeeper Shirley Aronson wrote to them, requesting the completion of the necessary forms. Mendelow, the architect and project manager, kept assuring me that the paperwork was coming from Harold, who did the actual construction work.

At the same time we learned that the *Globe and Mail* was preparing a story on NCJW's political activities. Rumours were reaching my ears that NCJW insiders were speaking to the press.

At the NCJW board meeting in mid-January, I reported on the situation and went back, step by step, over our political activities of the past five years. There were several questions, but no concerns were raised. Former NCJW president Edith Sobel asked if we had contributed to all three parties. When she was told that we had, everyone seemed satisfied.

Lesley Miller and I had discussed what I should say at that board meeting, and she agreed that a total recap of our activities should be given again, just to make sure everyone was on side.

A few days later I went down to Queen's Park to alert them to the *Globe*'s inquiries. When I spoke to David Peterson about my concerns, he dismissed the importance of the newspaper, saying they were number three in the dailies and had very little clout.

But they were continuing to put pressure on his government to call an inquiry into certain developers' activities in York Region. Marco Muzzo, Fred DeGasperis, and Rudy Bratty were being singled out. I knew them through Angelo DelZotto. Occasionally one of them would join us for lunch at either Monte Cassino or Le Parc (owned by Fred DeGasperis). It was fascinating to watch them in action, discussing land purchases and making deals with each other, for the most part verbally. Once, Angelo wrote out the numbers of a particular deal on a napkin, everyone shook hands, and that was it. These gentlemen were active philanthropists and at the forefront of many social issues that affected everyone, not just the Italian community. The press never mentioned that during their attacks on them.

Globe reporter Jock Ferguson, who had already finished off Al Duffy, former mayor of Richmond Hill, was now raising questions about the Goldfarb-Muzzo connection to the Peterson family's business interests. David was bitter about their "fucking innuendoes."

✦ One day when I was at Queen's Park, Gordon and I decided at the last minute to go to Il Posto for lunch. I was sitting around his office waiting for him to "freshen up" when his phone rang persistently. His secretary Sue Callum had already gone out for lunch.

"Get it, will you?" he called from behind the washroom door. "Pretend you're my secretary, and try being humble."

"Good afternoon, Mr. Ashworth's office," I said in my most professional voice.

"Sue, it's David. Put him on, please," said the premier.

I didn't correct his error because his tone was brusque and it sounded serious.

I asked Gordon in a whisper if he wanted me to leave the room. He simply shook his head and pointed me to his armchair.

During his phone conversation with David, which lasted about five minutes, all the colour drained out of his face.

When he got off the phone, he put on his coat, grabbed my

A Visit from the Globe

arm, and off we went. Usually I drove to wherever we were going, but this day, Gordon wanted to walk up to Hazelton Lanes instead, despite the biting wind.

"What was that all about?" I asked. He didn't answer. We kept walking.

"How well do you know John Eakins?" he asked. "And his assistant?" (Eakins was minister of Municipal Affairs.)

"Reasonably well," I answered. He and his assistant had been very helpful with Ontario Place when Eakins was minister of Tourism and Recreation.

"There's going to be increasing pressure to call an inquiry into York Region," Gordon went on. "Certain people are getting nervous."

"What certain people?" I asked. "The developers I know and love aren't concerned."

"That's what they tell you," he replied. "Everyone is very edgy. We've got to put a stop to this."

"Eakins wants an inquiry," Gordon said. "And he's not backing off. And I think his EA is pushing him too."

We continued talking about it all through lunch. I told Gordon I thought he was crazy to get involved in heading off the inquiry. The *Globe* was after these guys, no matter what, and if the *Globe* ever got wind of any of this, it would be all over but the shouting.

Gordon then told me about the relationship between Martin Goldfarb, his brother Stanley, who was Muzzo's partner, and Hershell, who was now working for Molson's. He made a comment about the tremendous cost overruns in the building of the Skydome. He also mentioned that Muzzo, Bratty, et al. were part of the conglomerate. Paul Godfrey was the key mover and shaker there and at the same time had a top position at the *Sun*, where Rudy Bratty was a director. He reminded me of the government contracts Goldfarb's company had been awarded and who had recommended them. Gordon then told me it was Goldfarb who had arranged for Muzzo to buy C.M. Peterson & Co., for substantially more than some people said it was worth.

As for Hershell, despite having left Queen's Park months earlier, he spoke with David almost every day. Most people admired and respected Hershell, including me. He had been a diplomat in External Affairs before joining Peterson's staff. He had worked tirelessly in the political "outback" during David's years as leader of the Opposition, and he commanded the respect of politicians from all three parties. It was Hershell who had orchestrated the accord with the NDP that brought the Liberals to power for the first time in forty years. He was a brilliant academic who would have been successful whatever he had chosen to do.

"So I gather Eakins isn't cooperating and David wants you to twist his arm?" I asked Gordon.

When he didn't answer, I went on. "I'll see if I can find anything out."

At breakfast at the Novotel hotel in North York a week later, I asked some ministry insiders about rumours concerning developers in York Region and the possibility that Municipal Affairs was going to call an inquiry. Since NCJW was building a new housing project, I said I was concerned that any problems might affect us.

I was told about an inquiry "in the works." I remembered the comments I had heard about the Waisberg Commission and how it had hurt so many people.

"You know, guys," I said, "these things often turn into a witch hunt. You start out with the right idea, but somehow you end up catching little fish. The major players will have covered their rear ends, for sure. Why not leave it to the police and forget the other stuff?"

"It's too late. The wheels are in motion," was the response. They seemed gleeful, and I was uneasy. When I repeated the conversation to Gordon, I told him again that it was my opinion that he was crazy to get involved.

By now I was no longer a political neophyte. Working hand in hand with the Peterson government on the waterfront, in the election that saw Alan Tonks voted in as Metro chairman in December 1988, and on the Olympic bid, I had lost any illusions I might once have had about altruistic motives. It was business, pure and simple. Everything and everybody were simply tools to perpetuate the power of the government and their key players. Everyone, therefore, was expendable. It would be no different no matter which party was in power.

Gordon never told me what he was going to do about the York Region matter, for when we next met, Paul Henderson, the Olympic '96 coordinator, was in his office. There was concern, which David Peterson reiterated to me the next day, that the local NDP-backed social activists were going to screw up the united front so necessary for a successful Olympic bid. Toronto needed the jobs such an event would create, along with the millions of dollars in tourist revenue. A resolution of support from all levels of government had to accompany any final bid. Obviously, if that resolution were unanimous, or almost so, our bid would have a stronger impact.

The waterfront bombshell was still being kept under wraps. It was our feeling that to avoid a lengthy and costly legal battle over the lands, a compromise would be reached with the feds, allowing the province to fully develop the long-range plan for the waterfront as envisioned, including the Olympics. The two components David felt were essential to his plan were Alan Tonks and getting some NDP municipal councillors on side.

Dennis Flynn, the current Metro chairman, was a Tory, but a supporter of the Olympic bid. He was also a long-time politician who had served his constituents well. The initial straw vote on the election of a new chairman showed him as the winner by two or three votes.

Again the province began meddling in municipal affairs. When I was asked to help swing the vote to Tonks, I refused at first. Though I liked them both, Dennis Flynn, as an experienced politico, had always been available when I wanted to talk politics, brainstorm on some municipal deal, or just shoot the breeze. I didn't want any part of ousting him, especially since he supported some of David's long-range plans by opposing Exhibition Place chairman Mario Gentile's attempts to influence waterfront development.

But then the reality of how deeply I was "in" was brought home.

Gordon reminded me of who I was in terms of power and position — thanks in large part to the Peterson government. My abilities were recognized only because they had provided me with the opportunity to show them.

"If you're part of the team, you play by the rules," he said. "We need to count on our key players to deliver. Sometimes you have to put your personal feelings aside. This is politics. It's nothing personal.

"One of the key votes, presently for Flynn, can be turned around, especially if you speak to her. Some of your non-Italian connections won't get involved if you don't ask them to. And we want you to ask them."

That was it. Simple. No explanations necessary. I understood. If I wasn't strong enough to walk away from everything I'd come to enjoy and the security I thought it provided, I'd have to go along with them. And I did. I felt awful, but I did it and felt guilty for a long time afterward.

Alan Tonks was elected Metro chairman by two votes. If Flynn knew of my involvement, he never let on.

The article in the *Globe and Mail* that began the downward spiral of so many lives started off quite simply. The reporter called my office at Council House early in 1989 and asked Ruby to set up an appointment to discuss the politics of non-profit housing.

It was a quiet Friday afternoon when the reporter arrived. I'd done interviews before, and at first nothing unusual was in the air. We made small talk, she was very pleasant, and I answered some of her questions about NCJW's upcoming Ridley project. Suddenly, with no warning, she began asking personal questions about the DelZottos. I was shocked, but tried to hide my feelings.

A Visit from the Globe

I refused to talk about them, and everything went downhill from there. The politeness and cooperation were gone. She became quite demanding, asking the next question before I had a chance to answer the first one. I started to get nervous, and all I could think of was that this reporter was attacking me. I didn't know why.

She had a leather case which she began to rummage through, quite carelessly, or so I thought. Then I saw it! A photocopy of one of NCJW's ledgers showing some of the journal entries relevant to the political events we had attended. I recognized Shirley's handwriting. But Shirley (the NCJW bookkeeper), would never have given anyone that document. I suspected who had, however.

Before the reporter left, I told her that if it was I or the DelZottos the *Globe* was really after, then please leave NCJW out of it. "It's the organization you'll destroy, not us," I said.

When the article came out, it was a classic in the art of media manipulation. It contained off-the-cuff comments I had made which were reported out of context. NCJW's political activity in fundraising events was reported, and in the next paragraph were comments from Revenue Canada's senior staff (Charities Division) on the repercussions that *could* befall any charity that engaged in illegal political activity, including losing one's charitable number. To me, and many of NCJW's members, the implication seemed clear. This official was referring to us, the Toronto Section.

But he wasn't.

He called me from his office in Ottawa the next day. I was at Ontario Place. He assured me that he had been answering a series of *hypothetical* questions the reporter had been asking. He went on to say that he had *never* referred to NCJW specifically, and had stressed that point, very forcefully, to her. He was surprised and angry that there was no clarification in the article.

As a result, many of NCJW's general membership assumed we were about to lose our charitable status because of our "illegal" activities. This created panic, and Council House was inundated

175

with calls. It was also the first opportunity some of my detractors had to attack.

From that first day, the interviews given by them only fanned the flames. And the articles kept coming. Other community members then started to get nervous about their own organizations' attendance at political events, especially those in which I was involved. The more people reacted, the wider the ripple effect.

But the executive of NCJW, Toronto, was still supportive. They knew of Revenue Canada's reaction to the article and suggested that we all call around to our different associates to reassure them, and that we be available at Council House to respond to any calls of concern we might receive from our general membership.

A week later I got a call at home from Eric Slavens, my CJC "boss." (At this point he was treasurer, and I was assistant treasurer.) He said he was calling to reinforce the support of the Canadian Jewish Congress. Some of their executive had just met and they wanted me to know before it was announced officially that I would be invited to serve another three-year term as an officer.

But I had to keep silent about this newspaper article, he said. "Put your head down, Patti. We're all behind you. If you fight back, it will cause 'us' more harm than good. Besides, you're so high profile, you make an easy target. If you get hurt, so do the rest of us."

I then faced the executive of the Toronto Section of the NCJW for the first time since the article had appeared. Included in my comments to them was the conversation with Eric. The attitude of the executive was still supportive, but I noticed, for the first time, the way both Lesley Miller and Marsha Slavens avoided looking at me. I was uneasy, very uneasy. Nonetheless, I went on to suggest that we hire an outside lawyer and accountant to look over our records and give us another opinion regarding our political activities.

A Visit from the Globe

I, along with some others, was asked to come back to the next meeting with some appropriate recommendations.

✧ At the end of February I hosted a dinner in honour of Alan Tonks at the House of Chan. David Peterson, along with most of the mayors of surrounding municipalities, local councillors, some Cabinet ministers, and many political wheeler dealers were there, including Dennis Flynn. David suggested I use this dinner as an opportunity to invite some of the NDP city councillors who were opposed to the Olympic bid. Within this social setting, which included politicians from all three parties and all three levels of government, some lobbying and networking could take place. I agreed.

In his comments that evening, David dismissed the article's importance and went on to charm everyone in a speech that lasted twenty minutes. It was more fun than serious and he cut up most everyone there, in a delightful way, as only David can when he wants to be delightful. The dinner was a tremendous success, made even more so by the fact that it was kept out of the press, at least until the inquiry. There was so much lobbying going on that it was hard to keep track of who was cutting a deal with whom and for what.

David wrote a wonderful note of appreciation, as did most of those who were there. Later, during the Starr Inquiry, those in attendance that night were listed as part of the evidence given for the public record. Also on record was the fact that I had paid for this dinner personally.

After that dinner Vince Borg took over the job of lobbying these politicians for the Olympic bid, which he continued to do until 1990. Unfortunately, the vote on holding the '96 Olympics in Toronto was heavily split. Many believed the bid was hurt by the demonstrations and dissension urged by the so-called activists, partly led by Jack Layton, the losing NDP candidate in the election for Toronto mayor.

The jobs lost by their actions could have become a lifesaver for so many. What benefit did these militants provide to our city anyhow? They didn't lose their jobs when our economy took a nosedive, since many were, and still are, on the payroll of agencies receiving public funds.

✦ That same week, Jane Pepino suggested I meet with her and one of her colleagues, Peter Atkinson, to assess the situation at NCJW. She also suggested that a couple of our key executive members attend to discuss a counter-strike.

I still had no clue of what was in store for me, though I was angry over some of the excerpts of my conversation with the reporter and even more with the interviews some of our NCJW national members were now giving to the media.

Two of the NCJW executive and I did meet with Jane and Peter, in one of the boardrooms on the upper floor of Aird & Berlis on King Street in downtown Toronto. When we walked in, Jane and Peter looked as though they had already been meeting. I was wearing the brown Gideon Oberson suit I had bought for the Tonks dinner, and I wanted to get the girls' opinions on it. Peter excused himself and said he'd be back in fifteen minutes, since one of his clients was having a crisis.

Jane sat at the head of the boardroom table. She looked at me for a few moments and then said, "*Mea culpa*, Patti. That's what I think you should say. And then resign from NCJW. You always believed you were acting in the best interests of the organization. If you've been wrong, you're sorry. *Mea culpa*. And then you leave, head up."

I felt something, deep down somewhere, that I couldn't put my finger on. It passed in front of my eyes in the fleeting of a second, like what a drowning person must feel near the end. But like an old prizefighter, I also heard the bell ringing for the next round, and I instinctively put on my gloves and went into the attack position, as I had done so often over the past twenty-five years. Why, oh why, didn't I follow her advice?

Eveline Berger, NCJW treasurer and incoming president, spoke up.

A Visit from the Globe

"Don't be silly," she said. "Why should she quit? We're finished with our political dinners anyhow. The Ridley project is almost ready. If she resigns, then she admits being guilty of something, and if she's guilty, then we all are."

Jane sighed, took out her notepad, and started writing as we discussed the kind of official response the officers of NCJW, Toronto, should make to its membership. A draft letter was developed by Jane and Eveline Berger that would be taken back to Council House for discussion with some of the other executive members.

A few days later it was sent out to NCJW's membership, expressing support for me and reinforcing our earlier decisions on political activity. This letter was entered later in the record during the Starr Inquiry, but it was ignored by the press.

When Peter Atkinson returned to the meeting, the other girls left. We discussed the situation again, including my political involvements and my personal financial interests. He wanted to know if I had ever taken any money from NCJW.

"Are you crazy?" I snapped. "I'm a volunteer. I don't get paid for my services."

For the next few minutes he kept asking me variations of the same question. When he asked, "Have you ever been reimbursed for any out-of-pocket expenses?" my answer was yes.

In twenty-five years, I had submitted two chits. One for $4,000, which was for a table at the federal Liberal's 1988 Confederation Dinner. The girls had attended with me and knew that the foundation would reimburse me.

The other one was for $25,000, an accumulation of five years' out-of-pocket expenses incurred on behalf of the foundation, including the disabled workshops and seminars in Boston, Atlanta, and Montreal that Lesley, Nita, and I had attended. There were backup chits attached. The $25,000 also included petty cash expenses for the Ridley project, which the girls knew of, in detail.

There were also two cheques for a florist, written in July 1988, totalling $4,035. Since the florist had done work for NCJW previously, the staff assumed they were a foundation expense when the bills came into Council House and simply included them in a batch of cheques for my signature. I signed them without noticing they were my own personal expenses.

It wasn't until our accountant submitted the fund's draft financial statements in December 1988, two months before my meeting with Jane and Peter, that I saw it and realized the error.

When Nita Goldband, Eveline Berger, Marsha Slavens, and I went through the fund's expenditures line by line, we saw that Ruby had already marked the cheque stubs as a personal expense to be reimbursed by me. The mistake was no big deal, considering the thousands of dollars my husband and I contributed to NCJW's projects every year, and no further thought was given to it.

"Put all the money back, right away," Peter said.

"You mean the $29,000?" I asked. "I most certainly will not!" For the next hour we argued about it. I was adamant that with the exception of the $4,035, the expenses incurred belonged to the fund. Why should I have to pay for them? I had already donated thousands of dollars to NCJW over the years. Jerry's fiftieth birthday party raised $8,000 for NCJW's projects and my B'nai Brith dinner another $10,000. Besides, everyone knew about it.

"These chits aren't worth the paper they're written on," he continued. "You girls have been running the organization's finances like amateurs. Save yourself a headache and do what I tell you. Put all the money back right away!"

So I did. But I made a terrible mistake. Instead of writing two separate cheques for the $4,035 florist's bill, which was personal, and for the $29,000 bill, which wasn't, I wrote one cheque for the entire amount.

That mistake would send me to jail.

Peter then recommended that the NCJW executive hire Clifford Lax, of Goodman & Goodman, to represent us. At the time I didn't realize that the "Goodman" part referred to Eddie Goodman. Peter knew Cliff well and felt that they could work closely together. As an officer, I would be part of this larger group, but it would be wise if I retained my own counsel as well, given the diversity of my involvements. Peter would also begin looking into a lawsuit against the *Globe*.

When I spoke with Cliff shortly thereafter, I was impressed and recommended to the executive that they hire him right away. Once Eveline Berger and Dody Rudson, the new executive director of Toronto Section, met him and concurred, he was retained on behalf of NCJW, Toronto.

Some weeks later, Cliff asked me to come to his office on a Sunday afternoon, along with the new accountants he had hired in order to take them through every item in the Capital Fund, including reimbursed expenses that dated back to 1983. Peter Atkinson came with me. More than once during that four-hour meeting, Cliff was referred to as my lawyer on NCJW matters.

We went through all the cheque stubs and my personal, handwritten notes. I explained the rationale for all the expenditures and what our strategy had been at the time. He and his staff made detailed notes.

I felt very comfortable sharing all the information, including all my recollections, with him. However, Peter was not so comfortable, and he began making comments of concern, about something he couldn't "put his finger on." He thought we might start rethinking my position and raised, for the first time, the possibility that NCJW might soon see their interests as different from mine.

I scoffed at the suggestion, thinking he was doing the usual lawyer tactic of creating conflict. He would turn out to be so right, and I would be so wrong.

During this time of upheaval, Nita Goldband, Marsha Slavens, and Lesley Miller met with Eveline Berger and me one morning in Council House. They told both of us that the three of them had retained separate counsel for themselves. It was like a bomb dropping on my head. Eveline and I looked at each other, stunned.

Marsha Slavens did the talking. "They" felt that "their" interests might now be different from ours. This episode might grow, and they were distancing themselves.

"Why can't we all have the same lawyer?" Eveline asked. "This is a team. We're all in this together."

"No," Marsha said, "we're not." Lesley and Nita said nothing.

After all, Marsha went on, their husbands were all professionals and shouldn't be held responsible for anything I did.

To her great credit, Eveline Berger became angry, questioning their decision. They had obviously been planning this for some time. They had already retained a lawyer, Donald Carr, of Goodman & Carr, who was known to all of us as one of the leaders of the Jewish community.

"And why didn't our lawyer Ron Miller speak up before this if he had a problem with any of our activities?" she asked. "And why are you now the ringleader?" she asked Marsha. "You aren't even an officer of the foundation yet. Do you think this 'distancing' is going to help you with the other girls?"

For my part, I just sat there stunned. I could hardly speak. Nita, Lesley, and I had been a team for ten years. We had been pregnant together. We had worked together, advocated the issue of special needs housing accessibility together, stood together against the bias and disinterest we encountered within the Establishment. We had worked together creating the documentation on so many of NCJW's projects. I'd do the typing because they couldn't, and they'd store our records in the computer because I couldn't understand how a computer worked. We had talked about men, sex, and life. We had gone on perennial diets together, had travelled together by car, train, and plane to advocate on behalf of the disabled.

And now we were splitting up. It was all over. There was nothing more to say.

Eveline made their decision known to the others, and in the

next few days, they were almost completely ostracized. Pretty soon Nita resigned as president of NCJW, Toronto. She and Lesley opened another office elsewhere for Futurac Consultants (the company they had formed), and then they left, for good.

And the world we had once known began unravelling, surely and steadily.

CHAPTER THIRTEEN

The Daggers Are Unsheathed

At an NCJW board meeting in March 1989, almost two hundred members were in attendance to get an update on the situation and ratify the appointment of Clifford Lax as our lawyer. I was there, but didn't speak. The national members showed up in force.

Donald Carr represented the interests of Nita, Lesley, and Marsha. Cliff Lax had told Peter Atkinson that it wasn't necessary for him to attend. I was being "looked after."

Donald told the board that we had to form a wall of silence. He went on to say that leaks and interviews would fan the flames of anti-Semitism. The other lawyers present practically begged "those who are using this opportunity to pay back old debts" to stop spreading stories and talking to the media. Cliff would hire an independent accountant and a full report would be forthcoming. Until such time, a united front was critical.

Despite the warnings, and the show of hands in support of silence, most of the details of that board meeting were in the hands of the *Globe* by late afternoon. The reporter called me at home for my comments. I had none. So much for a united front.

And now, strangely, I started to get calls and letters of support from politicians, CEOs, former NCJW colleagues, and from Queen's Park. Even strangers would come up and speak to me about what was happening with words of encouragement.

At about this time NCJW had a front row table, again, at the premier's Heritage dinner. Several of the girls attended, including

Eveline Berger and Rochelle Reingold. Their husbands were sitting elsewhere in the back of the hall. Eveline and Rochelle had also attended my dinner for Alan Tonks a few days earlier. I was inundated with words of support. Even the lobbyist Ivan Fleischman, Art Eggleton's close friend, came over to commiserate, having been a victim of the press himself during the Elinor Caplan scandal. I began to believe that "this too shall pass" and started getting defiant again.

Along with Ron Barbaro, president of Prudential Life, and Toni Varone, president of Columbus Centre, I co-chaired a St. Patrick's Day luncheon honouring the Lord Mayor of Dublin, who was in town. The function also raised money for Jewish and Italian charities.

This brought more publicity, which I thought was a smart move. After all, it reinforced how unperturbed we all were by the allegations. But it was another act of stupidity on my part, only inciting my enemies more.

Days fluctuated from being okay to awful, depending on what was in the press. I came to dread reading the newspapers, and in fact, stopped. Of course, everyone called to give me a blow-by-blow report, along with their personal analysis.

The *Canadian Jewish News*, long the information arm of the Jewish community across Canada, was covering this story from day one in a way unlike anything it had ever done before, or would ever do again. They repeated the allegations carried in the other dailies, along with the comments of "unnamed sources." This was particularly hurtful to me. I eventually gave them one interview, which was so edited that it bore no resemblance to what I had actually said. Specifically, any mention of Nita Goldband, Lesley and Ron Miller, and Marsha and Eric Slavens, was removed.

Some time later, I called the new editor of the *News*, Patricia Rucker, to complain about the coverage I was getting, and to ask why the paper was singling me out for crucifixion as though no one else was involved.

I had known Patricia for years. When she joined the Liberal

government as political staff to Ken Keyes, solicitor general, who represented Kingston, she called to tell me about it. We had kept in touch and in December 1986, she asked if she could bring Keyes to a Chanukah luncheon Tridel was throwing at Monte Cassino for the NCJW team. She wanted to impress him with her contacts by introducing him to some leaders of the Jewish and Italian communities.

As a converted orthodox Jew, Patricia insisted that her food that day be served on a paper plate. It was. We also gave financial support for Ken. As with all political dinners, it was discussed among a group of our executive. In 1987, NCJW sent $2,500, to purchase tickets for Keyes' fundraiser. Since no one from Toronto intended to go to Kingston, Patricia requested permission to give these tickets to local seniors who would attend instead of us. We agreed. She sent a nice letter of appreciation to Council House.

But now, it was two years later. Even though almost everyone else was suddenly suffering from amnesia where their political activities were concerned, how could she rationalize the paper's attacks on me when Ken, at her suggestion, had benefited from NCJW, Toronto, by way of contacts and money for political purposes?

She just hung up. I don't know the answer myself, but one thing is for sure: no one else in our community — lawyers who have been disbarred or even others who have been cited for being slum landlords — has ever received the negative coverage in the *Canadian Jewish News* that I did, week after week.

In April, our NCJW group, minus Lesley and Nita, realized things were not going to get any better. Eveline Berger continued to be loyal, but the incessant media coverage was starting to take its toll, and I was getting scared. We decided that no matter what happened, we had to save the Ridley project. Given the disarray of our group, and the absence of Lesley and Nita, who were so important to Ridley's success, we decided to approach the Establishment within our community, the Toronto Jewish Congress, to ask them to take over the project.

It was another one of those days that I'll always remember so clearly. I walked down the street from Council House to the TJC-CJC building for a scheduled meeting with some of Congress's officers. The meeting had been arranged by Les Scheininger, who would later become president of the Canadian Jewish Congress. Les was one of the few senior community leaders whose voice of support on my behalf never wavered.

I was carrying all the documents on Ridley, including the recently arrived approval from the Ministry of Housing. In the package were our notes, our committee structures, needs, and demand surveys — in short, two years of research and development. My heart was full. I was reminded of a TV show I'd recently seen, in which a terminally ill mother tries to find a good home for her child before she dies.

When I got to the meeting, I was overwhelmed by the sensitivity shown me. Some of these people had not been supporters of mine, and too often had been on the receiving end of my barbs regarding their inaction on social issues. But I saw sympathy in their eyes, as though they knew what was coming. Yes, they would love to take over Ridley, they told me. We didn't need to worry. NCJW volunteers would remain a part of it. TJC wasn't afraid of any press jabs at Tridel, since the Prince Charles project was testament to both their construction skills and our volunteer management. We should be proud of what we had accomplished to date. They were proud we had asked them to take over Ridley and work with Tridel to complete it.

I thanked them and left. I cried all the way back up Bathurst Street to Council House. Somehow I knew I would never be part of this project or my community again.

✦ May 1989 was the beginning of the end. The media weren't letting up. All the confidential information being reported to the NCJW board was being leaked. This included breakdowns of who exactly attended the dinners as far back as 1984 and how the receipts were allocated. Lost in the shuffle was the fact that all this information was clearly documented — hardly the action of women who thought they were doing something illegal. These stories used the word "illegal" in all references to me, or the Fund, or even NCJW. There was a clear implication that our actions were secret, when in fact they were not and never had been.

I kept waiting for someone to come forward and diffuse some of the controversy. Many could have lent support with their prior knowledge and professional opinions on the Capital Fund. But they didn't.

During the first week of May, I flew to Montreal for the plenary convention of the Canadian Jewish Congress for what turned out to be two days of contradictions. Many people came up with words of encouragement and support. But a great many more were very cold. I encountered silent stares, whispering and pointing, and obvious snubs. The knot that had been in my stomach since January got worse.

A close friend who from day one had encouraged me to just let this blow over now turned his head away when he saw me. Maybe I am being too sensitive, I thought. But when I walked right up to him, he looked me in the eye, turned on his heel, and left.

That evening, at an officers' reception, where once again pointed stares and turned backs greeted me, I insisted that someone tell me what the hell was going on.

Their answer horrified me. They had been told that I had "stolen" money from NCJW. I stormed out of the room and went looking until I found Frances Mandell, NCJW national member, Jewish National Fund president, daughter of financier Joseph Tannenbaum, and volunteer colleague for twenty-five years. I asked her if she could shed light on the origins of these rumours.

"Well, I heard you spent $100,000 on your son's Bar Mitzvah and paid for it with NCJW's money," she whined.

"Do you know what slander and libel are, Frances?" I said. "I'm going to sue whoever is spreading these lies."

"Well," she said, "I heard it from some of the others who have all the facts."

"Who are they, Frances?" I demanded.

"Oh, you know, the ones who don't like you."

The Daggers Are Unsheathed

"Frances, I've known you since I was a kid. How could you hear this and not ask me directly whether I had done something like that?"

"I'm sorry I took you under my wing twenty years ago," she answered, her voice rising. "You should be ashamed of yourself. Stealing money from Council House." She turned and walked away.

I wanted to scream and kick the walls. I wanted to lash out, but of course, I couldn't. My head felt as if it would explode. I had been tried and convicted on whispered innuendoes. For the first time since all this started, I realized that I could be cast out from my community, no matter how many years I had volunteered and despite everything good I had been part of, period.

Both Gordon Ashworth and Hershell Ezrin attended the last day of that convention. I got the feeling that Hershell was avoiding me. He certainly wouldn't look me in the eye whenever I did get a chance to speak to him. When I asked Gordon about it, he told me to stop being paranoid.

On the plane back to Toronto, I tried to figure out what I should do. I didn't know where to turn, or who would help me anymore.

✧ Six months earlier, Eric Slavens and I had attended a small reception for Barbara McDougall at the Albany Club in Toronto. Jane Pepino had joined us. We discussed the imminent federal election, and strategized how our combined group of Liberal/Tory backers would work to ensure the election of both Barbara, a Tory, and Jim Peterson, a Liberal. On the drive back up to the House of Chan, where I was meeting John Bitove, Sr., and Eddie Cogan to hear their suggestions about the expansion of Ontario Place's Forum, Eric and I talked about his upcoming campaign to become chairman of the Ontario region of the Canadian Jewish Congress. He asked if I would help coordinate it. Of course I agreed.

He mentioned how tired out I seemed to be and suggested easing up after the Ridley housing project was under way. I appreciated his concern and gave him an update on NCJW's activities.

"Eric, we'll soon have two dynamite housing projects, along with our other community services, which are flourishing. Council House's renovations, including the addition of a special needs elevator, has enabled us to expand our outreach programs to seniors and the disabled. Obviously the Capital Fund has served NCJW's purposes, thanks to you. Its assets are going to provide ample security for NCJW's administrative costs. There'll be less enthusiasm on the part of most of the other girls to continue going to the political events once I'm gone. But we've already begun winding down anyhow, so it won't matter much."

We then discussed the fact that Lesley and Nita had formed Futurac Consultants and wanted to leave NCJW when Nita's term of office was over in May 1989.

That would be the right time for me to retire as well.

"What a party the community will make for you, Patti," he said enthusiastically. "B'nai Brith's tribute dinner will seem like a tea party. Then you'll really see exactly how much you mean to us and how the community shows its appreciation to a person who gives so much of themselves, as you have. I'll be the chairman."

And now, six months later, they were really showing me, all right.

But I resolved that no matter what happened, no one would ever see me cry or appear to be afraid. At least I would hold my head high and deprive "them" of the satisfaction of seeing me suffer.

That same week, a dinner was hosted by David Peterson for the governors of the Great Lake states. I went with Gordon. When we got there, David and Vince Borg stopped us for a brief chat. David was concerned about the media, and warned me not to speak to them under any circumstances. We discussed the innuendoes concerning improper political activity and my conversation with the Charities Division of Revenue Canada.

Vince confirmed that all of NCJW's contributions were clearly noted in the files of the Ontario Liberal party. I had already sent them copies of the Lax report on the Capital Fund's expenditures and the documentation on which NCJW's opinions had been based.

I also alerted them to another *Globe* article coming out the next day with more details of our Capital Fund, which had been leaked to them. Again David insisted that I keep quiet, since no matter what I said, the media would twist it and take it out of context.

I assured him that when the reporter had called me for a comment, I refused to give one. Too bad, because in hindsight, I should have. At least some of the truth might have been printed somewhere, before it was too late. After dinner, Gordon and I drove down in my car to the *Globe* building on Front Street to get the next day's paper. There I was, on the front page.

The article was something else. I didn't know who was giving the press the information, but I did know that the report was getting wider circulation than I was comfortable with. For example, Cliff Lax had warned me earlier that Dody Rudson, on his instructions, had allowed Betty Stone back into Council House to read his confidential report to the board (the Goodman & Goodman report) on NCJW's Capital Fund expenditures, the details of which I had provided.

So Dody left Betty alone for forty-five minutes to read all the material. Cliff said, "Dody was sure Betty didn't take any notes because the door was kept open."

At the time, I, along with some of the other girls, had raised an objection with Cliff about allowing anyone in to see the report who was not on the board. Betty was not then, nor was she ever, a member of the board. But Cliff said it would be better if she was allowed to see the report. He didn't say why.

"But I'm the one being crucified!" I cried to him. "Don't my wishes count?"

"My responsibility is to the executive of NCJW," he replied. "Even though you're one of them, the greater interest has to prevail."

And now Gordon and I were reading the *Globe* article, and there was a glaring error. The article alleged that the NCJW Capital Fund had given Chaviva Hosek $10,000. Absolutely untrue.

With Gordon beside me, I called Jane and Chaviva from my car phone. "Does this mean I could file a lawsuit, finally, against the *Globe?*" I asked Jane.

I had wanted to do this earlier, but each time it was suggested, the advice given was that such an action would create more press. This evening, however, Gordon was adamant about suing and starting to fight back, despite what David kept saying.

"Leave it alone, it'll die out," was the constant direction I had been getting. But it wasn't stopping; it was getting worse.

Jane said she would reach Peter Atkinson the next morning early and tell him to file a notice of defamation and libel against the *Globe*. In the meantime, Chaviva should issue an immediate denial.

Finally, I would be on the attack.

When we then spoke to Chaviva on the car phone, she asked me if NCJW had ever given her $10,000. Gordon rolled his eyes skyward and I spit out an obscenity in Hebrew so Gordon wouldn't understand what I was saying. But he guessed anyway and started to snicker. "Well then," she said, "an immediate denial will be issued." Gordon and I drove around for another hour discussing the situation.

One of the subjects of our conversation was Hugh Paisley, of the Office of the Public Trustee, which was investigating whether NCJW had committed a breach of trust by its activities. The public trustee in Ontario is responsible for monitoring the activities of charities as they apply to public funds received or donations solicited. They also look after bequests, trust funds for minors, and anything that involves wills and estates.

But neither Gordon nor I knew then that since 1988 the Office of the the Public Trustee itself had been under investigation by the OPP for misuse of public funds. In 1992 the authorities said it would cost the taxpayers hundreds of thousands of dollars to conduct the investigation properly, so the matter was ended by finding the trustee's office "remiss."

In May 1989, however, the trustee's office weighed in heavily. It began pontificating when the Starr Affair started to fly, and ended up deflecting attention from itself by going after me.

By the following Monday, Chaviva still hadn't issued a denial regarding the $10,000, and the media were now on this like vultures.

Her silence was surprising, in light of the support I had given her before and after her election to office.

"Chaviva!" I beseeched her. "You can't ignore this. You've got to speak out. I'm on the ropes!" She promised to speak to Vince and have him handle it.

It would be another week before a letter to the editor was printed in denial. But by then it was too late. The damage had already been done.

✦ That same Monday afternoon, I received a call at Ontario Place from David Peterson. Gordon was with him. I was in the Trillium Restaurant, looking out over the clear, blue water, watching people getting their boats ready for the upcoming season.

David felt the press were really going to go after me as long as I was so high profile. The trustee's office was getting antsy.

"David, do you want me to resign?" I asked, my heart not beating.

His response was, "No, absolutely not."

He went on to suggest a leave of absence, which would remove me from the public eye and allow matters to cool down. It would also give the trustee time to prepare a report that showed the real numbers in terms of political fundraisers for the provincial Liberals, not the inflated ones being bandied about.

"Then you'll be able to come back, better than before," he said.

In one week, Ontario Place was to open its eighteenth season. Our new attractions and improved facilities were almost completed. This was to be the culmination of two years' work, and now I was being asked to step aside. Once again, I would have to give up something I had worked so hard for and loved. I felt as though my resolve to be strong would soon melt away.

"Okay, David, you make the announcement," I said, barely able to hold back my tears.

Before I left Ontario Place that afternoon, I walked through every inch of it once more. I wanted to keep its image, as it was for me then, indelibly in my memory. I called my husband from the car, then Ruby, my sweet and loyal secretary, Jane Pepino, and Angelo DelZotto. Then I drove home, crying and sobbing all the way with frustration, rage, and a broken heart.

Jerry and the children were waiting for me. They gave me their unwavering support, though Randy, our youngest, was worried that he would never be able to play miniature golf again.

Paul Godfrey phoned up the next morning to express his friendship and support, and that of my colleagues on the Molson Indy board of governors. (As chairman of Ontario Place, I was a member of that board.) However, notwithstanding my leave of absence, which he was sure would only be temporary, the group had asked him to call and let me know they still wanted me to continue. Paul also said that Jerry and I were still expected to be part of the group going on our annual trip to the Indianapolis '500, courtesy of the *Toronto Sun*. His call made me feel so much better — even hopeful that things might still work out.

At the end of May, we all met at the Toronto Island Airport to go on our second trip to the Indianapolis '500. Included in this group were Mayor Art Eggleton and his wife Brenda; Cabinet ministers Monte Kwinter and Hugh O'Neil, along with their wives; Paul and Gina Godfrey; Ralph Lean and his wife Marcelle; Jeff and Sandy Lyons; Hal Moran, CEO of Molson's, and his wife; and Jerry and me, along with assorted Molson executives.

We flew directly to Indianapolis on a private Dash 7. All our expenses were covered. We all stayed on the same floor in the hotel and as a group had lots of fun, especially since this was our second year together. I hoped to forget some of my problems, especially since we spent the day of the race in a private box supplied by one of the sponsors. We had a betting pool, into which everyone put ten dollars. Art Eggleton won both years in a row.

We were also right in front of a horrific crash that happened at the beginning of the race. It was really hard to fathom, since your brain denies what your eyes are seeing and it's much different than on TV. The noise was deafening.

On the final day, over drinks in the bar, I had a meeting with Monte Kwinter and my "boss," Hugh O'Neil, the minister of Tourism and Recreation. Hugh, as always, was supportive. He had heard that I was considering reimbursing the Capital Fund, personally, for all political expenditures, in order to enable the trustee to close its books. Then I could be reinstated at Ontario Place, which was still his ministry's responsibility.

That suggestion had been made to me earlier when Peter Atkinson and I were in Cliff Lax's office listening to Cliff on the phone with Hugh Paisley, the public trustee. Cliff suggested that the money could be put into a trust fund, which he would administer. He thought that might satisfy Paisley.

At the time, I was happy to do it, but Peter, thank goodness, wouldn't allow it. He was getting more concerned about the vibes he was beginning to get. He couldn't put his finger on it, but he felt that such an action would concede some wrongdoing on my part, as well as isolate me from my NCJW colleagues. But he also emphasized that Lax's duty was to the executive and not just to me.

So Hugh O'Neil, in his usual caring way, was concerned that day in Indianapolis that I would be left high and dry, which he felt wasn't right. Monte, for his part, started ranting about the press again, and Chaviva Hosek in particular.

"See how loyal she is to you?" Monte asked, quite agitated. "I told you not to stick your neck out for her." Chaviva and Monte had never gotten along at all, and on more than one occasion I had been caught in the middle. Once, in a dispute over her treatment of Monte's friend, developer Rudy Reimer, I had stepped in.

He also reminded me of the number of times he and Wilma had told me to get out of my volunteer commitments, especially back in February and March. That's why they avoided volunteer organizations themselves, he said, citing backstabbing and disloyalty.

But he told me not to worry, because of all the friends I had in government, including David Peterson and, of course, Monte himself. He then urged me to continue my "no comment" stance.

On the plane ride back from Indianapolis to Toronto, I sat with Ralph Lean. He was still part of NCJW's law firm, Robins, Appleby, Kotler, though he did not work with Ron Miller. Although the controversy in which I was embroiled had arisen over whether a charitable organization like the NCJW could buy tickets to political events in lieu of spending its money to travel to lobby politicians, Ralph appeared to have little knowledge of what was going on.

"Cut the garbage, Ralph," I said. "You and I have been involved together politically for the last six years. I still have the letters you wrote asking NCJW to buy tables for Tory fundraisers. And when NCJW did buy a table, and you got the cheque under our letterhead, you didn't have a problem taking the money. If you thought there was a problem, why didn't you raise a red flag? So don't play dumb now."

I went on to express my disappointment at the silence of Ron Miller and Eric Slavens.

"All they have to do is tell the truth," I went on, clutching Ralph's arm with both hands and trying to keep my growing fear of being abandoned under control. "They gave us their best opinion. If it wasn't the right one, so what. It wouldn't be such a scandal if they admitted that we had discussed it with them before we did anything."

He was silent for a few moments and then removed my hands from his arm. "Do you have any instructions, in writing, from either one of them telling you girls to write the cheques or attend the dinners?" he asked.

Oh, my God, I thought. That's it. That's why they haven't said anything. They're going to leave me hanging out to dry. But they couldn't do that. Their wives had attended the dinners and been reimbursed by NCJW for cheques they had written.

Or could they? I didn't know anymore.

CHAPTER FOURTEEN

"I'm Through Sneaking"

In June, excerpts from Cliff Lax's report were being released to the press, outlining the details of the Capital Fund's expenditures.

For some reason, these disclosures didn't include any portion of his report which confirmed that "officers of NCJW, Toronto Section, were aware of the Fund's activities, that Patricia Starr did not act alone, and that as volunteers, the executive's actions were motivated by what was thought to be the best interests of the organization."

By now, Eveline Berger was the new president of NCJW, Toronto Section. Some of our mutual friends told me about the pressure being put on her by the national office to distance herself from me and withdraw her previous support. She had worked hard to become the president and had wanted the position very badly. If she continued to be supportive of me, then her presidency might be in jeopardy. And as icing on the cake, some of the girls also said they were being encouraged along the same lines, stressing that such a course was now in the best interests of the organization.

As long as no one from NCJW had any recollection of my alerting them to the florist's bill ($4,035), then I had committed a breach of trust, which was a criminal offence, meaning that I no longer deserved their loyalty. By washing their hands of me, NCJW could then move forward with Lax's recommendations on how the foundation should operate in the future. It's too bad they didn't give more thought to how their abandonment of me would appear not only to the public, but also to some of NCJW's general membership. I believe their actions hurt the organization much more than anything I ever did. I doubt if anyone out there really believed that no one knew anything, especially given all the political events we had attended as a group over the years.

And now the media really went off the wall. Articles and broadcasts, almost every day, with wildly inflated numbers and allegations, kept the scandal going. I'd never even met some of those giving interviews about me. Anything and everything was given its day in the press, always tempered by the word "alleged."

Patrick Gossage, PR consultant for the Liberals, continued to try to help and was in constant touch with Queen's Park, specifically with Vince Borg. Finally, it was suggested I consider resigning as chairman of the board of Ontario Place. The public trustee was still vacillating and the premier's office was under tremendous pressure. And still no one knew about the ongoing investigation of the public trustee's office itself.

As long as I was still tied to the government, so the reasoning went, the press wouldn't let up, but if I was really gone, then they would probably back off. This was another blow.

My life had become full of anguish, and Jerry and the kids were all that was keeping me together. Our wonderful friends and family kept calling all the time, dropping in, and just being there.

Many of the politicians I had worked with municipally sent notes and telephoned.

But still, it was a nightmare. I couldn't sleep. I didn't know whom to trust anymore. I was frightened. After my recent conversation with Ralph Lean on the plane ride home from Indianapolis, any hopes I had of vindication were shattered.

So one morning in early June, I drove down to Queen's Park to hand in my letter of resignation to Gordon Ashworth personally.

He looked awful, pale and haggard. His eyes were red, and if I didn't know better, I'd have thought he had been crying. But not Gordon Ashworth, the premier's front man who it was rumoured had icewater in his veins. Very few people had ever seen the warm and fun side of him, the devoted father and churchgoer. But I had, and for a few moments I tried to comfort him, telling him I was okay, and not to worry.

He turned his head away quickly, and then said the press were camped outside and if I wanted to sneak out the back way, that was okay.

"I'm through sneaking," I told him. "It's only made things worse. Maybe I should have hired a press agent, and held a news conference to give my side of the story before it was too late. And now it is too late. I hope that whatever happens with the waterfront, you'll keep an eye on it for me."

"Listen, Patti," he said. "There's more to this than you know. But soon it'll be over. The Skydome scam is going to break soon. The financial picture there is catastrophic, and David's ass is really on the line. Cost overruns, the hotel–health spa addition that was never budgeted, expense accounts, the works. Nixon's trying to keep it quiet, but he won't be able to for much longer. The press is going to have a field day, and you'll be old news.

"We're not saying anything publicly, for now, about the ownership questions on the Lakeshore. It's still too hot. But your record at Ontario Place is written in stone. I think you should know that Hershell was against your appointment in the beginning, and I had a real battle over it. But I'm proud of you, and proud of what you've done, and . . ." He choked up and turned his back.

I got up to leave. He put his arms around me and we held each other, in silence, for a few minutes. Then I walked out of his office and into the arms of the press.

✦ Two weeks later, Betty Disero and I left for her parents' home in Florida. Every day we were there, phone calls kept coming about the ongoing "revelations" in the media. Betty had to fly back to Toronto for a day to attend an important City Council meeting. Many of her colleagues knew she was in Florida with me.

She told me that Tom Jakobek advised her not to return to

Florida, but to leave me there alone; he thought it would be bad for her political career to be seen with me now. She ignored him and returned the next day.

Jane and I were on the phone daily. The stories hadn't let up, and the premier had finally called for a police investigation, which he hoped would stop the press speculation.

I couldn't care less, because I had nothing to fear from the police. Or so I thought.

One morning before Betty and I left for the beach, Jane called. "Patti," she said very gently. "I think you have to resign from the Committee of Adjustment. The press is planning to attend any future meetings you attend. Larry Wynn is giving interviews trying to get in on the publicity. I talked to Mel Lastman. He says he'll stick with you all the way, but some of the others think you should withdraw."

It was happening again. I had been on that committee for four years, and I loved it. I had learned a lot, made lots of friends, and developed an appreciation for the planning process.

First Ridley, then Ontario Place, and now the Committee of Adjustment.

Betty was standing there with me when I faxed my letter of resignation to the North York Commissioner of Planning. By now I was almost numb.

We walked along the beach. Betty put her arm around my shoulders and we didn't speak. She had shared every moment of my anguish since the onset of this nightmare, and despite the fact that she was fifteen years younger than me, I was leaning on her as if she were the mother I didn't have. Her loyalty was unwavering.

Jerry had decided to take the kids out of school when I got home and take us all to Vermont. The media were now coming to the house looking for me.

On our drive to Vermont we kept turning off the radio station every hour when the news came on, to prevent the kids from hearing my name, along with the allegations. I tried not to think about what was still happening, but every night when we called home to speak to my daughter, who had stayed in Toronto because she had a job, she would read off the list of messages, mostly from the press. My stomach would turn every time.

Vermont is one of our favourite places, and we stayed in a country inn, played tennis with the kids every day, and did a lot of sightseeing. Then one morning I got a frantic phone call from Peter Atkinson. Jerry was standing beside me.

Gordon Ashworth had resigned over a refrigerator and paint job that weren't paid for. Tridel was being accused along with me. The press had gone beserk. David Peterson had called an inquiry. Later he would name Mr. Justice Lloyd Houlden to be its chairman.

"I don't give a shit what David Peterson has called," I said to Peter. "I didn't give Gordon Ashworth anything."

"Well, he admitted he didn't pay for the fridge," Peter answered, "and the press release out of the premier's office points the finger at you and Tridel."

"But I didn't give him anything," I insisted. "I just sent Dyanne Ashworth to a wholesaler."

"Well, the allegation is that you did. Anyhow, I don't do inquiries. You'll have to look for another lawyer. Jane is also worried that in light of this revelation, her position has become untenable, given that she has acted for Tridel."

Until this moment, I had no idea that the fridge hadn't been paid for. I believe that whatever happened in terms of this nonpayment was an innocent oversight, not worthy of creating the Starr Inquiry. I believe Gordon was set up by those in the premier's circle who wanted to get him out of their way.

In order to deflect media attention from David Peterson and protect his interests, the fridge became the rationale for destroying Gordon's career and my life as I had once known it.

When we returned to Toronto the next day, Jerry dropped me off at my aunt's house so he and the kids could go home without me. The press were camped outside and if they didn't see me, they would assume I was still away. Later my aunt drove me home;

I lay on the back floor of her car so none of the press could see me.

That same day, Jerry's father, who had been very sick for several months, died. At the funeral the next day, the press was camped outside our house, the funeral parlour, and the cemetery. We received many calls from politicians we had considered friends. They knew we understood why they couldn't show up at the funeral, given the presence of so many reporters.

The day after the funeral I received a registered letter from my accountant stating that given the circumstances, which he didn't elaborate on, he would no longer act for my personal companies.

Revenue Canada notified me that as a result of the inquiry being called, a special investigation would be conducted into all my personal business affairs.

Peter Atkinson then confirmed that he could not act for me any longer. He mentioned that Jane Pepino was distraught over this situation.

"Listen, Peter," I said again, very quietly. "I didn't know Ashworth didn't pay for the fucking fridge. If I had, I would have paid for it myself. But so what? He wasn't even a civil servant at the time. He didn't do any favours for me or Tridel or anybody that I know of. Maybe no one ever sent them a bill. Or maybe Dyanne misplaced it. Politicians take freebees all the time. Ask any developer. Why is Gordon being thrown to the wolves like this? It's all completely crazy!"

He didn't answer.

"Okay," I said, "thanks for all your help. Send me your bill."

He did, and I paid it.

The next day, Jamie Pearson, Jane's husband, called to offer his condolences and words of encouragement. I didn't hear from Jane Pepino again.

CHAPTER FIFTEEN

"They'll Never See Me Cry"

By July 1989, any press articles on any subject that could possibly include my name or Tridel's continued. It seemed that everybody and anybody who ever knew any of us was giving interviews, usually full of hot air. All the old innuendoes about the DelZottos were rehashed.

In the Legislature, Ian Scott had denied giving any support for Elvio's appointment to the Ontario Police Commission.

The media seemed to be so excited about the inquiry, scheduled for September. I still didn't have a clue about what was coming, other than what I had heard about the Waisberg Commission. And it was time to face Angelo.

Our meeting was highly charged.

I was devastated by the damage being inflicted on his family and his company, and felt largely responsible because of my refusal to throw in the towel months earlier. Perhaps if I had, none of this would have happened.

I also knew, no matter what he said, that the notoriety associated with my name would be permanent. That meant that any hope of a continuing, long-term career within the Tridel group of companies was now over.

Anonymity, one of the keys to success in this business, had been lost. And nothing could bring it back.

On the day of our meeting, Angelo was, as he had been the first time I met him five years earlier, elegant and eloquent. His words were full of reassurances and support. But I knew the rules of the game. And he knew I did. After all, he had taught them to me.

When I left Tridel's offices that last time, another sad page in my life was turned.

And now our friends and family who were lawyers themselves kept insisting that I needed a criminal lawyer.

"But I'm not a criminal," I would protest. They felt that the inquiry might lead to other problems, though, and advised me that I needed protection. They believed my political "friends" would abandon me in a second once there was any chance they might be implicated in anything themselves.

Bloodlust for the Italians, and the DelZottos in particular, was being promoted in the media. When David Peterson allowed Vince Borg to publicly humiliate the DelZottos by demanding their resignations from volunteer boards under the government's aegis, I called Austin Cooper, one of Canada's leading criminal lawyers.

After paying him an initial retainer of $15,000, we spent two hours discussing my community and political involvements and the current situation. He was reassuring and confident. I felt terrific.

As he was deeply involved with the Joe Burnett tax fraud case, still ongoing after six years, he retained another outstanding criminal lawyer, Earl Levy, to join the team, so I would always be covered. His younger partner, Peter West, would work hands-on with me as well.

The Tridel team of lawyers consisted of Earl Cherniak based in London, Ontario; Michael Moldaver; Alan Gold; and Julian Porter, who represented Elvio DelZotto personally. This was a high-powered, brilliant, but very expensive team. The terms of reference for the Starr Inquiry had been drawn up by Attorney General Ian Scott, and Mr. Justice Lloyd Houlden of the Ontario Court of Appeal was named as the commissioner. When these terms were made public, a pow-wow was called by all the lawyers without me present.

I learned later that Gold, another top criminal lawyer who was specifically representing Mario Giampietri on behalf of Tridel, considered the whole process an outrage and advocated stopping it with an application under the Charter of Rights and Freedoms. The rest of Tridel's lawyers concurred. Since I was the individual named, they felt that I would have to be the principal applicant, in order to have the best chance of success.

But Austin was uneasy at first, because his primary concern was me, not Tridel. He wasn't so sure they might not try to stab me in the back, as others had, if things got too hot.

For the first time in Canadian history, an individual, Patricia Starr, had been named in a judicial inquiry. When Austin's former client, Susan Nelles, had been involved in an inquiry, it was called the Grange Commission; its terms of reference were generic, and her name had not been used. The press frenzy around me reminded Austin of the Nelles Affair, however. He was growing more concerned that in order to justify the millions of dollars an inquiry would cost, pressure would be put on the police to get me for something.

Furthermore, some of the wording in the terms of reference for the Starr Inquiry was taken verbatim from the Criminal Code. By pointing a finger directly at me, especially with an ongoing police investigation, the inquiry had effectively removed any presumption of innocence for me.

Austin suggested, however, that ironically, the Peterson government, which was continuing to hide behind a veil of self-righteousness, might even reap some benefits if the inquiry was quashed, since they'd have a hard time explaining their backroom activities in a public inquiry.

I had already been told by some Liberal party pros, including Monte Kwinter, that David's calling of the inquiry was a kneejerk reaction to media pressure, especially after their Muzzo-Goldfarb allegations, and he now regretted it. This made sense to me, knowing the individuals as I did. But I still could not understand the Gordon Ashworth business, because the fridge was not a secret, and it had happened two years earlier.

Austin, however, remained wary of trying to get the inquiry quashed. He felt that no matter what was said during it, when my turn came, any evidence I gave would be immune from prosecution. As a result, others had more to fear than I did. But Tridel had lived through an inquiry before. They didn't want to do it again. I cared about them and understood their anguish.

On the other hand, it was my life on the chopping block. I was still unsure about appealing, especially after Austin warned me that the judges were an old boys' network who often took appeals personally.

An inquiry of this kind would put Lloyd Houlden's name in the history books, something he would certainly want. Though his expertise was in bankruptcy law, he felt qualified to run an inquiry. Austin was concerned that an attempt to stop the inquiry at the outset might not sit well with him.

In the meantime, Earl Levy and Peter West were trying to figure out what kind of criminal charges I might face. But the information and backup documentation they had on my activities reinforced their confidence that the whole matter was a tempest in a teapot. Knowing this also reinforced my belief that this was a political witch-hunt, and had to be handled as such.

It was agreed that we would take it one step at a time. An appeal would be filed the first day of the inquiry to protect our future options. If it was turned down, we would decide whether to go on. By now, I was hoping it would be turned down. I wanted to fight.

My aunt and uncle had taken my personal notes and files out of my house during our recent trip to Vermont, which I then turned over to my lawyers. As Peter West and I started going through them, my resolve was growing, along with my confidence in being vindicated.

I was still in contact with most of my political associates and I made no secret of the fact that I was looking forward to my day in court. The higher up they were in the power structure, the more surprised they were that a legal challenge was not a given, and that in fact, Austin wasn't so sure we would pursue it at all. I did not fail to note their reactions.

And then, one day in July, Austin got a call from my former lawyer Cliff Lax, who was still representing NCJW, Toronto. He had heard talk about the Council House renovation grant being the hook for criminal charges. Cliff didn't have details right then, but he'd let Austin know.

Again, my stupid reaction: righteous indignation. "Good, let them," I said. "Every grant I ever did for the last ten years will be under scrutiny. They were all done the same way. Then they'll see that I've never gotten one cent for my efforts."

But I forgot that it was only the NCJW renovation grant that I had actually signed. The others had been signed by staff.

◆ A week later I got a call from Marty Mendelow and we met in the parking lot of the Nymark Plaza in the Sheppard and Leslie area of North York. I was unprepared for what he told me that sunny afternoon.

"The investigators have been around," he said, "and I had to tell them that we couldn't match all the donated labour and material for Council House's renovation. I also told them we had never intended to."

I nearly fell down right there. And of course, I knew then what Cliff Lax had been trying to tell Austin about fraud charges on the grant. "And the contractor is doing the same thing," he went on. "He has submitted an amended statement of costs which are reduced by almost half the original numbers on the application."

I just stared at him, unable to speak.

"Patti, I'm sorry," he said, "but we have to look after ourselves and our businesses. Besides, nothing will happen to you; you're only a volunteer."

"Marty, don't you think you could have called and warned me about what was happening so I wouldn't be left here dangling in the wind?" I asked. "At least I would have had a chance to alert the ministry and adjust the numbers before an investigation was called."

Memories of my conversation with David Silcox about the renovation grant now came back to haunt me.

"Marty, we spoke to people several times from day one about how you guys were going to match the funding," I said. The original documents had reinforced those numbers. And the interim submissions, accompanied by Verdiroc's statements, had backed up NCJW's reports.

"How could you do this to me?" I was practically sobbing. "And why? If you guys pretend you didn't prepare the numbers, it'll look like I made them up. And that's fraud."

"I'm sorry," he said, eyes on the ground. "Everyone is edgy now. We've got other ongoing projects that can't be jeopardized."

"I worked as a volunteer for you!" I cried out at him. "I helped you — and your two kids. You people were supposed to help us renovate Council House. We discussed it several times."

When he didn't answer, I went on. "I didn't get paid for any of this, but you people did. Are you giving back your fees? You've left me to die in the desert."

I turned and left, never to speak to any of them again.

On Monday I went through the grant documentation with Austin and Peter. They were still hopeful that nothing much would happen, since every cent was accounted for. And in a normal world, nothing would have happened. But this was a political witch-hunt, and there were no rules.

A couple of weeks before the inquiry was to begin, Austin, Peter, Earl Levy, and I had dinner at the House of Chan. Monte and Wilma Kwinter were there with some friends. Monte came over for a big hug and kiss and chatted for a few minutes with the lawyers. He then asked to speak to me privately for a moment.

"Don't worry," he said, "everything will be okay. Just keep mum. You know we're all with you."

What I didn't know was that Monte had already given the police a statement.

I reported the conversation back to my lawyers and we went on to chat about frivolities over our steak and lobster dinner. Everyone was looking forward to the inquiry's opening day.

I was prepared. Right down to the details of how to dress and behave. Sedate and no comments. Period.

When the day finally came, the three of us — Austin Cooper, Peter West, and I — walked over to the courtroom at 180 Dundas Street West from their offices on Queen Street. I felt confident and was anxious to get on with it. When we got inside, though, we were shocked to find an entire floor taken over for the inquiry, including a media room twice the size of the courtroom.

TV cameras, reporters, and microphones pushed in our faces — the whole media blitz. For twenty minutes we sat waiting for the judge to come in. Photographers were snapping pictures from every angle.

"Speak only to me," Austin said in a very quiet voice. "Don't look at anyone, don't smile, just concentrate on me until the judge comes in. I'm sure he'll stop this. By the way, there's a TV camera trained on you. Don't forget it's on, so any facial expressions you make or any comments you might make to either me or Peter will be picked up. But I'm sure the judge will have that removed."

From the moment Mr. Justice Lloyd Houlden came into that room, the inquiry, in tone and approach, became a witch-hunt, a circus. Houlden had no problem allowing live TV coverage of an inquiry where there were relaxed rules of evidence and little restriction on unsubstantiated allegations. He refused to have the cameras removed, despite the request of our lawyers. His rulings allowed into the record rumours, innuendoes, and, worse, third-party hearsay. The evidence any witnesses gave could not be used against them in other proceedings.

This also meant that whatever was said could be reported in the press, with no protection for me from libel or slander. I didn't like the way Houlden was looking at me. My political instincts told me that this man knew a lot more about this case than he was supposed to. Before that first day was over, I told all the lawyers that Houlden didn't like me and I was in trouble. My sense was that he had already made up his mind.

But they all smiled at me as though I was nuts and suggested I was a touch paranoid. Only Earl Cherniak didn't smile.

The next day was the beginning of a nine-month nightmare. From the first day, when the press printed pictures that made me appear cross-eyed, while depicting Austin as a Fagin-like character, nothing was spared to present a negative visual image to go along with the articles.

The inquiry was supposed to look into the relationship between Patricia Starr, Tridel Corporation, Tridel vice-president Mario Giampietri, Gordon Ashworth, and certain elected and unelected officials. Simple. Or in other words, what the hell was going on between Patricia Starr and the politicians?

But Houlden had other ideas.

The first weeks consisted of personal attacks on me.

Our group of lawyers, which now included Gina Brannon, representing Gordon Ashworth, became very concerned. They had assumed the issues to be investigated would be relevant to the terms of reference and would deal primarily with elected and unelected officials.

Instead, we heard about personal hostilities towards me by ex-NCJW employees, one of whom had worked for us for only three months and whom I barely knew. The taxpayers were footing the bill to hear Betty Stone's complaints about her treatment by NCJW executive officers and me in particular. They also heard of her displeasure with the settlement she had agreed to concerning her wrongful dismissal suit against NCJW.

Add to that her unsubstantiated allegations about threats to her daughter, money laundering, payoffs, etc., and the press were given a field day. The inquiry, to some, was reminiscent of the McCarthy days.

And it was all carried on live TV. And then reported in the press, every day. A couple of the more creative headlines were: "STARR DICTATOR" (*Toronto Sun*) and "EVIL LET LOOSE" (*Toronto Star*).

For the first time, Austin Cooper was becoming angry. Until now, he had told me to put my faith in the judicial system, which he lived by and had believed in for his entire career. Before the inquiry began, and even a couple of days after it started, he kept telling the rest of the team not to worry, that Houlden would rein it in.

But Houlden never did.

"Charles Dubin he ain't," became the daily synopsis during the first couple of weeks. (Charles Dubin was the judge who had conducted the inquiry into Ben Johnson's alleged use of steroids in Olympic competition.) Our lawyers had gone into this one assuming it would be conducted in a similar fashion.

And so Austin decided to go along with the urging of Tridel's legal team: to proceed with a legal review of the terms of reference of the inquiry. Even though I still had some doubts, I agreed.

By now, all pretence of separate interests between the main cast of characters — Tridel, Mario Giampietri, Gordon Ashworth, and me — was dropped. Many times during cross-examinations, the other lawyers would speak out on my behalf. Earl Cherniak was particularly eloquent.

It was clear that all the lawyers had a great deal of respect for each other, and I enjoyed listening to them plan strategy.

Earl, the most dapper dresser, wore wonderful hats and ties. Corporate litigation was one of his specialties. Julian Porter, one of this country's most prominent slander and libel lawyers, is a tall, distinguished-looking gentleman who gave us a dissertation every morning on the previous day's press, highlighting the potential slander and libel actions that could be filed. Of course, no one wanted to bother anymore. His explanations of how the word "alleged" is used by the media as protection from lawsuits was most chilling, especially since it was me he was using as an example of its abuse.

Michael Moldaver, who would be appointed a judge a year later, was warm and friendly, always smiling, with encouraging words for everyone, every day.

Alan Gold was the force behind the primary focus of the court challenge. He had a relaxed and hang-loose manner, until you looked into his eyes, which looked like steel pellets, especially when he was angry. Alan always carried his portable phone in case of emergencies, and it would often ring during the hearings. It was his opinion, from the first moment it was called, that the inquiry was tantamount to a criminal investigation without any protection under the Charter of Rights for those named.

Austin Cooper was tall and nearly bald. He could be quite intimidating, but when he wanted to be charming, he was delightful. His young associate, Peter West, was enthusiastic and confident, but somewhat unsure as to how to attack the allegations made by the "old ladies" without creating sympathy for them. They both decided to go easy on them, rather than risk the further wrath of Houlden.

Every day during the proceedings, this team of lawyers kept mumbling to each other, "This is a witch-hunt, a lynching. It's a zoo. To have to fight to get copies of documents being entered into the record by the commission's staff is outrageous. . . . No rules of evidence — hearsay, rumours, innuendoes — I've never seen anything like it."

"What has this testimony got to do with either the terms of reference or the intent of this inquiry?" Austin demanded of Houlden a few days into the proceedings. "The taxpayers are footing the bill for a personal vendetta. I'm requesting limitations on the unsubstantiated allegations being allowed into the record."

Houlden refused his request. And the press, with no information to the contrary, came up with one liners that forever cast a shadow over my volunteer career: "STARR USED THE CHARITY'S MONEY TO MAKE ILLEGAL POLITICAL CONTRIBUTIONS," or "CHARITY MEMBERS DIDN'T KNOW ABOUT STARR'S ACTIVITIES." My own lawyers told me I'd have to wait until my day in court before any response could be given on my behalf. By then, I wondered, would anyone care anymore?

For me, it was the smirks on the faces of Betty Stone, Gloria Strom, Eleanor Appleby, and Dody Rudson, the four horseladies of the Apocalypse as they came to be known, that bothered me the most — not what they were alleging. But in fact, they did me a favour. For the next two years, whenever I wanted to burst out crying in a courtroom, or in press confrontations, I'd remember their smirking faces and know how pleased they'd be if I did break down.

"Never," I vowed, "they'll never see me cry." And they never did.

And as long as the allegations continued, the press gave them front-page coverage.

But when, after a few weeks, some of the other members of the NCJW executive, like Phyllis Moss, Rochelle Reingold, Donna Zener, and Shirley Aronson, our bookkeeper, testified, their evidence was carefully edited in the media.

The problem, from the media's point of view, was that these women disputed a lot of what had been said by the others. Shirley Aronson, especially, showed another perspective that included criticism of Betty Stone's behaviour and her complicity in the grant process. They also confirmed the fact that other NCJW colleagues knew of our political activities and admitted, quite readily, that many of the girls had attended the dinners over the years and been reimbursed. Anything remotely supportive of me was generally ignored in the media. Even the TV coverage, carried live during the day but edited for the evening rehash, cut out most of their positive comments.

Gradually, the other lawyers, especially Alan Gold, Earl Cherniak, and Michael Moldaver, began looking at me with sympathy in their eyes. And I hated that. I wanted to fight back, but there was nothing to be done, at least not until my turn came.

And then Hugh Paisley, the public trustee, had his day. As mentioned, none us knew that his office was under investigation itself for negligence in the handling of trust funds. The press, caught up with me, missed him. I wonder how much credibility his testimony would have had if that information had been known.

Every day became more devastating than the last. I'd get up at

6:00 a.m., have a bagel with my kids, who were usually watching cartoons, remind myself how lucky I was to have them, and dress for the day's torture. Determined to show no concern or fear, I would steel myself by conjuring up those smirking faces.

Every day I parked in the same Richmond Street parking lot. The attendant would save me a spot in the front row and wish me luck. As I walked along towards Cooper's office, the construction workers would whistle, wave their hardhats, and yell, "Good luck, Patti. Give 'em hell, Patti."

Jerry and the kids were very courageous and never showed any concern, other than for me. The teaching staff at both Windfields Public School and York Mills Collegiate kept a close eye on the boys. Jerry and I received great comfort from their assurances that no negative comments were being made by the other students. Our friends called every day, most often leaving cheerful messages on the answering machine.

But the ordeal was taking its toll.

On one occasion, I lashed out at both Austin and Peter about their approach. I gave Austin a list of dirty laundry, wanting him to fling it back at Betty Stone, Gloria Strom, and the others.

"Do something," I would cry.

"Mrs. Starr," he said, "Cooper, Sandler and West has never, nor will we ever, sink to the level of some other lawyers participating in this inquiry. We believe in the sanctity of the law and the dignity of the court. Our successes are based on respect for the process, which ultimately prevails. If you wish anything different, you'll have to find another legal firm."

I backed off.

By the first week of December 1989, three months into the inquiry, a recess was called. Betty Disero and I went down to Florida.

✧ I was a mess. Consumed with rage and a burning desire for revenge, I couldn't sleep. Unfortunately, it didn't stop me from eating, and my perennial diet took a turn for the worse.

"What good will my day in court be?" I'd ask her. "The way

the press are selectively reporting things, nobody will even hear my side of it. Austin says this can take another year, at least. By then, who'll care anymore?"

"Hang in," she'd say. "Remember who you are and what you've accomplished. You can't give up."

By then, the combined legal team on the appeal was finalizing its submission to the Supreme Court of Canada, with the hearing scheduled for January 1990. We all flew to Ottawa.

The chambers of the Supreme Court of Canada are awesome. Two massive doors are opened, an announcement is made — just the words "The Court" in French and English — then seven men and women, the court of last resort, come marching in, single file.

The presentations of all three lawyers designated to make the submission — Austin, Earl, and Alan — were brilliant, inspiring, and articulate. And they were all talking about me.

Well, I thought. If nothing else, my name will go down in the history books. I hope it's not on the losing side.

During the proceedings, Peter and Austin turned around to smile at me. Suddenly, their eyes fixed on someone behind me and their smiles disappeared.

At the break, I asked what was going on. Apparently, two senior OPP officers were sitting right behind me. The police investigation, which was supposedly halted back in June when the inquiry had been called, was still ongoing.

So what? I didn't care and couldn't understand why they did.

But care they most certainly did. When Peter went over to talk to them, I sauntered along behind him. Their conversation had to do with the weather and Ottawa in general. Finally Peter asked them if they had any plans to act if the court should rule immediately that the Starr Inquiry was unconstitutional, and therefore quashed. Their answer was noncommittal. They were just there observing, they said. Good, I thought. Observe me close up. I walked over, introduced myself, and sat down right next to them.

Austin, at the next recess, really let me have it.

"Don't you ever talk to the police again without my presence and approval," he snapped. His face was white and his eyes burned into mine. "This isn't a game, not one of your political manoeuvres. This is serious, and anything you say to the police, no matter how innocent you think it is, can, and will, be used against you."

Finally the arguments were over. The court was reserving judgment. We all went out for lunch.

For the first time, the team of lawyers asked for my opinion and I was happy to give it.

"This is, and has been from the beginning, political," I said. "You people have a lofty view of the judicial system. You forget that judges are political appointees, many of whom lobbied, cajoled, contributed to campaigns, did favours, and indulged in all the usual activities needed to get appointed.

"Now think about it. Who has the most to lose if this inquiry goes forward? Not me and not Tridel. The Peterson government, that's who. They've seen the personal attacks and slurs I've been getting and they'll be next. Politicians on the receiving end of benefits, backroom decisions, even David Peterson's personal and family business interests will become public property. And like me, they'll have no protection under the rules of evidence either, at least not the way Houlden interprets them.

"And these same government people have already heard of my ambivalence concerning this appeal," I went on. "So if I were still in my old political insider seat, I'd be advising the powers that be to look for some way to persuade me to do just what we've done — try to stop the inquiry."

They were all listening, very quietly, no one speaking.

"So I think Lloyd Houlden did them a favour," I continued. "If he hadn't let the inquiry be so petty and vindictive, allowing unsubstantiated hearsay evidence, then no one could have persuaded me to file this challenge and miss my own day in court. And if I hadn't filed the challenge, the inquiry would have gone on to its natural conclusion. And who knows where that might have led?"

TEMPTING FATE

I rested my case.

Austin responded by saying that judges, especially higher court judges, never let politics affect their decisions. If I was suggesting that Houlden was being intentionally helpful to the attorney general and the Peterson government by the way he conducted the inquiry, I was wrong. Lloyd Houlden was an excellent judge.

"Well, I don't agree," I interjected. "And mark my words. I'll get charged for something if this inquiry is quashed. Peterson will have to do something to keep the public's confidence while at the same time destroying my credibility. You just wait and see!"

The other lawyers were silent as Austin reiterated his deep and abiding faith in the system.

"Besides," he said, "your analysis is too Machiavellian for most people to ever dream up."

Maybe. Maybe not.

✦ On April 5, 1990, overturning both the Divisional Court and the Court of Appeal decisions, the Supreme Court of Canada quashed the Starr Inquiry as unconstitutional, by a vote of six to one.

Chaviva called me at home to express her regrets and sympathy. She also alerted me to the fact that I would probably be charged criminally. Terror shot through me like a knife and I burst out crying in the arms of my friend Betty Disero, who was with me at the time. I never heard from Chaviva Hosek again.

A week later, Austin called.

"Mrs. Starr, I'm sorry to tell you that Inspector Roy Teeft of the Metro Toronto Fraud Squad has requested your presence at the police station," he said. My heart stopped beating. "You're being charged with one count of fraud relevant to the renovation of Council House."

I drove down to Queen Street to pick up Austin and Peter, who would escort me to the police station. I couldn't find Jerry to warn him, but Betty said she would track him down so he could get the kids out of school before the news hit the press.

They got in my car, both looking very sad.

"I told you," I said. "Now my credibility is gone too. My political 'friends' must be having a good laugh. Who'll ever believe anything I say again? I'll be a criminal, with a record."

"Mrs. Starr," Austin said, "have more faith in the criminal justice system. It doesn't allow hearsay, innuendo, or vindictive attacks. All prosecution evidence must be submitted in advance, so we'll be able to examine everything. There'll be no surprises. But at least Roy Teeft is a top-rated cop. He'll be very thorough and follow up every lead. But he won't be vicious and he won't use the press against you the way others have."

Every nightmare I'd had was now coming true. Partway along Queen Street I had to go to the bathroom. I pulled up the car in front of a restaurant, which turned out to be a drug-pushing establishment. The press, already alerted, were following my car. So were the police.

I ran out of the building fast when I saw some of the characters in the restaurant. The whole scene was like a Mack Sennett movie. There I was, driving my Cadillac with two of Canada's top criminal lawyers sitting in the back, being followed by a stream of cars carrying the police and the press.

Once inside the station, the process took over. I was fingerprinted, had a mug shot taken, and was then read my rights and the details of the charge.

Austin and Peter stayed right with me because, despite my attempts to play it cool, I was shaking. But I was determined not to cry.

I was so afraid.

There I was in a police station, for the first time in my life, and being charged like a common criminal.

And for the first time, I looked over and saw a prison cell, up close. And then I did start to cry.

CHAPTER SIXTEEN

Scapegoat

By May 1990 I had begun to hope the worst was over. My lawyers felt we had a strong case on the grant. It was anticipated that a preliminary hearing wouldn't happen for another year, and by that time, the press hoopla would have died down.

"Don't worry, Mrs. Starr," Austin Cooper would reassure me, "this time you will be protected under rules of evidence. Without the glare of the media, there won't be as much pressure to make an example of you."

Austin always called me "Mrs. Starr" rather than "Patti" because he wanted to keep our relationship strictly professional.

One afternoon, a few weeks after I was charged, I got a call from Betty Disero. She had just spoken to Gordon Ashworth.

"Call him at home," she said. "The two of you should get together and talk."

I drove to Gordon's house in the Lawrence Park area of Toronto and we walked over to the park nearby. At first we just sat on a bench, neither of us saying anything. Then he put his arms around me and gave me a hug.

"They betrayed me," he said, very choked up, "and they crucified you, even after I agreed to resign." We spent the next two hours talking through everything that had happened.

He said that lobbyist David MacNaughton, CEO of Hill and Knowlton in Canada, and campaign chief for the upcoming provincial election, had pushed Bob Nixon, treasurer, who had pushed Ian Scott to go public on the fridge. "I think they were worried about me," he said. "After the York Region stuff, and then Borg's shot at Marlene DelZotto, I was really pissed off."

Marlene was Elvio's wife, an outstanding community volunteer who was admired by everyone for her kind and generous personality. Borg had publicly demanded, on behalf of the premier, that all the DelZottos resign from the various board positions they held. But Marlene had refused.

"Some of the others were getting nervous because they were afraid I wouldn't cooperate with keeping the lid on the Skydome scam and the government's involvement in killing the York Region Inquiry."

"Which others?" I asked.

He wouldn't say.

"Listen, Patti," he said. "There's a few things I need to tell you. Monte Kwinter isn't your friend. He's been talking to the police, distancing himself from you. Don't trust him."

So much for our good friends the Kwinters, I thought.

Then Gordon said, "Senator Grafstein keeps saying, 'I told you so' to anyone who'll listen. Maybe he sees this as payback time."

I can't say I hadn't been warned.

"Kathy Robinson (president of the Ontario Liberal party) told me that a person with inside information on NCJW's activities has been giving info to the party and the press since 1988. It seems this person resents Elvio because they think he is standing in the way of their getting a Liberal nomination to run in the next federal election."

I knew who he meant. You little worm, I thought. I wished I could stomp on his pimply face.

"Gordon," I said, "you're still not explaining to me why you resigned. It couldn't have been that stupid fridge. Were you still trying to protect me?"

"David assured me that if I resigned, the whole mess would be over," he answered. "The media would leave you alone, and after a while, I could quietly start picking up the pieces."

Gina Brannon, Gordon's lawyer, had warned that the finger should not be pointed at Tridel in the press release announcing Gordon's resignation. But she was ignored and told to "fuck off." And in addition, of course, they had called the inquiry.

Bastards. What a setup, I thought.

"They knew that the Starr Affair would keep the press happy and away from their other problems if a real bomb was dropped," he went on. "The fridge episode, and the way it was handled, provided the fuse. We were both expendable."

"But who is that smart, Gordon? Someone has to be orchestrating this."

Gordon didn't answer.

"By the time an election was called, you and I would be long forgotten," he said, "but it didn't work out the way they had planned."

After a few moments, I said, "A complaint was filed by the Ministry of Culture and Communications to the police about the renovation grant for Council House. And now there are rumours of the Commission on Election Finances getting in on the action too." Suddenly every antiquated regulation was being examined to see if I could be nailed for some infraction, no matter how minor. And that commission had Peterson appointments on it. More legal costs.

Gordon took up the thread. "David's enemies see their opportunity too. They hope you'll go off the wall and start pointing fingers if criminal charges are laid against you, so they start pushing the police, who are happy to comply because they want to nail a few politicians and developers and figure you might be the weak link. But you spoiled their plans and didn't break. I knew you wouldn't — and that's why I wanted to talk to you and maybe help you deal with all this."

"Listen, Gordon, you know how much I regret what you've suffered, as well as Dyanne and the kids. You've been a loyal friend. I wish I could undo some of the stupid things I've said and done. But one thing is for sure, I don't deserve what's happening to me and my family, and neither do you. It's cost me over $200,000 to date in legal and accounting fees and I've got a criminal charge over my head. You've had your career wiped out and I'm sure a lot of your savings as well. And all because of a few gutless wonders you and I used to know. I want to go after them for our costs. Your statements today would really make a difference. How about it?"

He said he'd think about it and let me know. We then talked about his family and his plans. He kept his arm on my shoulder as we walked back to my car. Before we got in, he looked at me and said, "You know, 'they' couldn't have done anything to you if your former friends had stuck with you. The police could hardly have charged a bunch of volunteer ladies who never took any money for their efforts."

I had no answer.

Then, no more words, just a warm embrace.

When I got home, I called Barry Swadron, my civil lawyer, and discussed part of the conversation I'd had with Gordon. He didn't think Gordon's lawyer would let Gordon talk to me again, much less confirm our conversation. But I knew Gordon would call. His principles were strong.

And sure enough, the very next day Barry got a call from Gordon's lawyer and a meeting was set up with Gordon and her. As a result of the statements made at that meeting, Barry Swadron and Marshall, his son and associate, prepared the documentation necessary to file a lawsuit against David Peterson, Ian Scott, Vince Borg, et al., on my behalf.

Before any action was taken, though, I got a call from some former associates tied to the Liberal party who'd heard that I was considering a lawsuit. They said they were concerned about the negative results such an action might bring upon me. In appreciation for all my hard work and loyalty over the years, they wanted to arrange for a reimbursement of my legal and accounting costs to date. Of course, no payment could be made until after the upcoming provincial election, which was scheduled for the first week of September.

They went on to speculate that the Commission on Election Fianances was possibly only posturing about charges. As well, they had it "on good authority" that if matters were allowed to settle down quietly, there would be no further criminal charges either.

I told them that if they were serious about all this, it would have to be confirmed, verbally at least, with my lawyer. Otherwise, I could only assume that this was a ploy to avoid any further controversy before the election.

But in any event, they didn't represent Peterson, Scott, Borg, et al. So Barry Swadron attempted to negotiate a settlement with the government's lawyers before any lawsuit was filed, in order to forestall my filing a lawsuit, referring to my earlier discussion about settlements with party insiders. However, they showed no genuine interest.

At the beginning of July, I filed a lawsuit against the government, David Peterson, Ian Scott, and Vince Borg, claiming, among other things, damages for the calling of the Starr Inquiry.

Despite all the analysis and commentary by the media about why David Peterson had chosen to call an election only three years into his term, I understood his rationale. He was concerned that those issues lying dormant during the hoopla of the Starr Affair might come back to life, especially if I chose to raise them. He anticipated that after the fraud charge was laid against me, I would go off the deep end.

As long as his mandate hadn't been renewed with an election, he would still be vulnerable. But if — and this was his strategy — if his government was re-elected despite the Starr Affair, then he wouldn't have to worry about anything else concerning me. And he could stonewall on the other matters too.

The criminal charge already against me would be of assistance to him, since my credibility would now be in question and the press wouldn't be interested in covering anything much about me any longer, even if I did "go to pieces" and start babbling.

He'd be home free and I could whistle Dixie.

But the people of this province weren't that stupid. They knew something was fishy by his calling an election only three years into his mandate. Many interpreted this as the ultimate act of arrogance and were suspicious about a hidden agenda. And they gave him their response by throwing him out of office, along with most of the Liberal party. Unfortunately, we then wound up with the New Democratic government, albeit by default.

Despite all his self-righteous rhetoric in 1989, Bob Rae put the lid on any further inquiries about politicians when he took office in September 1990. He also began filling the bureaucracy with NDP hacks, despite his promises of financial restraint. He created several new Crown corporations and commissions and increased the number of consultants hired by the government. Those receiving his largesse, at salaries in excess of $100,000 each, included Dale Martin, former NDP councillor; John Sewell, losing mayoralty candidate; and Jack Layton, another losing NDP mayoralty candidate.

Furthermore, some of those NDP civil servants within the Ministry of Housing who were most responsible for the millions of dollars wasted on non-profit co-op housing allocations have been moved quietly into other ministries.

Only time will tell who was worse for this province.

✦ In July the Commission on Election Finances filed more than one hundred charges against the National Council of Jewish Women, Toronto Section, and me, among others. Then the Crown prosecutor laid an additional ten criminal charges against me, most of them variations on the same theme, namely, the renovation grant.

In the meantime, the police investigation of my activities, called Project 50, continued full steam ahead under the supervision of Inspector Roy Teeft. Friends and former colleagues were being interviewed, along with government bureaucrats, many of whom I did not know. I suspected my phone was tapped (it wasn't) and I was being followed (I was).

The police were accumulating evidence that consisted mostly of taped interviews. Until these recordings were turned over, which they eventually were, Austin Cooper and Peter West could only guess at what they might contain. From July 1990 until March 1991, two major defences were being mounted on my behalf — one on the criminal charges, the other on the election finance ones.

On the criminal matters, the police started turning over the cartons of transcripts they were using against me. How can I describe the bitterness and despair I felt as I read some of the comments of former colleagues? They "didn't remember" our discussions about political contributions and had no recollection of the details concerning the renovation grant, despite the documented board minutes. Some insisted that only Nita Goldband, who had signed the grant with me, knew about it, which wasn't true.

To my absolute horror, Dody Rudson, the recently hired NCJW staff person, was telling the police investigators about the florist's bill. According to Dody, I had reimbursed the money only because I knew I'd get caught.

For anyone to even suggest that I would ever take a cent from NCJW for myself was unbelievable. The silence of the other girls who were with her at the time of the interviews was another knife in my heart.

But why? Dody had been working for NCJW only seven months when I left and barely knew our operation. I'd known her for almost thirty years. I'd offered my sympathy, friendship, and support through times of personal difficulty. Was she trying to win points with the national organization? Did she think this would endear her to the membership? When I complained to Austin and Peter about it, they promised to deal with all of this during their cross-examination of her at my trial.

Nita Goldband and Lesley Miller refused to speak to the police at all, and under the law they did not have to. But their statements would have changed nothing anyway. I was the driving force behind that grant — and many others obtained for my community over the past twelve years. I had looked for the loopholes that would allow us to apply for funding that would otherwise have been out of our reach. Matching grants with "in kind" donations was a common practice. Simply put, for every dollar the government put up, the organization had to match it. Using volunteer hours and donated labour and materials in lieu of cash was permitted, in moderation. But once Marty Mendelow and company agreed to donate labour and materials to match NCJW's portion of the grant, the amount was steep.

Nonetheless, the bureaucrats within the Ministry of Culture and Communications, all the way up, had known about it. And they had approved it.

When the charge was laid, my defence was, and still is, common knowledge, along with common practice. But the letter of the regulations, rather than the spirit, was now being applied to me as punishment for all the other allegations that could not be substantiated. My lawyers felt we had a strong case. In addition, I was a volunteer, and every cent of the grant was accounted for. So something more, something obviously worse had to be found to make prosecuting me more palatable to the public and, more importantly, to the press.

Enter the $33,035.

Remember, there were two cheques in reimbursed expenses over a five-year period that totalled $29,000 ($4,000 for the table at the federal Liberals' 1988 Confederation Dinner and $25,000 representing five years' out-of-pocket expenses plus petty cash expenses for the Ridley project). There were also two florist's bills totalling $4,035.

Without knowing any better, I had reimbursed the Capital Fund for all four items using one cheque. Once again, the letter of the law came into play.

When my former colleagues "couldn't remember" my telling them about these expenses, or seeing the cheque stubs for the florist that were clearly marked as a personal expense to be reimbursed, I was charged with breach of trust, on the entire amount of $33,035.

The police claimed that by writing one cheque as reimbursement for all four items back in February 1989, there were reasonable and probable grounds that everything, not just the $4,035 florist's bill, was a personal benefit. The fact that the cheque had been written on the Capital Fund in error didn't matter. Once the money had been out of the account "for even ten seconds," no matter what the reason, charges of improper use and breach of trust could be laid. Since there was no attempt on my part to hide these expenditures (the cheque stubs were clearly marked and the money had been reimbursed more than two years earlier), my lawyers felt the defence on this charge was even stronger.

But it was the most painful for me. To even suggest that I had received any financial benefit for my volunteer activities was horrible, but knowing about the whispering campaign being conducted by some national NCJW members to justify their disloyalty made it even worse.

So to try to keep some perspective and avoid self-pity during this period, I returned to my first love, volunteering. Luckily for me, the Volunteer Centre sent me to the Canadian Occupational Therapy Association (COTA) as a girl Friday to their director of volunteers, Carissa Urquhart. COTA worked with disabled individuals who were living independently, helping them cope with the problems they encountered every day. It is a wonderful organization that took me into their family of volunteers despite the notoriety surrounding me.

Other organizations would not. In fact, the day after I had been sent to another well-known community agency as a volunteer, I received a call from one of their senior directors telling me not to come back, because some of their board members objected to having me around. They were concerned that my presence as a volunteer would hurt their fundraising campaign, given the perception that I had misused "some poor charity's money."

This took me a long time to get over.

◆ For several weeks in June and July, the press, especially the *Toronto Sun*, were reporting on the fact that the Commission on Election Finances was preparing non-criminal election finance charges against me and several others. These charges were separate from the renovation grant charges. Included in this speculation were reports of Ontario Liberal party president Kathryn Robinson, one of Cliff Lax's associates, having correspondence with a member of the commission. The commission members, despite being political appointees, were supposed to be non-partisan. There were rumours of deals being made not to charge any politicians who had received the monies, but to concentrate on NCJW and me.

My lawyers subpoenaed the *Toronto Sun* and its Queen's Park bureau chief, Ann Dawson, for the material being used as the basis of the press reports. We eventually got them and discovered just how much politics had to do with the commission's decisions. The documents showed that both the Crown and the police had the view that the commission might be "stretching the net to catch Patti Starr in circumstances beyond the intended legislation."

We also learned that Ben Hutzel, my former fundraising colleague, was one of those under investigation and that his colleague, John Campion, a member of the commission, was declaring a conflict of interest. The commission ultimately decided not to charge Hutzel. The documents also showed that Kathryn Robinson had been in direct communication with the commission and had been receiving inside information from Daniel Murphy, one of its Liberal members.

So after these weeks of wild press speculation and screaming headlines, it was almost a relief when the charges were finally filed in July 1990.

There were more than one hundred of them, but eventually the case boiled down to eight cheques, mostly for political fundraising events. Eight cheques. And the "crime" had nothing to do with whether the act of writing the cheque by NCJW was illegal, but simply the methodology used. According to the commission's regulations, amended in 1986, and which none of us knew about, all cheques had to be "legibly printed" rather than handwritten. Since our new, printed cheques hadn't arrived from the bank yet, we used counter cheques to make the contributions and wrote them out by hand. Who knew anything was wrong with that? Why hadn't the cheques been returned if they were "illegibly printed"?

These same regulations also stated that the onus was to be put on those soliciting and accepting the monies — not simply the contributors (such as the NCJW) — if there was an irregularity. And according to the confidential minutes and documents we had subpoenaed, this was exactly the position of the police, who kept discouraging the commission from pursuing a case against me at all.

But during the Starr Affair no one else counted, especially the politicians who had benefited. In order to get the biggest "bang for their buck" in the press and to reach a "respectable" number of charges, which would justify their existence to the public, the commission originally laid eight different charges relating to *each* of the cheques — four charges against NCJW for writing them and four charges against me for aiding and abetting them.

When the affair was finally over, the cost to taxpayers was more than $1 million. I was fined $3,500 for eight breaches of the Election Finance Act. All the other charges were thrown out of court.

◆ The charges on one of the cheques represented the final straw that broke my spirit and will to fight on. At issue was a $500 cheque to Monte Kwinter's driver Bob McGillvray, an upbeat and pleasant man, who would often drive us to political functions.

When the 1987 provincial election was called, although the girls were sick of going to dinners, we wanted to do something for Monte, who was very close to our organization. (He knew many of the NCJW members and had helped us with grants.) We agreed to pick up the costs for Bob during the election campaign, since it was illegal for a Cabinet minister to use a government car or driver for anything other than government business. The amount required was $500, which was considerably less than a table at a fundraising dinner, so we were happy to contribute that amount for Monte to be able to use his driver during the campaign.

Just prior to the trial on these election charges, the police turned over transcripts of Monte's statements made to them back in 1989. He had said that he had no recollection of receiving this contribution. He had also had his lawyer write a letter to the commission confirming this.

During the trial, sworn evidence given by Bob stated that Monte had told him about this $500 cheque, before the fact. He also corroborated my statement that Monte had accepted the cheque from me and then handed it over to him while both couples — the Starrs and the Kwinters — were in Monte's car being driven to an event.

The judge, after hearing the evidence Bob and I gave, still found me guilty. It was immaterial to him whether a Cabinet minister had played a role or not — a minister had not been charged and I had. The judge said I should have sought out the right official to ascertain the correct procedure, even though I had no idea who that official might be or that the procedure was wrong in the first place.

Even though he expressed "some sympathy" for my situation, it was his opinion that I didn't exercise "due diligence" and that "ignorance of the law" was no defence, at least not for me. So that was it. No matter what the circumstances and extenuating circumstances, I was shown no mercy. I alone was the culprit.

Deep down in my heart, I knew then that I was gone on everything else too.

The hypocrisy, the double standards, and the selective application of the letter of the law towards only me made it clear that fighting on was useless. My lawyers' initial optimism had turned into skepticism. At each step along the road, their expectations of the results had not been realized.

So in April 1991, when Austin Cooper asked me for another $100,000 in anticipation of the start of the preliminary hearing on the criminal charges, I balked. I told him the time had come to take another hard look at my prospects.

By this time we had mortgaged our home so that Jerry could

buy another business to support us. I had already spent close to $300,000 in legal and accounting bills. To spend any more would probably bankrupt us. And if I won, what exactly would I win?

Nothing would remove the cloud of scandal around me or give me back the credibility I had earned over twenty-five years of community service. The damage had already been done, and it could not be undone. I had signed the grant; I had never denied that. I had known, along with everyone else, that NCJW had not raised their share of the money in hard cash when I had signed it. I had never denied that either. But the complicity of others had been ignored to this point, and there was no reason to expect that to change. The letter of the law was being applied to me and only me. I had to accept that.

Sadly, my lawyers now agreed.

✧ One beautiful, sunny day in April 1991, I walked along Queen Street towards the offices of Cooper, Sandler & West. I had parked my car in Barry Swadron's lot as I usually did during court appearances or consultations with Peter and Austin.

The Swadrons continued to provide great encouragement and support, even offering to take my criminal case forward if the only reason for my giving up the fight was money.

But money wasn't the only reason. Austin and Peter had warned me that my trial would take at least six months. Since the Crown presents its case first, all the allegations and negative testimony would be fully covered in the media before my side was heard. My family would have to endure it all over again.

The inquiry had been a nightmare for all of us. The trial would probably be no different.

"I've never learned when to fold my cards," I told the Swadrons, after I had expressed my appreciation of their offer. "It's time I did. If I had listened to Jane two years ago, I wouldn't be here today."

When I arrived at Cooper, Sandler & West, Austin was out and only Peter was there to speak to me. I sat across from him, and got a sick feeling in the pit of my stomach at the look on his face.

He'd spoken to the Crown prosecutor, Peter Griffiths, about cutting a deal in the criminal case.

"Griffiths is asking the court for jail," he said, very gently, "but he's prepared to settle for six months, which means two, if you get paroled.

"One charge of fraud, and one charge of breach of trust. The other nine charges will be dropped. He also intends to enter into the record the fact that your former NCJW colleagues had prior knowledge of your activities and that you never received any personal financial benefits."

Big deal, I thought.

Peter went on. "He says there's no way the attorney general's office will accept anything less than a jail sentence, given Bob Rae's stance on the whole Starr Affair."

"But nothing happened to David Peterson and the rest of them," I cried out. "It's only me!"

"Peterson was defeated," Peter chortled. "That's a lot to happen to him, at least from his perspective. And Bob Rae now thinks of himself as the knight in shining armour. He doesn't want the public to think he created a political scenario for himself out of smoke and mirrors, so there must be at least the perception of illegal activity to justify all the time and money spent. Besides, the police are insisting on jail, though they said they'd go along with the Crown's recommendation of only six months."

"Only!" I shrieked at him. "Austin said I'd never go to jail! I'm afraid to go to jail. I've never been in jail. I'll have a criminal record. I didn't take any money. Every penny is accounted for."

"I'm sorry, Patti," he went on. "Austin and I never thought it would come to this. But the pressure is on to make an example of you. You're too high profile, perceived as rich and powerful. If you're given a suspended sentence, the press will go beserk, screaming about special treatment. Breach of trust is usually a mandatory jail term, which is why the Crown is insisting on it.

"However, Griffiths does recognize your years of community service. I don't think he's too happy about this case altogether.

He's agreed to let me choose any judge I feel will be the most compassionate and if a suspended sentence is imposed, he won't appeal it. He's also suggested we time things so that your youngest children will be away at camp just in case I'm not successful.

"Of course," he went on, "if you want to talk to the police, and the information you give them is helpful, all charges against you will be dropped."

There it is, I thought.

I wasn't surprised that Peter had raised this option, since others had over the past year. In fact, some had urged me to give the police something, anything on the Petersons, the DelZottos, or a politician or two, to take the heat off me.

But I didn't know anything to tell, and even if I did, I wouldn't. I told Peter I'd think about it and rushed out of his office.

✦ For the next two hours, I walked back and forth along Queen Street between University Avenue and Yonge Street, thinking of all that had happened to me and trying to make sense of it. But I couldn't think beyond my terror of jail and how to tell the kids. I tried to concentrate on the future, tried to look beyond the immediate horror, but all I could do was envision a cell with me in it.

No one's ever been charged, much less sent to jail, for signing a grant, I fumed to myself — especially when they didn't take any money. I was so full of hate and frustration at that moment that it gave me a start. If I didn't stop it, I'd wind up with ulcers or a heart attack.

Maybe the judge that Peter picks will consider all the good things I've done and show some compassion, I thought.

Get real, Patti, the other side of my brain answered. You're living in la-la land. Nobody cares anymore. You're on your own. Get a handle on yourself. Remember the smirking faces. The kids can't see you afraid. And neither can Jerry, or everything will fall to pieces.

I walked back into Peter's office. "What do you think my chances are?" I asked.

"Fifty-fifty."

It was time to tell my husband and children.

How can I describe the pain I felt in my heart as I watched their faces fall? I could not make them bear the full brunt of what Peter and I had discussed. And so I lied to them.

"Try not to worry," I said. "Peter thinks my chances are good. After all, I didn't steal anything, and I've been a volunteer for twenty-five years. Lots of people are going to write letters on my behalf.

"Look, kids," I went on, "I signed the grant. Nobody made me do it. I knew the information wasn't all true and I was wrong to do it. It doesn't matter that other people have done it too, or that it was for a good cause. I'm the one who signed it and now I'm being punished. Remember that the next time someone tells you it's okay to do something you're not sure about.

"Now I may have to go to a detention centre for a while as punishment. (I couldn't bring myself to say the word jail.)

"But I'm sure it won't be so bad. I'll be doing volunteer work and it'll be nice not to have to go anywhere. I'll do a lot of reading."

"Hey, Ma," my youngest son piped up, "are you going to a real jail, with a real cell with bars? Can you bring home some handcuffs? When are you coming home? Will you be here when I get back from camp?"

Luckily for me, the two youngest seemed to accept the situation with very little trauma. My older children were much more upset, because they understood the reality of what was coming.

Jerry took it the hardest. His bitterness at former friends and colleagues almost provoked him into going to see a few people and letting them have it — but reason soon prevailed. He called Austin Cooper, which I didn't know about at the time, asking him to do something. Of course, nothing more could be done.

For the next two months I waited, sleeping barely more than a couple of hours a night. I visited my parents' grave every other day, looking for some solace. Jerry and I kept our spirits up thanks to some wonderful friends and family who called and visited almost every day, and our new business, Reid & Lyons, was keeping Jerry busy. He was happy to be an entrepreneur again. Getting the kids ready for camp helped keep me occupied as well.

But time marched on, and June 27, 1991, soon arrived. And you know the rest of that story.

SEVENTEEN

Timberlea, June-July 1991, Vanier Centre for Women

I awoke in my cell that first morning, hot and sweaty, with the sunlight streaming in. There was a torn sheet on the window, which I assumed was a substitute for drapes, but it wasn't very effective. I heard the grinding clang of my door being unlocked from some distant place and then a loud click. I tentatively tried it, and it opened. I could hear talking coming from somewhere, so I got dressed and followed the sound.

I found myself in a central lounge area, which contained couches, chairs, some tables, and a TV set. Some guards were sitting behind a glassed-in cubicle. Off this lounge was a communal kitchen and dining area. Three corridors branched off to where the inmates slept and had washroom facilities. There was one communal shower stall and bathtub for the twenty-four women on the unit. Paint was peeling off all the walls, the tiles were broken, and the shower had a torn curtain that didn't stop the water from pouring all over the floor whenever you took a shower.

The bathtub didn't have a stopper, so the drain had to be plugged with a washcloth, which really didn't stop the water from seeping out; it only slowed it down. There was also a shredded shower curtain on the tub, which didn't provide any privacy. The male guards could see us in the tub or shower when they looked in through the glass window, which they did quite often. They could also look in the windows of our rooms and watch when we used the toilet. There was nothing we could do about it.

"Never complain" was the motto. Anyone who has ever been in jail knows it.

As soon as I walked into the lounge, someone named Linda, a rather robust person, shrieked, quite loudly, "Holy shit, it's Patti Starr! Hey, girls, look who's here! Hey, Patti, how ya doing? My boyfriend told me you were coming here."

The other girls came over and introduced themselves. Cathy was in for eighteen months for killing her newborn, though she had no memory of doing it. Lizzie, who assaulted her abusive husband with a bowling ball, dropping it on a sensitive spot when he was sleeping. Sandra, who spent more than $10,000 through credit card fraud before she was caught. Lenore, an assistant to a bank manager, had transferred more than $100,000 from inactive accounts before she was caught — her boyfriend had most of the money and he had disappeared, naturally, when she was arrested. She had spent three months in jail, no bail, waiting for her sentencing. It was "dead time," meaning it wouldn't count when her sentence was finally given.

One girl in particular, Lori Pinkus, attached herself to me. Lori was originally from Ottawa and was twenty-four years old. She thought she was Jewish. She had vague childhood memories of dinners where people ate big crackers (probably Matzo) and sang happy songs while the men pounded the tables. I was sure she was referring to a Passover Seder.

Her mother had once called a rabbi, asking for someone to come and see Lori during one of her stays in prison. But no one ever had. According to Lori, her mother was quite elderly and she didn't remember her father. Her brother, to whom she felt close, had just died from a drug overdose the day before.

"What?" I said, "aren't you getting a pass or something to go to the funeral?"

"No, they won't let me," she said. "I've been crying for two days and John (a guard) told me that if I don't stop, I'll get a misconduct."

I put my arms around her.

"And a misconduct is worse than a poor effort," she went on. "If you get three poor efforts, they can add a day on to your time. If you get any misconducts, they can add a day to your time and if you get more than one, they might put you in SNU."

"Oh God, what's SNU?" I asked.

"SNU is the worst," she answered. "Isolation. You're kept in a cell, sometimes with a dry toilet, no sheets, and only a nightgown. No privileges, no activities, nothing. Twenty-three hours a day you sit on a cot."

"What do you have to do to get one of these poor efforts or misconducts, and who decides?" I asked. "Don't you get a hearing? I can't believe you can get punished for crying too much over your brother's death."

"The COs (corrections officers) have the power," she said. "You can file an appeal, and the guards have to put the stuff in writing. But if you argue with them too much about it, they'll put 'bad attitude' on your file, and then you're in even more trouble. Jeff said I was bothering the other girls by crying. They gave me some medicine to help me feel better. But I don't."

She started sobbing, "I got nobody now, nobody!"

"Lori," I said as gently as I could. "I'm sure there's an ombudsman, or a human rights commission that helps people who are being treated unfairly and who have nowhere else to go or anyone to help them."

"Yeah, sure. Wait till you're here for a while. The girls are always calling the ombudsman's number for help. They never answer. In all the time I'm here, I ain't never heard of no one getting called back, even when they leave plenty of messages. Nobody gives a fuck about us. It's all for show."

I knew that the Office of the Ombudsman and the Human Rights Commission were supposed to be more responsive, especially considering the extent to which they were funded by the taxpayers; they were supposed to help those whose options had run out. I made a mental note to ask, when I got out, why they weren't responding to these calls for help.

"What are you in here for, Lori?" I asked.

"Hooking, and drugs. I've been doing drugs for years. But this time I'm going to quit, for sure. Turning tricks for the money to shoot up is getting more dangerous. One John beat the shit out of me and then didn't pay. If I keep on, I'll have to get a black pimp, you know the guys that come from the niggertown out east."

She was referring to a town in Nova Scotia that was once known as Africaville.

"They got a hold on the trade, and they take almost all your money. Sometimes you have to give free blow jobs to them and their friends. . . . I want to start over. My Ma is really old now, and I'm gonna to try to make it all up to her." Lori turned to me and searched my eyes. "Hey, do you think things are gonna get better for us with you here, cause the brass is afraid of the press? Are you really one of the Mob? Can I stick with you?"

Over the next two months Lori and I kept in daily contact, even when she was moved to the drug rehab cottage. She worked in the Vanier laundry, and I was in charge of washing the pots and pans, both located in the same building, so we were able to talk. She was most interested in learning about Judaism and the community. Our discussions about our mutual heritage gave me an opportunity to remember my Orthodox background.

Lori always looked and acted somewhat stoned, but this was because of the medication she was given to keep her calm and help with her withdrawal symptoms. She had very little memory of her childhood.

I wondered what had happened during her young life to drive her to drugs. She was broken down and scarred from needles, her brain nearly fried, and her future bleak at age twenty-four.

What a sad waste of a human life. I resolved to keep in touch with her after I got out.

I never got the chance. In September 1991, just after she was paroled, Lori Pinkus was found brutally murdered in a parking lot. When I called the police to ask about the circumstances, they told me she was listed as a prostitute and guessed it was either a

John or a pimp who had killed her. They had no leads, and no one has ever been arrested. Rest in peace, Lori.

During that first morning, no staff spoke to me, and I relied on the other girls to show me the ropes. After the initial interest, they settled into their usual routines. Almost everyone smoked. Tobacco from old cigarette butts was accumulated and then recycled into new "smokes." It was a constant activity. There was lots of chit-chat, and I enjoyed listening to the stories the girls told about their "careers," most of which were illegal. Hearing about the life most of these women had endured made me stop feeling so sorry for myself.

The guards stayed in the glass cubicle most of the time but occasionally came out to talk to us. Most of them were pleasant and tried to be helpful, but a couple were sullen and hostile.

The Vanier Centre for Women began operations in 1968. The only provincial institution for women in conflict with the law, it consists of three adult medium security "cottages" — Timberlea, Hochelaga, and Kon Tiki. There is also one minimum security "cottage," Ingleside. Up to forty women can be housed in each of these facilities. During my stay, approximately twenty-five women were kept in Timberlea and twenty in Ingleside. There is also a young offenders' unit called Invictus, which houses up to forty-five teenagers of both sexes — fifteen males and thirty females — in an integrated environment.

Of the 56,000 inmates in provincial jails and detention centres across Canada in 1990, 4,800 were women (8 percent). Approximately 75 percent were under the age of thirty-five. Of the 9,100 offences these women committed, only 69 were violent, while 2,500 were related to unpaid fines.

It costs the taxpayers approximately $4,500 *per month* to keep one woman in prison.

✦ During my first few days, there were no activities, and no up-to-date reading material was available. On occasion, the staff let us read their newspapers. All references to me were cut out. The absence of reading material was all the more frustrating because there was nothing else to do.

From the Friday I arrived until the following Monday afternoon, I was not allowed out in the fresh air. The explanation: that the recreation staff were on vacation and no one could process me. I kept fighting off the urge to start screaming and pounding my fists against the locked doors.

I paced back and forth in the lounge, trying to keep myself exercised. Funny the things we take for granted. Opening a door and going outside, getting a glass of water, sitting down with your feet up — freedom.

All choices were gone now.

During the first three days, we sat in the lounge from 8:00 a.m. to 10:00 p.m., doing nothing. There were no clocks on the walls, nor was anyone allowed to wear a watch. We tried to gauge the time by watching the sun. Minutes seemed like hours.

Printed information relating to programs supposedly available were not accompanied by any explanations as to how to go about applying for them. The same was true for the list of rules we were given, which were often ambiguous. One guard would give you one ruling and another would contradict it.

Staff, for the most part, sat in their glassed-off room talking, reading the paper, eating pizza, drinking Cokes. This was particularly hard on the younger inmates, who were always hungry and thirsty — especially for pizzas and soft drinks, which many of them hadn't had in months.

The first weekend I was there, a cottage meeting was convened. This was supposed to be an opportunity for complaints and suggestions to be aired openly between inmates and staff, with no threat of reprisals. Betty Jo, one of the head honchos, conducted the meeting. I had been warned by the other girls to keep my mouth shut, no matter what I heard.

Betty Jo began by calling us all "fucking assholes" who were the scum of the earth. All the while she was staring at me. She complained about an earlier incident and said that if any one of us "pissed her off," we would be slammed into the door. "I give out misconducts like popcorn," she said. "You better wise up."

She said "fuck" almost every other word. I had never heard a woman use such vile language, especially in mixed company (there were male and female guards on duty regularly). And she was senior staff, a role model who, I assumed, was to set an example for her "fallen" charges.

One of the agenda items for this meeting was staff's insistence on the removal of the torn sheets on our windows being used in lieu of drapes.

A couple of the girls objected, tentatively, to removing the sheets, saying how hot it was. The sun would beat directly into their cubicles and they would have no privacy. I was lucky. My room only got the sun in the morning, but for the others who got it all afternoon, their rooms were like a furnace.

"Why can't we wait until new ones come?" asked Lamb Chop, a young woman with a wonderful sense of humour. She also happened to be a prostitute.

"Listen, you fucking shit, don't you question me on anything I fucking tell you to fucking do," was Betty Jo's response. "Anyone who doesn't take those fucking sheets off the fucking windows and turn them in by Tuesday morning is getting a fucking misconduct."

I couldn't believe it. Where did these so-called professionals come from? Surely there had to be standards for custodial staff, some kind of psychological testing and educational requirements.

Prison is not a picnic; we were there as punishment for crimes. But Betty Jo's conduct was outrageous. She had no concern about being reported or reprimanded for her behaviour, or at the very least, her language. It's hard to believe the Ministry of Correctional Services would give their blessing to this kind of treatment.

I looked at the faces of the other COs. They all avoided eye contact with us and each other.

For her final blow, Betty Jo reminded those present that paroles were never guaranteed, and a poor report from her would go a long way towards delaying them.

She also told us that she could hold up TAPs by giving us negative reports. (TAPs are temporary absence programs, whereby inmates who have jobs leave Vanier a few hours a day to work, returning in late afternoon.) Most of these reports did not have to be documented or backed up.

At my sentencing, it had been recommended by Mr. Justice Wren that I be given a TAP as soon as possible. Betty Jo's threats were particularly worrisome, since she kept looking at me.

I had met another inmate, Victoria, that first morning in Vanier. She became my friend and confidante. We were stunned by what we were hearing. I had already been warned that I would be watched closely and my room searched, so we agreed that she would document this and any other significant events. When we got out, we were going to do something about this.

Victoria managed to keep her notes hidden till we were freed and then she turned them over to the Ministry of Correctional Services investigators, hoping they would be used to help the girls still there. That investigation is still ongoing.

My next encounter with Betty Jo occurred a day or two later, after a meal, when it was discovered that a fork was missing. This created tremendous anxiety among the girls, and the guards came running.

Victoria and I couldn't figure out what difference a missing fork could make.

"Okay, you fucking shits, find that fork!" Betty Jo shrieked at all of us. "Until you do, all privileges are cancelled and you're in lockup."

This meant no phone calls, no mail, no TV, and bed at 6:00 p.m.

I felt sick. I wouldn't be able to see or talk to Jerry and find out how the kids were. I was terrified about what was coming next.

The other girls were becoming agitated, and two guards I had never seen before showed up. Victoria and I decided to speak to Betty Jo directly to find out what was going on. Before we could, a couple of the girls started screaming, "Brenda, if you've done this again, we'll break your fucking neck!" With that, Brenda took off to her room.

"Look, Betty Jo," I said, "I'm sure there must be some intelligent reason for locking up twenty-four women indefinitely because a fork is missing. Perhaps you could explain why?"

"Who the fuck are you to question my orders?" she snarled. "You're not with your political friends now. Here you're just a fucking crook like everyone else. You're nobody."

The other girls went quiet and edged over, forming a semicircle behind me.

"Organizing the cottage, are you, you fucking bitch?" she whispered through gritted teeth when she saw the other girls moving. "That'll get you SNU for sure." A vicious smile formed on her face.

I began taking very deep breaths. I had to keep calm.

Fortunately for me, one of the other guards, who realized I didn't understand what was going on, came forward. I was playing with fire and I was going to get burned.

"Look, Mrs. Starr," she said, "eight years ago an inmate stole a fork, filed down the edges, and attacked a couple of other inmates, causing a lot of injury. Since then, there is a cutlery count after every meal, and if any are missing, we take strong measures. Cutlery can be used as weapons."

That made sense. I had never thought of spoons and forks as lethal weapons, but in jail, anything is possible. I turned to Betty Jo. "I would like to apologize for my reaction," I said. "I didn't understand what was going on, but now that I do, I'd like to ask if there's anything we can do to help search for this fork?"

Another guard, standing behind Betty Jo, signalled me by waving her finger and then putting it to her lips.

"Okay, ladies, start looking for the fork," said Debbie, one of the guards who was liked and respected by the girls. She, along with her colleagues Mary, Kim, and Joyce, were responsible, polite, and caring. Unfortunately, they were not in charge and had to follow orders.

We emptied all the garbage cans and went through the refuse, piece by piece. Then we went over every inch of the common room. I was starting to get panicky again, thinking of not seeing

TEMPTING FATE

Jerry and being locked up even more. Finally, just as an individual room search was to begin, Linda said, "I'll be right back."

She rushed down the hall toward Brenda's room. The fact that she was allowed to go alone, with no guard, was unusual, until she returned with the missing fork.

Then even I figured it out.

It all seems so trivial now, but back then, with the tensions, fear, and despair so prevalent in everyone's life, the incident was earth shattering.

✧ Finally, Monday afternoon arrived. We were looking forward to a walk outside. I could hardly wait, thinking of how the sun and fresh air would remind me I was still alive.

Suddenly the girls began running to the main entrance, chattering excitedly, "Big Mama's back. She's coming, she's coming. Now we'll have some order in this dump."

Victoria and I stayed in our chairs, watching. All we could see when the main doors were unlocked was the top of someone's head as she came in, accompanied by a guard and surrounded by the other girls.

"Where is she, where is she?" yelled a familiar voice. "Hey, Mrs. Starr, my girls treating you okay?"

My God! It was Coco — the woman I had met at the Metro Toronto West Detention Centre after my sentencing. I couldn't believe it. I thought she was going to Kingston. I ran over to her and gave her a big hug.

"Cool it, man," she said, somewhat embarrassed. "Do you want everyone to think I'm back into broads, especially an old Jewish mother like you?"

She smiled broadly and lifted her hand for a "gimme five," which I didn't know was customary between good friends in jail. She grabbed my wrist and smacked her palm against mine.

"That's the hello," she said. "You'll learn who to give it to, now that I'm here."

"How's Isobel?" I asked.

"She's still in the West," Coco said. "All dead time. Her

fucking lawyer forgot to file some papers and she won't get a hearing for a few weeks. She's trying to get bail, but who knows — she's been nailed too many times."

The guards knew Coco, of course, and she was treated like a welcome house guest, rather than an inmate. I introduced her to Victoria, who came from a proper Scottish background and looked it.

"Oh, Christ," Coco laughed, "another fallen lady. What did you do, Vicky baby?"

"The same as me, Coco, sort of," I answered. I knew Victoria didn't want to talk about what had happened to her. She had two sisters and wouldn't let them come to see her. She told me, often, "I intend to wipe this experience from my psyche, and I don't want to have anything to remind me of my past while I'm locked up here. If my sisters come, I'll go to pieces for sure."

At 4:30 on Monday afternoon, Coco, Victoria, and I, along with the other girls, were let out to walk around the inner courtyard that passes by the Vanier Centre buildings. The air never smelled so good, and the sun never shone brighter. I breathed deeply, and Victoria and I started to jog.

All of a sudden, loud whistles were blown and a couple of guards came running up to us.

"No sudden movements, no running, just walking, with space between you," they said. Why the hell didn't they tell you the rules *before* you did something wrong? Was it policy to try to get us in trouble in order to give us a poor effort, or say we had a bad attitude? Maybe the other girls weren't as paranoid about the COs' power trips as I had originally thought.

But it was so wonderful just being outside. Even though there were guards all around, I just turned my head to the sky and enjoyed the moment before reality set in again. I was introduced to at least fifty other inmates during that thirty-five-minute exercise. Questions, comments, even requests for my autograph (I declined) kept coming. Victoria and I kept looking at each other saying, "No one will ever believe this," as we kept walking, by now surrounded by quite a large group. I had dragged Lori outside with us so she would get some fresh air and she was enjoying all the action.

"No loitering, no groups of more than three together, no whispering," barked a female guard who looked like a hairy bulldog.

"Let's go in," Victoria said. "There seems to be some agitation going on and we'd better diffuse it. Now that they've seen you, you'll be of less interest. Let's not cause any more disruptions."

We went back inside. The next few weeks were going to be very informative and challenging. The women's interest in me continued unabated. They were so diverse, with such different backgrounds. With Victoria keeping notes, we hoped something could be done to help them when we got out, especially when it came to the behaviour of some of the staff.

That night, for the first time since I'd arrived at Vanier, I actually slept through the night. Jerry had come to visit, and told me all our kids were doing great. He had spoken to the two youngest, and they were so excited about being in camp, which they loved. They hadn't seen any of the headlines, obviously, so my sentence wasn't as traumatic for them as it might have been.

The older children were still taking it much harder, but as usual they behaved admirably.

Coco's spies who worked in the yard told her that Jerry had started to cry by his car when he arrived at Vanier that first time. Seeing the barbed wire fence and then passing through steel doors and being searched must have been a shock to him.

His visits three times a week became the thread that held me together. Like Victoria, I wouldn't allow any of my friends or any other family members to come and visit. I didn't want them to remember seeing me in jail.

The next morning I was called into a tiny cubicle off the main lounge. There, in the civilian clothes that she usually wore, was Betty Jo.

"Listen, you fucking Jew, you're no better than the nigger cunts we have here. You may think you're special, but here you're nothing. If I had my way, I'd make you eat the fucking food we serve, and not the Jew food you're getting." (I had requested kosher food, which comes in TV dinner form from the male prisons nearby. It was not an unusual request, at least not among the men.)

"I don't like your fucking attitude," she continued. "I'm in charge here."

"Listen, Betty Jo, I don't think you're allowed to talk this way to me, or to any other inmate. I've apologized to you publicly for my reaction to the fork incident. Why don't you leave me alone?"

"I've been here twelve fucking years," she snapped. "I have seniority. Nobody can do nothing to me. You and your fucking political friends. Here you're like a piece of shit on the road. You think you're going to get a TAP soon? Forget it!"

"But the judge said so," I said, almost crying.

"Forget those fucking judges. They don't run this fucking place. We do. He can only recommend. We decide. You think you're going to get paroled in two fucking months, eh? Well, don't count on it. We tell the parole board who they should let out, and they usually listen to us. Your fancy fucking lawyers can't help you now. Only I can."

For a minute, it sounded like Queen's Park and a political deal in the making. I almost asked her how much she wanted.

Instead I asked, "What do you want me to do?"

"There's nothing you can fucking do. People like you get away with fucking murder. Fancy clothes, fancy cars, lots of money. I'll bet you pocketed plenty from that $750,000 you stole."

"I didn't steal anything, Betty Jo," I said. "I signed a grant on behalf of a charity to renovate their building. Both the judge and the Crown agreed that I received no personal financial benefit."

"Bullshit. I know all about it. It's time you learned your fucking place. I'll be watching you. Now get out!"

Okay, I thought. This is like a movie. Walk calmly, don't react. What can she really do? Visions of isolation in a dungeon, bread and water, no light, beatings, passed through my head. Grow up, Patti, this is Canada. She's trying to scare you. I'll tell Coco. She'll know what to do. I'll tell Victoria. She'll make notes.

◆ The next day as I was walking down the hall to my room, I heard a slurping sound, and as I looked into a neighbouring cell, I saw the back of a male guard (the door was slightly ajar) and the top of the head of someone who was kneeling in front of him. It was obvious what was going on. I started giggling, a ridiculous reaction, and rushed back into the lounge.

I saw Lori first.

"Lori, you'll never believe what's going on down the hall." I started giggling again and told her what I'd seen.

"Mrs. Starr (Lori refused to call me Patti, saying it was disrespectful, especially since I was old enough to be her mother), I hope you didn't let them see you. Sex, especially oral sex, goes on all the time. Wait till a couple of the girls go at it. You can hear them all the way down the hall."

Again, I stupidly burst out laughing. Lamb Chop walked over.

"Mrs. Starr has just seen her first blow job," Lori said. "I think she's shocked. Tell her, Lamb Chop."

That afternoon, on our yard exercise, Lamb Chop and some of the other girls told me about sex behind the walls. There was sex between inmates and guards, male and female, often for favours like cigarettes, good reports, and, as it was rumoured, drugs. This took place in the fields behind the cottages or in the rooms themselves. Victoria and I saw body language and flirtations that we believed indicated intimacies.

Sex between women was more common, and that included some guards. Loneliness and longing for any kind of affection are usually the reasons. Most of the women, especially the prostitutes, view sex with another woman as a welcome diversion from sex with men, which is done for money or drugs. Most often the men, or Johns, are nasty and violent. There is none of the tenderness they can often get from a woman. This doesn't mean they don't like men, but when none is available, a woman sometimes fills the void.

"Have you ever tried it with a woman, Patti?" Lamb Chop asked.

"No, though I've seen it in movies," I answered.

Timberlea, June–July 1991

"Would you like to try it?"

"No, thank you," I answered with a nervous laugh.

"Too bad. A couple of the girls from other cottages are asking about you."

Oh my God, I thought, what if someone grabs me?

Seeing the look on my face, Lamb Chop started to laugh.

"You gotta stop thinking this is a made-for-TV movie you're in. Rape is only for punishment or a grudge. Besides, the word is out to leave you alone. Keeping your mouth shut to the cops really won you points here. Everyone hates snitches. Elaine got a broom shoved up her ass for pointing a finger at a drug stash going down. She's still in SNU for her own protection. Besides, I think there's too much press and too many people watching you. Last night they caught two reporters trying to get in over the fence. They said they were trying to find you for an interview."

Lamb Chop was quite short, with long blonde hair and a fair complexion. She wore two pony tails most of the time, but when she let her hair down, she was very sexy looking.

"By the way, I hear Coco's gonna introduce you to the 'guys' tomorrow. Nothing happens without their okay."

✧ The next afternoon, while all the girls were having their smoke break outside the main building, Coco and I joined them. Walking towards us were three women, as muscular and powerful as I'd ever seen, wearing construction boots. Their hair was cut short in front and longer in the back. Their shoulders were very broad, obviously from the weights they lifted every day. They gave me the high-five greeting.

"Nice to meet you, Mrs. Starr," they said.

"My name is Patti," I said. They looked at Coco, who nodded.

The brass had put these girls in charge of the grounds, and they were allowed to move freely around the whole site. In this way, information and messages were quickly available throughout the facility. Anything that happened at the main building was known throughout the cottages within fifteen minutes.

Drugs were usually the downfall of the large numbers of women who were returned to jail. It drove them to robbery, assault, and prostitution. Aside from their well-toned bodies, most of them looked ten years older than me, and they were all at least fifteen years younger.

Crack cocaine dulls the hair, blotches the skin, and turns teeth dark grey. So many were missing teeth, not from fighting, as I originally thought, but from the side effects of drug use.

As long as they were careful about what they were arrested for, they could keep coming back to Vanier rather than going to P4W (the term used for Kingston's federal Prison for Women). Any sentence of two years less a day meant Vanier. Anything over, and it was the "Pen," which everyone feared.

For too many of these women, Vanier represented a clean bed, regular meals, and showers. They showered three and four times a day, washed their clothes after each wear, and stuffed themselves with bread at every meal. The food being served wasn't too appetizing, but it was better than what they got on the outside, where many of them lived in hostels, which they described as hellholes, or on the streets.

Linda, who was only nineteen, said she had been on the street since she was twelve. Her mother was a prostitute, her father an alcoholic who had "given" her to his buddy for a bottle of wine when she was eleven years old. Her younger sister was into crack. Notwithstanding the abuse and lack of love in her life, she still longed to go home and be with her family, hoping against hope that things would get better. The statistics said they wouldn't.

I expected hostility from these women. Given Betty Jo's reaction to me, and she was a guard, I thought the inmates would surely feel the same, or worse. But they didn't. Their view of life was live and let live. I encountered very little anti-Semitism.

In fact, I was surprised by how much they knew about Judaism. At first they were all interested in what kind of food I was getting, but after seeing me eat meatballs almost every day for lunch and dinner, they decided kosher food wasn't so hot.

Every day they asked so many questions about politics, people they had only read about, and the world in which I had once lived. Their assessments of certain politicians were right on — besides being hilarious.

Their interest gave me a chance to share what I had experienced during the Starr Affair and the feelings I had tried to keep hidden for so long. They listened with great empathy; their comments were nonjudgmental and very comforting.

These girls equated a lot of what had happened to me with their own experiences. They believed, as I did, that I had been betrayed and abandoned by my community, and they valued loyalty above all else. It was a sacred trust. Anyone who broke it was dead meat.

As their own bodies started deteriorating and they became less desirable, their "old men" would take up with someone new and throw them out, often penniless. For many of them, the only friends they had left were those they met in jail.

A few of the girls were prostitutes. The going rate for a good one was about $1,500 a day. None of them paid any income tax and most of them were still independent. They didn't need to work the streets yet, as their customers contacted them through a phone service. But as their bodies began to become less attractive, they were dreading the day that was sure to come. Streetwalking. The money was less, the dangers greater.

After months in jail, they were drug free. Their thinking processes were clear. But once they were back on the street, most of them would slip back into the drug habit that was destroying them. Very few, if any, would be able to resist the urge to buy more drugs with every cent they made.

That didn't stop us from discussing, and them from fantasizing about, what they'd do with their money when they were older. They were so intense about it and almost childlike in their belief that this time, for sure, they were going to stay clean and begin to salt something away for their old age. (Later I was to bump into Lamb Chop in the hall outside the College Park provincial courtroom. She was under arrest again. The first thing she told me was that she still had the T-bills she had bought when she was last paroled. I hope she still does.)

Parole was the most important thing in our lives. We talked it, thought it, planned it, lived for it. It was the only ray of light in an otherwise bleak existence. To have the best chance of getting it, one had to "graduate" to Ingleside, the minimum security cottage on the outer edge of the grounds, near the gates.

Despite my background and my clean record, I was afraid the high profile of my case would place added pressure on the parole board not to be seen to be giving me special treatment. Nonetheless, I read everything I could about it, as preoccupied by freedom as everyone else.

With no programs available, I, along with the others, tried to keep busy by working in the main building of Vanier. Various jobs in housekeeping and maintenance were assigned to us. My job, washing the pots and pans, helped the time pass and didn't require me to think. It also gave me an inside view of the kitchen operation.

Food was prepared by the inmates under the supervision of staff. All aprons, gloves, and hair coverings were cleaned every day. The cooking equipment was clean and functional. Working on food preparation was a job most everyone wanted. It meant eating on the job (if no one saw you) and "lifting" stuff to take back to the cottages, like extra sugar, tea bags, fruit, and cookies.

The vegetables were canned. So was some of the meat. So was most of the fruit, though there were fresh apples, oranges, and peaches on rare occasions.

Not enough, though, especially in the summer months. One can't expect food in an institution to be good, but fruit and fresh vegetables would have gone a long way, especially for the pregnant women on special diets and the Moslems who couldn't eat pork. We used to kibbutz together about them ordering a kosher diet, but the rules of Vanier would not have allowed it, even if they had been brave enough to do so.

In the restricted environment of the cottage, bonds developed between the girls. There was tremendous loyalty, as I would learn over the next few weeks, and real risks were taken to protect each other.

Before a transfer to Ingleside was granted, a psychological-comprehension test was given by the head psychologist. When mine was finished, he congratulated me on having the highest score in the twenty-four-year history of the Vanier Centre.

"Does this mean I'll get transferred to Ingleside and then be paroled right away?" I asked.

"No chance," he said. "The cottage supervisor makes the recommendation. In your case, this result will probably increase her hostility and resentment. Be cooperative, do everything you're told, and don't ask questions or talk back. That's my advice."

I was dejected. I knew what Betty Jo would do, and she did it. Since she could not stop my transfer, given the test results and my clean record, she made sure I was put in a closed program at Ingleside, which meant I would be confined another four weeks without getting a TAP. "Bad attitude" was the reason given.

I went back to the kitchen and cried over my pots and pans. The supervisor, who had already heard what happened, came over and tried to console me.

"Look, you've got a life when you get out of here," he said. "Most of the other girls don't. I know it seems like forever, but it'll soon be over. Hold your head up, don't let anyone see that it's bothering you. This too shall pass."

✧ Three days later I was transferred to Ingleside in the closed program. Victoria had already been moved there, and Coco, strange as it seemed, given her record, was going too. As happy as I was, I knew I would miss some of my Timberlea friends, and the day I left, I tried to tell them how much their kindness had meant to me.

"Forget about us, and forget about this place," Sandra said. "You won't be back. Most of us will. Put it out of your mind and get on with your life."

I was still afraid of what Betty Jo would do, but I felt the first twinges of hope at the prospect of going to Ingleside.

During the three-hour processing, I was kept in a cell in the main building. Sitting on the hard bench, sweat pouring off me in torrents, staring at the cement walls and watching the newcomers arriving, I began to think about the past for the first time since I'd arrived. Was anyone thinking of me or wondering how I was? Did anyone care what had happened or even feel bad? What did Ian Scott think now? Did Jim and Heather Peterson ever try to help me? Did Hershell?

I was all alone, in a cell. Did I really deserve it? I could barely remember anything before the day I was sentenced.

I had been loyal to a lot of people, just like the girls were here. Why wasn't anyone loyal to me?

I thought about the way I had waded into the political scene, full of enthusiasm for getting things done, even though I was uneasy about how many manipulated the formal, and informal, process.

The informal process is well known, and it's a system of *quid pro quo*. *Quid pro quo* (Latin for "something for something") is a phrase that has several meanings in politics: payoffs, influence peddling, blackmail, greasing the wheel, or just favours asked for and reciprocated among friends. It does not always denote corruption, and not all politicians are involved in its corrupt forms. But it is as much a part of government as the bureaucrats who push the paper.

The "price" goes up from bargain basement municipal deals to much more munificent federal greasings of the wheel. The more powerful the politician, the easier for him to solicit favours, or donations, or payoffs. If he has a trusted aide or friend who can do the actual soliciting on his behalf, he can then distance himself from any illegal benefits received should any problems arise.

The more powerful the contributor, the more people he has around him to ensure that the favour, or donation, or payoff, travels a circuitous route into the hands of the recipient.

The name of the game is delivery. Whether it is rezoning for increased density on a development project, the awarding of co-op housing allocations to a consulting group, the appointment of a private consortium to do major construction for the government, or the selection of a site on which to build some facility at the taxpayer's expense, the necessary votes must be delivered. And when the stakes are high and the gains even higher, eveyone wants to get in on the action.

A politician can deliver only if his colleagues cooperate. After all, with so many playing the game, no one can be the quarterback on all the plays. So deals are made. Votes for or against a certain issue (for example, at City Hall) on the clear understanding that the favour will be reciprocated when requested. This explains why some politicians, especially municipal ones, sometimes support issues that do not seem to fit their usual positions.

The benefits can be a case of whiskey, a trip to Florida, ownership in a condo (in trust, or in the name of a relative), a couple of hookers, cash. The cash gifts usually range from $500 to $3,000 in small bills in a plain white envelope. The occasional Cabinet minister appreciates receiving $5,000 in one-hundred-dollar bills.

More often than not, an intermediary handles the actual transaction, taking a cut as their fee for service, or an appointment for a friend or relative on a board or commission that pays a per diem, or a city job — especially if the politician is a member of an important subcommittee.

Politicians who take gifts, at all three levels of government, prefer the cash, which is untraceable. A favourite place of deposit is the household freezer, where the money is wrapped in newspaper and marked as "steaks," with the date of expiry clearly marked.

But power can be truly corrupting, and very often a politician will begin to believe his own rhetoric and think he is infallible. He starts asking for cash directly, not wanting to share with those whose job it is to protect him, who earn a good part of their income from their cut and whose job it is to take the fall should something go awry.

When a multi-million-dollar project is on the drawing board, the money at stake in terms of benefits can be staggering. Several people want to get in on the action. So there is serious competition among the politicians to show the developer, or the lobbyist-lawyer, exactly who the real power brokers are.

The only fly in the ointment happens when the stakes get so high that greed comes into play. Deals that have been made, always verbal, start crumbling. One or more of the players decides their cut isn't high enough, and they want more. They might threaten either the benefactor or a colleague. Everyone starts getting nervous. In order to keep things on track, promises are made on future deals or votes, often without a real ability to deliver. And if one ever reneges, their ability to be part of the action in the future is damaged.

Greed also breeds stupidity. Chances are taken with flamboyant lifestyles sure to draw attention. The aphrodisiac of power prompts men to start flaunting their power, making no secret that "they" are the ones to see if any deal is made. Women, usually younger, almost always single, become part of their lifestyles, quite openly. Philandering husbands, womanizers, whatever one wants to call these politicians, are never "outed" in the press, despite the high level of office some of them hold.

I'd been told stories about the lobbyist-lawyers who provide call girls as part of their services to politicians. In one case, a man had to be lifted onto the bed by two of his lackeys — good for a few laughs among the guys at a couple of political fundraisers.

Some provincial and federal politicians are the same as some municipal ones, only they've earned the right to play the game at a "higher" level. Again, the payoff most often is cash. But now the politicians also seek favours for their friends and family, by asking for jobs or executive positions for them in the private sector. They can reciprocate, *quid pro quo*, by virtue of their influence on the process of appointments to government boards and commissions (such as royal commissions and task forces or the Ontario Muncipal Board) that pay handsome per diems.

Other examples include the National Parole Board, citizen court judgeships often given to unskilled wives of powerful players, and the provincial chair of the police board.

The infidelities of these politicians are more discreet. They are less inclined than their municipal counterparts to take benefits that can be easily traced. They have political dinners and fundraisers that allow for the appropriate gratitude to be shown them. Any personal benefits are usually handled through another trusted politico with as much to lose if their activities are exposed.

I have referred to men in these matters because with two exceptions that I know of, most of the *quid pro quo*, whether muncipally, provincially, or federally, is practised by men. And that's probably the way it's been since the beginning of time, since women have had so little opportunity to exercise real political power.

Women have traditionally been uncomfortable with duplicity, manipulation, and corruption, a fact of life in backroom politics. There is also a perception that women are gentler, less able to lie with a straight face, less able to intimidate and threaten, and more likely to crack under pressure. Not necessarily so. The militants who have overtaken the women's movement attest to that.

I thought back on how women had resented me. What in men they saw as ambition and assertiveness, in me they saw as ruthlessness, my not fitting into the female mould. They felt I had left the sorority to join the fraternity. Men, meanwhile, resented me for not fitting their stereotype of a "real" woman. They felt threatened, that their turf was being invaded — particularly on the waterfront issues.

When things got tough, I wasn't really one of the boys, and therefore was not deserving of the supportive network they provided for each other, no matter what the situation. As for my female associates, I was beginning to suspect, sadly, that many of them delighted in my downfall. Resentment over my personal power, the belief that I had strayed from an acceptable role for a woman, and my own shortcomings were all contributing factors.

TEMPTING FATE

So in the end I was alone, not belonging anywhere.

Maybe it was time for me to start thinking about it all again, and see if I could find the answer that would give me some peace of mind. I wanted to move on, but I was too confused. Maybe the next few weeks would give me a chance to sort it all out.

EIGHTEEN

Ingleside Cottage, July-August 1991, Vanier Centre for Women

When I finally got to Ingleside, after sitting in a hot cell for three hours, I was close to tears. I don't know why, but I was.

The cottage was a one-floor structure with two corridors of rooms and a large eating and kitchen area, lounge, and separate TV room. There were communal toilets, as well as showers and a bathtub. Everything was run down. The paint was peeling, especially in the rooms. Once again, the showers had ripped curtains and the tiles were cracked. Taps were leaking constantly. The place was shabby and depressing. But I was away from Betty Jo, so I didn't care.

Here the rules were different. The rooms weren't locked, and we were allowed to walk outside every day for limited time periods. On weekends we were even allowed out in the afternoons.

Visitors came to visit on-site. We no longer had to go to the main complex. After an assessment period, we were permitted a limited amount of personal effects, including clothing, jewellery, and a watch. Ingleside was the first step to freedom.

There was a head count every hour at Vanier, so whatever we were doing or wherever we were, we had to come in for the count. Twice during my stay, inmates escaped and it was the count that alerted staff. Everyone ran around, and for a short while afterward, we were all watched even more closely. At Ingleside we were responsible for serving the meals, for cleaning up afterwards, and for the general maintenance of the cottage and the grounds.

Ingleside should have provided some preparation for the outside world. Most of the girls had completed rehab or detox programs at Hochelaga or Kon Tiki before coming to minimum security, but the lack of any productive activities was worse than in the maximum security Timberlea.

The day started at 7:20 a.m. After breakfast and cleanup, we sat in the lounge, reading old books and magazines or knitting till 12:00. At 1:00 p.m., after lunch, we sat in the lounge until 4:00 p.m. We did absolutely nothing all day.

There were no programs, no classes, nothing. Any books or magazines that were available were very old. Occasionally there would be some sports activity for an hour or two. On two occasions a social worker conducted a discussion on children.

A basic computer training course was supposed to be available, but when Victoria asked about it, she was told the computer was down. The only up-to-date equipment available was in the male facility next door, the Ontario Correctional Institute. Most of the men incarcerated there were sex offenders and child molesters. The women in Vanier would have to go there if they wanted some kind of skills training program, though the only one I ever heard about was woodworking. It seemed unfair that the one and only female provincial institution was so run down and poorly equipped while a well-equipped one just next door was home to men who had victimized women like those incarcerated at Vanier. Most of the girls refused to go there and expressed their feelings to the staff. But nothing changed.

Ingleside's one electric typewriter was broken, apparently forever, according to the girls. One of them spent hours working on it and eventually fixed it. It should have been used as a training tool for some of the girls to help them get a job on the outside, but there was no one available to teach them. All the skilled personnel were next door at OCI.

There was one social worker for every twelve inmates at OCI, but at Vanier, there were three to look after one hundred and seventy-five women. Talk about reinforcement of one's lack of worth. If the kind of men who had perpetrated much of the abuse against these women were getting preferential treatment within the penal system as their "punishment," then the implication was very clear. Women deserved whatever they got, and any abusive treatment was probably coming to them. I wondered where the feminists were.

Most of the staff Victoria and I spoke to agreed that the situation was unfair. But women make up only 8 percent of the prison population, they said, so we get only 8 percent of the programs and services. I think something's wrong with that formula.

If these women were given life skills training that could be practically applied in the workplace, the money spent on welfare would be dramatically reduced. It is true that not everyone wants to work. Many of the girls I met had no intention of ever getting a job, but others did hate living on the dole. They said they only knew how to lie on their backs and wished for the opportunity to learn something else. Prisoners are a captive audience, and ignoring the potential for some skills development was a wasted opportunity.

During my stay at Vanier, only five of the girls I knew were *not* on welfare. They couldn't apply for the TAP program because they didn't have jobs, and they couldn't get jobs because they had no viable skills.

There had once been a cooking class which had also covered healthful eating habits, but it had not been available for a long time. Once or twice an arts and crafts instructor came, and some of the girls made bracelets and necklaces. I made some for my kids.

There was a fledgling hairdressing class that I had gone to while I was in Timberlea. It had no funding and only one staff person, who did the best she could. Many of the black women said how much they'd love to learn the specialized techniques needed to give hair care to their own people and how lucrative it could be. Disinterest from the ministry, along with the lack of funding, which was being funnelled to OCI, prevented this program from taking off. Another opportunity missed for a realistic alternative to the welfare cycle.

✦ Once at Ingleside, we could no longer work in the main complex; the risk of passing things between Ingleside, which was not fenced, and the rest of Vanier was too great. So I couldn't kill any more time washing what I had come to view as *my* pots and pans.

I assumed the relationship between the screws (guards) and us would improve. I was wrong.

To my horror, one of the senior staff at Ingleside was as bad as Betty Jo. Her name was Alice, and she prided herself on being the daughter of a cop. She would sit in the staff office and screech at the top of her lungs anytime she wanted something or didn't like what was going on. If the radio was too loud, she would scream out to us, "Turn that fucking radio down, you scums (or shitfaces, sluts, or whatever other name suited her at the time), or I'll turn it off for good." The other girls were afraid of her, and when I arrived at Ingleside, Victoria took me aside and warned me that she was worse than Betty Jo.

If she didn't like a look, or a response, or anything, she would give the girls a poor effort. She wouldn't allow inactivity, which was strange, given the lack of any available. So we had to sit in the lounge pretending we were reading. Some of the girls held their pocketbooks upside down to see if she'd notice. She didn't. If we started to gossip or put our heads back and just daydream and she caught us, we got a poor effort.

She inflicted strip searches regularly. We were taken into a room off the main hallway with at least two other female staff (though I was told by the other girls of the occasional presence of male guards), told to take off all our clothes, made to lift our arms high, open our mouths wide for inspection, turn around and lift one leg, then another, followed by bending over. If the screws really wanted to be mean, they would make us jump up and down with our legs spread wide and then make us do squatting knee

Ingleside Cottage, July–August 1991

bends. It never got any easier, no matter how many times you were subjected to it.

Drugs were being smuggled into prison either by visitors or the inmates themselves. In the case of women, the hiding spots were obvious. Searches were necessary to try and stop it, or at least control it. But many times I felt these searches were being used in a punitive way, to exercise power and inflict humiliation. Some of us had never, nor would we ever, use drugs. But I was lucky. I wasn't put through it almost every day like some of the others.

Food continued to be awful, though I was still eating my kosher TV dinners, mostly meatballs. But after two of the Moslem women complained about the lack of fruit, we started to get peaches, apples, and oranges regularly. One of the new inmates who was working in the kitchen was allowed to make chocolate brownies for all of us. That was the end of my diet.

Two of my cottage mates were working outside during the day. They, like me, had been recommended for a TAP when they were sentenced, but unlike me, had been allowed to go to work within a week of their arrival at Vanier.

There were more male guards at Ingleside than at Timberlea. I didn't like it, especially since some of the other girls would become restless when they were around.

Victoria, Coco, and I would go out everyday at 4:00 p.m. for a walk around the cottage. It was very hot, and we would often sit on the bench in the back under a tree. Most of the guards were kind and flexible, allowing us to stay there during the count, as long as we were in view of their office.

One afternoon, Victoria and I were sitting on the bench outside the back door when a car pulled up. Inside were three black men with dark glasses and Penny, a former inmate of Ingleside, who had recently been paroled. It was a contravention of her parole to be on Vanier's grounds without permission.

The car stopped and they all stared at us for a few minutes before the car door opened and Penny staggered out. She proceeded to put a package under a bush outside one of the bedroom windows. Victoria and I froze, afraid to move. Penny staggered back into the car and they took off. But instead of leaving the grounds, they kept circling. The two of us were terrified. And yet we were angry too. This was obviously a drop of some kind. All of us were now in jeopardy. Penny was the lover of one of the girls still here and we assumed whatever was in the package was for her. But snitches were the lowest form of life. We dared not say anything.

On the other hand, Victoria and I, despite where we were, were law-abiding citizens whose first instinct was to run inside the cottage and call the COs. But the repercussions would be horrific for us if we "sang." We grabbed each other and very slowly, arm in arm, walked back inside, whispering about what we should do. We decided to try to alert the guards to the car circling the cottage, in the hope that they would recognize Penny and react. This would trigger a search of the cottage and the surrounding grounds, and they would find the package without our having to say anything.

In hindsight, our behaviour was comical. We kept telling the COs to look at the beautiful blue sky outside. Then I told them that I thought the press were trying to find me for an interview again. Wasn't that a car circling the driveway? The CO in charge was disinterested, and now we were left with the option of spilling the beans or keeping our mouths shut. We chose the latter.

Two days later the drugs were found on one of the new girls after she was caught staggering around with glassy eyes. A CO had called for help and a raid took place at Ingleside. All our rooms were searched and so were we. Lucky for us, all privileges weren't pulled because the person involved was a new arrival.

There was a positive result, though. At an open forum discussion that evening between the inmates and the staff, a lot of hostility was expressed, by the inmates, towards those who would jeopardize all our privileges for their own selfishness. The consensus reached was clear and simple. No more drug drops. If anyone else did it, we (the inmates) would deal with them and make sure the screws found out who they were. I was told that this was an unusual stance. Perhaps the remembrance of lockup, isolation, no phone calls or visits, restricted privileges, and risk of violence did the trick.

✧ I was appalled at some of the men who came to visit the other inmates. Bedecked in gold chains, fancy clothes, diamond rings and driving expensive cars, they often brought several crying toddlers with them, which agitated the girls.

I learned that many of the women inside had taken the fall for the jerk who had just come to visit. These guys were pimps and drug pushers who for encores smuggled stolen goods over the U.S. border. Since women usually got lighter sentences, their "old men" persuaded them to take the rap. Children too often represented for the men and women an additional welfare payment from the government rather than a life to nurture and love. Few of the women were legally married and all worried that their old men had other old ladies on standby.

When Victoria and I asked some of the guards about the potential for some lifeskills counselling for these women, they were extremely sympathetic. They told us they had requested these kinds of programs many times, because they believed the women would then be better prepared to face their problems on the outside. Unfortunately, funding was not available.

Weekenders — those who had been allowed to serve their sentences from Friday night to Sunday night — came to Ingleside almost every week. These were the only occasions when I saw racial tensions. Most of the weekenders were black, and as soon as they arrived, the Ingleside regulars who were black would adopt the weekenders' patois dialect and become hostile to the rest of us.

There was a lot of pushing and shoving, and these "visitors" would take over the TV room and turn up the rock music. Cracks were regularly made at the white broads, and most of us just avoided them. Luckily, the weather was good that summer, so we spent most of the weekends sitting in the back of the complex.

Too bad Alice was never around. Neither were most of the

senior guards, who I am told were afraid of these militants and would rather not have to deal with them. So Ingleside was often short-staffed on the weekends, and most of those who were working were inexperienced.

I had one bad experience when an article written about me was marked up with comments about the "Jew Starr" and passed around. I didn't intend to be subjected to religious slurs by anyone, so, with the article in hand, I walked into the TV room full of weekenders and turned off the set. They all stared at me and then everyone but the two biggest bullies took off out of the room.

These two were confident that their behaviour would continue to go unchecked. Vanier, like many other government institutions, was terrified of charges of racism and would bend over backwards to avoid them. This permitted an unfair balance of power between the inmates when the weekenders arrived. Despite our complaints to the cottage supervisor, little was done.

So here I was, again, in a confrontation. The advantage I now had was notoriety. The press was still hanging around Vanier and the supervisors were well aware of it. Any incident that involved me was sure to be reported throughout the media. It wouldn't be so easy for these weekenders to push me around as they had the others.

They were too stupid to realize it, though. Both of them picked up a couple of ashtrays and started waving them, as though that was supposed to scare me. I just stood there, staring at them, saying nothing.

Then they heard, before they saw, guards from the administration building running down the road towards our cottage. Someone must have alerted the main complex. All of a sudden they dropped the patois and started speaking to me in perfect English. They hadn't meant anything, they didn't want any trouble, they were only having some fun. And my name was now Mrs. Starr, no longer "Jew broad." That was okay with me. I suggested they stay away from me.

One of my favourite COs told me the next day that the

Ingleside Cottage, July–August 1991

supervisor was so afraid the press would find out about the lax supervision on weekends if her famous charge was attacked and injured by weekenders, that she had started hyperventillating.

After that, weekends were better.

✧ And then, finally, I received a TAP which allowed me to leave Vanier to work during the day, five days a week. I left Ingleside at 6:00 a.m., went directly to our store, Reid & Lyons, located near Avenue Road in downtown Toronto, and returned at 4:00 p.m.

The rules were very strict. I was not allowed to go anywhere but directly to and from work. I had to stay within twenty feet of the store if I went outside for a break. Jerry brought lunch into the store every day, since I wasn't allowed to socialize or have anything to do with anyone not involved in my job. We enjoyed just being able to talk without someone standing over us. The children were in camp, so I never had an opportunity to see them at all that summer.

I was always careful to follow the rules exactly, so as not to jeopardize the privilege of working. They were my first steps to parole — and freedom.

When I returned to Vanier after work, usually half an hour early just to be sure no highway traffic would delay me, the other girls would still be sitting around the lounge, holding their books upside down, and knitting. For the first time, I saw envy in their eyes. It was understandable, but it reminded me how lucky I was to have a supportive network and a job to go to.

Every day when I came back, Coco and Victoria would be waiting. Off we'd go on our brisk forty-five-minute walk on the road surrounding Ingleside. Parole was uppermost in my mind and nothing anyone ever said to me gave me any comfort. I was terrified something would happen to screw it up. The thought of spending the full six months like this was awful. But Coco, with her irrepressible sense of humour and depth of character made it easier. She loved tormenting Victoria, who was such a straitlaced Scotswoman. When Coco finally provoked her into saying the "F" word, as it was referred to by Victoria, we started to cheer and clap. Victoria's face turned beet red.

Most often my thoughts were fixed on my parole hearing, coming up in two weeks. Under the law, any offender is entitled to apply for parole after serving one-third of their sentence, in my case two months. If it is a first offence, especially if no drugs or violence are involved, parole is almost guaranteed.

But I still drove everyone crazy, including some of the guards, by asking over and over again what happens, what should I say, how does it work, who did they know who had been refused and why. They answered the same questions over and over again, always in good humour.

✧ Looking for ways to distract me during this two-week wait, Coco opened up about her life. She seemed more like a mother to me than a peer. She was always hovering around, wherever I was, and on a couple of occasions caught me before I broke some cottage rule or was about to lose my temper.

I still couldn't figure out how she had got to Vanier, and then Ingleside, given her record and the fact that the current charge against her was assault with a deadly weapon. I thought that you had to stay at the West for charges like that if you didn't get bail.

The first surprise was that she was a Canadian, born in Africaville, Nova Scotia, which was razed in the early sixties. Known as New Glasgow today, it has the reputation for supplying most of the pimps in Canada. She used an acquired Jamaican accent when it served her purposes and had spent two years at a community college taking computer training. She was fluent in French.

Coco had dreamed of becoming a writer and a poet. Until she was twelve, life was good. She had parents and two younger brothers. But then, one night coming back from the library, she had been grabbed by two thugs, both white, and raped. She ran home hysterical and her father went out searching for them. Unfortunately, he found them. In the ensuing altercation, her father was kicked in the back, and after that, needed a cane to walk.

He found out, from his own sources, that the rapists were part of an international ring of pimps, many of whom worked out of Africaville. These two had come into town via Montreal looking for new recruits. Their approach was not uncommon; rape and assault are used to persuade young girls to become prostitutes. They are told they are now damaged goods and no man would ever want them for anything else.

When I questioned this, Coco insisted it was a common tactic.

"You have to understand the mentality of the people involved," she said. "How many times have you told me how it was when you were a kid, with your parents afraid you might go all the way with some guy and then become second-hand goods. This is the same thing, only from a different culture."

"Yes, Coco," I said, "but becoming a prostitute was never a consideration. Why would these guys assume that if a black girl is defiled then her only option is prostitution? Especially now. After all, it's not the fifties, and virginity doesn't mean anything anymore."

Coco smiled wearily.

"Many of my people have been conditioned over the years to see themselves as second class to begin with. Abusive treatment is a reinforcement of that perception because it is always accompanied by the assumption of being deserved. Add to that limited education and opportunity, and you have a failure waiting to be reborn.

"In my case, every time I looked at my father, I was reminded of what had happened. My mother worked as somebody's maid all the years and her whole attitude was one of self-deprecation. She never thought I would advance too much beyond her, but she hoped for my brothers. So all of her efforts, and those of my father, went to them. And they're really terrific kids. One is in law school in Halifax and the other works for the government."

"Coco, how old are you?" I asked. I thought she was a kid.

"I'm thirty-six," she replied.

"What?" I practically shrieked. "Who's your skin doctor? Where'd you get your face lift?" At least I wasn't old enough to be her mother.

Coco went on to say how she always felt tainted by what had happened to her and never wanted to talk about it. In her second year of community college she met a guy — "You know the kind that's no good but you can't resist him." When they got married, she didn't know he was already married. They had two sons, a year apart. When he took off, never to be seen again, he had already introduced her to cocaine.

Even though her mother was looking after the kids, she dropped out of school. Her drug habit was growing worse, and some of her new friends suggested hooking to get some extra money. She rationalized her addiction by blaming it on the earlier rape, but deep down she knew that was bullshit. Coco was a very strong-minded person. She was doing drugs because she liked it. She also wanted to forget the emptiness of her life.

At the time of their birth, she felt she was too young to really appreciate her sons, but she did know they'd be better off without an addicted parent. So she had left her home and family ten years before and moved to Toronto. She was arrested a couple of times for prostitution, trafficking, and once for assault while robbing a restaurant. The proprietor had called her a jungle bunny and she'd smashed him over the head with a giant bottle of Coke, when they were still made out of glass, to teach him a lesson.

After she was paroled, she decided to stay in Toronto and go straight. It didn't work. Again, bad influences and a poor choice of friends. But her intelligence and sharp wit stayed intact, and soon she was a leader rather than a follower.

Over the years, she wrote her boys through her mother and sent money, but never told them where she was. Her mother sent snapshots to a mail box drop. Her brothers and their families formed a protective environment for her sons as well.

No one in her circle knew any of this. As the time passed, she was becoming more protective of the sons she had last seen as toddlers and believed that if they knew what she was, it would destroy their lives.

Nothing I said could persuade her otherwise. She was making the ultimate sacrifice, she would say, freeing her children from the albatross of a mother like her. Coco understood, clearly, that drug addiction, like alcoholism, can at best be controlled, never cured. She didn't believe she would ever be free of its curse, and the risk of hurting her children's futures made her sacrifice bearable.

In 1990, while Coco was managing a call girl ring run by these same pimps from Halifax, a young girl, much like the one she had once been, had been brought in to work. Her story was the same as Coco's. And for some reason, Coco got very angry. One night, when the pimp came looking for his new protégé, Coco confronted him. Words, and then fisticuffs, ensued.

He pulled his gun, Coco kicked him between his legs, the gun fell, she picked it up and shot him, between the legs. She then took the girl and ran.

One thing the Metro Toronto police have is a good network. Apparently this pimp was one of their informants, so it was important to find Coco and make sure she paid for what she did.

Coco took the girl to London where she had a cousin, left her with some money, and returned to Toronto, never dreaming there was such a concerted effort going on to find her.

She was caught within a week and had languished in the West for three months trying to get bail when I arrived there. The Crown was showing no mercy, probably because the police needed to keep their network of informers happy. Insurrection on the part of these pimps' stable of girls could not be tolerated.

Her lawyer said he might be able to plea-bargain a five-year sentence. Even though good behaviour and parole might cut the time served to less than half, it meant P4W in Kingston, the end of the line for women in conflict with the law. Coco had been there before. It was a horror.

"You know, Coco," I said. "I know a lot of people. Maybe I can help you. If I get my parole, I'll be out of here by the first of

September. You have lots of skills, more than most here. Maybe you need a different lawyer. What about the women's movement? It's so in to be black right now. Maybe they'll take up your cause. You have so much potential for success."

"Anything like that will expose my kids," she answered. "It's better if they think their mother is dead, which is what I've been thinking about lately. They're happy in a secure family environment with grandparents, uncles, and cousins.

"There's no guarantee a background check wouldn't be done and the truth come out. My whole family would be exposed. I've spent too long learning to live without them to risk causing them shame by their finding out they have a drug-using hooker for a mother. No, let it go. There's nothing to be done."

I let it go, for the moment. But I had no intention of letting it go forever.

✦ Finally my big day arrived. The parole hearing. I hadn't slept for two nights before. I was terrified. My stomach was turning over constantly and I kept preparing myself for the worst, as I had that day in June when I faced the court.

I was having a hard time, even though one of the COs warned me if I was too controlled, the parole board would become suspicious.

The hour finally arrived, and one of my lawyers, Bob Bigelow, met me in Vanier's main building. As we were waiting to be called in for my interview, the sounds of screeching, followed by sobbing and wailing, reverberated around us. Suddenly, the door to the hearing room opened and an Oriental woman was led out by two guards, one holding each of her arms. Bob turned white, and I thought that I would pass out.

Her parole had been turned down. I can still hear her heart-wrenching cries. She couldn't speak any English, so when Mrs. Rashid, the wonderful social worker at Vanier, came rushing over to console her, she couldn't understand what she was saying. Eventually someone came over to interpret, and Mrs. Rashid was able to help her settle down.

Ingleside Cottage, July–August 1991

And now it was my turn. The sweat was pouring down my back as Bob and I walked into the room to face the three people who would decide my fate. I was holding onto his hand for dear life.

The three panel members were familiar with all the details of my case, including my volunteer background. Their questions were brief, but detailed. My prison record was on the table in front of them.

After about half an hour of questions, they asked me to step outside while they came to a decision. I was living in a time warp. I waited outside, so terrified I couldn't even swallow. It seemed like forever, but it was only five minutes till they called me back in and told me parole was granted. I would be free in two weeks.

I screeched with joy, jumped up and down, clapping my hands, and then I threw my arms around Bob. The panel members smiled at me warmly. The chairman wrote their recommendations on the required form and then spoke to me on their behalf. She questioned the point of my being incarcerated in the first place.

Bob's mouth dropped open when she said that.

She went on to say that a person with my background could be of real help in trying to sensitize the public to the conditions for the women still inside. The other panel members concurred. To that end, they were imposing no conditions of parole. I was free to advocate or speak out in any way I wished. And they documented their comments, for the record.

When I left the hearing, I skipped, just like a kid, all the way back to Ingleside. The roadway passed along the outside of the fence that surrounded Timberlea, Hochelaga, and Kon Tiki. It was late afternoon and a lot of the girls were out there on exercise. I guess the word had already gotten out, because as I passed by, waves, whistles, and cheers greeted me. I raised my arms like Richard Nixon used to and blew everyone kisses.

It was a happy moment, still frozen in my memory.

CHAPTER NINETEEN

Ingleside Cottage, August 1991, Vanier Centre for Women

The day I was granted parole was also the first time I was allowed out on a two-hour pass for a trip to the local donut shop.

Part of the process of release is the granting of off-site passes in order to assess whether or not an inmate is ready for the responsibilities and temptations on the outside. There are strict rules concerning time and behaviour.

No communication is allowed with *anyone* on the outside. Every cent of the limited amount of money allowed must be accounted for, accompanied by a receipt. There is no leeway in terms of time; if you're late, privileges are usually taken away.

That Friday afternoon, Victoria, Coco, and I went on our first outside pass together. It would be a celebration, especially for me.

As we walked out of Vanier along the roadway to McLaughlin Boulevard and then turned left over towards the donut shop, we were so excited about being "free" that we started skipping along the road. Anyone driving along McLaughlin Boulevard that evening would have seen three not so young women, one black, two white, hopping along like goofs. We were singing and joking — at one point we were all holding hands.

As we passed by the Ontario Correctional Institute on our way, I stopped and stared, because I could not believe my eyes.

This facility, which housed sex offenders and child molesters, was surrounded by shrubs and trees, green grass, and landscaping.

Ingleside Cottage, August 1991

It looked like a modern office building. Vanier, on the other hand, was on flat land and the grass was brown. There were a few flowers at the entrance to Ingleside, but no trees and no shrubs. Drab. Even the fencing around the facilities was different: Vanier's was imposing and noticeable, OCI's blended in with the landscaping. Why was there such a difference, especially since Vanier was the only provincial women's detention centre? No wonder the other girls felt worse off than the men. It really was so out of balance.

We started kibbutzing about writing letters to the editor, phoning radio stations, and creating messages to be sent by telegram to feminist groups. But on the subject of feminists, our conversation turned a little more serious. I was curious as to whether the women on the street felt any kinship with the women's movement or its leaders. According to Coco, they didn't — and that wasn't only those in conflict with the law.

"Most of the black women get a good laugh out of those do-gooders running around claiming to represent them," she said. "But we're learning to keep quiet and let their guilty consciences keep giving us more and more. Some of them are so busy kissing black ass they don't see how contemptible most women think they are. And I have always seen their patronization as the ultimate statement of contempt. Don't they think we're intelligent enough to work things through on our own?

"And some of those fat, fucking rich Jew dames — not you of course, Patti — who claim to be feminist leaders while their kids are in private schools and they use our people to clean their houses, really make us sick. Most of the ethnic and coloured women just sit around and wait, laughing all the while, as the liberal white folk fight over how much to hand over. I myself think it's going to hurt my people a lot in the long run, because taking handouts instead of working doesn't teach anyone anything."

Victoria saw the issue of pro-choice as the only valid reason to support the feminists. She had the same distaste for those women, at least those in Canada, as Coco, though her reasons were different. Her background was "gentry," and she considered the manipulation of the media for self-serving motives "beneath contempt." Women were on the move all the time, and the strides of the past twenty years had been tremendous. She believed that confrontation and abrasive behaviour, especially against men, accomplished nothing and created hostility, no matter how suppressed it might be. Equal opportunity should also mean equal responsibility, and one should succeed only if one had the ability, not by a reverse quota system.

"Okay, guys," I said, "let's lighten up. This is a day to celebrate."

Victoria, who had been on me from the first moment we met about writing a book, started in again, along with Coco. Of course, writing a book was out of the question for me at that point. I could barely think straight, much less remember all the pieces in the jigsaw puzzle. I wasn't even sure I could remember where I'd been before Vanier.

But then they got onto the subject of a mini-series or movie about my life, and that really started some funny scenario spinning, including which actors should play which of the major characters. The two of them were having such a good time, laughing and poking each other every time they came up with an outrageous casting idea, that I had to throw in my two cents' worth.

"Well, if there ever is a movie, I know who should play me," I said. "Sophia Loren."

With that, they burst out laughing so hard, that they bent over double, and Coco, pounding her thigh, said, "Even Angie would get a kick out of that."

In a flash she realized what she had done.

Our eyes met. She knew that I knew.

Victoria kept chattering on until we got back to Vanier and we split up to go to our rooms.

My God, I thought. Coco was a spy. Or worse, a snitch. She'd made a major mistake by speaking just those few words. Everyone called Angelo DelZotto, Angie. Only I never did.

During my time at Vanier, and even before, I had never

Ingleside Cottage, August 1991

discussed the DelZotto family in any way. The only mention of Tridel was in relation to NCJW's housing projects. Even with Victoria, who would often ask questions which I knew came out of simple curiosity, I never mentioned Angelo's name.

My instincts had gone on alert from the first moment Coco had shown up at Timberlea. But I had dismissed them. After all, I wasn't knowledgeable about the prison system, and all I knew was what the other girls told me.

One thing was certain, though. Coco's slip of the tongue left no doubt at all: she was there to watch me, either for good or not so good. Who had sent her?

Did I want to know? Should I confront her? What power was behind this? Whoever it was, they had obviously hoped that sometime during my incarceration I'd let down my guard and spill some beans, any beans, to Coco. But I didn't have any beans to spill, and even if I did, if I didn't spill them to stay out of jail, I sure wouldn't do it now.

They, whoever they were, had underestimated me and the depth of the wounds inflicted by my former friends. I was one of the walking wounded, with so much scar tissue covering me that nothing would ever get through to hurt me again. Nor would I ever trust anyone again, and that included Coco. Was it the police? Was it David Peterson's people, to see what I might say about them? After all, they still had a lot of power. Or was it someone else just wanting to keep an eye out for me?

That night, before lights out, I walked down the hallway to Coco's room. She was sitting on her cot, holding some papers and making notes on them.

"Do you want to tell me, Coco?"

"No. You know I can't."

"Did you really think that if I knew anything, which I don't, I'd tell you?" I asked.

"I don't know what you're talking about. I was only sent to Vanier because the West was overcrowded and I have a few friends around here myself. Pretty soon I'll be shipped back to P4W. And I'll forget I ever knew you."

I was silent, and just looked at her.

"Why do you always assume the worst?" she said, her voice rising. "Maybe you still have some friends out there who think you got a raw deal? Maybe someone was worried about how you'd cope in jail? Maybe someone who couldn't protect you on the outside felt they could on the inside? Can't you ever let your guard down? Or maybe it was the screws, wanting to nail you for something else. Maybe it was a trap, to catch you admitting complicity in some real fraud — or a payoff to some politician. In any case, you'll never know, will you?"

"Coco," I said, "you've made life bearable here, and your protection was like a security blanket. I'll always be grateful to you, no matter who sent you."

"Listen, you dumb Jew broad," she snapped. "Nobody sent me. Now get lost."

The next day, Coco escaped from Vanier, simply by walking down the road and away, during afternoon break. The whistles blew, guards ran around, everyone was interviewed, but nobody saw or heard anything.

Later that evening, as we stripped our rooms for a search, I found an envelope under my mattress. I hid it inside my bra until the cottage search was over. It was poetry Coco had written while we were at Timberlea. There was no accompanying note.

A week before I was released, the supervisor took me aside to tell me that Coco had been found in London, Ontario. Dead from an overdose.

I felt as though I'd been kicked in the stomach. I turned my head quickly so she wouldn't see how distraught I was.

Besides making my stay in Vanier bearable, Coco had taught me to appreciate how special the company of other women can be, especially in dreadful circumstances. The cut-ups we'd shared, the hours of walking around Ingleside talking about men, women, and life in general, the practical jokes we'd played on poor Victoria, and the comfort of knowing she was there, watching my back. God, how I'd miss her.

Rest in peace, Coco. You were right when you said this book

Ingleside Cottage, August 1991

had to be written. It's also been published, and so has one of your poems:

>MY IDEA OF MARRIAGE WAS HAPPINESS AND BLISS,
>CARING AND SHARING A HUG AND A KISS,
>WE STARTED OUT GREAT,
>THE WAY IT SHOULD BE,
>BUT IT CHANGED ALL OF A SUDDEN,
>WHEN WE BECAME THREE.
>HE STARTED TO VERBALIZE,
>A PUSH THEN A SHOVE,
>THAT'S WHEN I KNEW, THIS COULDN'T BE LOVE.
>MAYBE IT'S ME, I'M NOT DOING MY BEST,
>I'M WORTHLESS, I'M NOBODY,
>THIS IS WHAT HE'D SUGGEST.
>I'M IN JAIL RIGHT NOW,
>FOR DOING A CRIME,
>IT'S A LONG, LONG SENTENCE,
>IT'S A VERY LONG TIME.
>MY CHILDREN ARE GONE,
>AND I'M OH SO ALONE,
>I'M TIRED AND SO SAD,
>I THINK I'LL GO HOME.
>
>— Coco, *Timberlea Cottage,*
>*Vanier Centre for Women, July 1991*

CHAPTER TWENTY

Time to Move On

The day I was released from the Vanier Centre, August 27, 1991, Jerry and I took a long walk in the park around the corner from our house. We agreed that the past was behind us. No dwelling on what happened, no wallowing in self-pity and bitterness. We had to move on. Period.

I'd just received a letter from the Elizabeth Fry Society asking me to consider volunteering with them to sensitize the public to the conditions of women in prison. Their offer was like a gift from above. For the first time in a long time, I felt there was still a role for me in the community.

During my stay in Vanier, the society had provided comfort to many of us. Their volunteers were discreet and always held out hope, not only to me but to the other girls as well. Their halfway houses provide an opportunity for many women to start over, along with their young children. They have, for many years, been in the forefront of advocacy on behalf of women in conflict with the law.

I was invited to meet with their senior staff and discuss how I might best be of service. My notoriety and high profile might now be an advantage. Most people weren't interested in women who had been in jail, and getting visibility for their cause was very difficult. Using me would attract the press, and probably others who would otherwise not bother.

So I agreed to be available for public appearances. Over the

Time to Move On

next year I made some speeches on their behalf as well as agreeing to appear on the "Shirley Show," a local TV talk show. Even though I was the obvious target for some of the preselected, confrontational questions, the plight of women still in prison was brought to the public's attention. During the taping, I was also fortunate to meet some outstanding professionals in the field.

In November 1991 I got a call from the Crown prosecutor, Peter Griffiths. The preliminary trial of Marty Mendelow, who himself had been charged with fraud on the renovation grant some months earlier, was coming up. I was being subpoenaed as a witness for the prosecution.

I agreed to meet with him beforehand and asked that the police investigators who had run Project 50 (the Starr Affair) be present as well. It was time to meet them, face to face, to talk about what happened, and then put it to rest. As I walked a few blocks south to the College Street police headquarters building from our store on Davenport Road, I thought about the end results of the Starr Affair, played out in living colour for three years.

I had pleaded guilty and was jailed for signing a renovation grant on behalf of NCJW's Council House. All money had been accounted for and I had received no personal financial benefit.

I had pleaded guilty and was jailed for signing a $4,035 cheque, *written on the Capital Fund in error*, even though I had personally reimbursed the fund more than two years earlier.

Revenue Canada, after months of their own intense investigation, found no reason to take any action against either NCJW or me. How ironic that our initial interpretation of the Tax Act relating to political activity had been correct, or at least acceptable.

All those allegations whipped up in the media about "illegal political contributions" and "misuse of charity's funds" turned out to be just that, allegations. The Capital Fund, which had started out in 1987 with $250,000 from the sales tax rebate, still had $214,000 when I left Council House for the last time in May 1989.

The renovation of Council House enabled NCJW to rent out

its upper floor to offset its administration costs, including Dody Rudson's salary. The ESL, literacy, and disabled workshops are still going strong.

Eveline Berger was eventually driven from the presidency of NCJW, Toronto, by the national organization anyway, even after she joined the group who "couldn't remember" anything much about my activities. It must have been hard for her to continue withstanding the pressures she faced, but I wish she had.

The legal firm, Robins, Appleby, Kotler, split up. Ralph Lean went on to join the same law firm as David Peterson. Ron Miller is practising law on his own. Lesley Miller is a consultant for the York Region Board of Education. Nita and Sam Goldband are still in the development business. Marsha and Eric Slavens continue to be on the executive of the Canadian Jewish Congress.

Victoria and I speak to each other at least twice a week.

✦ The meeting with the Crown and the police turned out to be very interesting. We had met once before during one of my many court appearances. Then I had been sitting alone on one of the benches watching Austin Cooper and Peter West chit-chat amicably with them. They were all having a good time, and it had irritated me a lot. Those people were trying to convict me, and there were my lawyers being so friendly with them.

Knowing it would bother Austin, I walked over to the last row of the courtroom where Inspector Teeft and his cohorts were sitting, ramrod straight, with faces like stone.

"Well, Inspector," I said with a sweet smile, "why don't you come and sit with me in the front row? Then I won't have to worry about the press parking themselves next to me, especially with you there to protect me. That is your job, isn't it? To serve and protect? Besides, we can have a friendly conversation. I'm sure you can be most charming if you try really hard. I presume you're allowed to do that, aren't you?"

Roy Teeft isn't exactly a chicken, so, returning the same sweet

Time to Move On

smile, he got up and sat next to me. His colleagues just kept staring straight ahead.

The judge kept looking over at us until Austin turned around. When he saw us, the smile left his face. Too bad, I thought. Next time don't be so friendly with the enemy. If you can, I can.

I was in a defiant mood and I asked Teeft if he was having fun chasing around after me. "Who's looking after the drug pushers and murderers if so many of your senior guys are busy with me?" I said. "Do you appreciate the paper trail I've left you on all my activities? Isn't that what all criminals do when they have something to hide?"

After sitting quietly during my petty jibes at him, he turned, gave me a very pleasant smile, and suggested that if I wanted an answer to one or more of my questions, I'd better zipper my lips. He also suggested I shouldn't ruin my image of icy control by behaving the way a normal person would when faced with the same circumstances. "Stifle yourself, Edith," he said. I burst out laughing.

Well, what do you know, I thought. The man actually has a personality. Too bad he's the hunter and I'm the prey. It would have been more fun the other way around.

He went on to say that the police knew I wasn't a criminal but that I had done some "dumb' things. However, their job was to enforce the law, which I'd broken. He also added that it was too bad I hadn't spoken to the police way back when. My explanations might have gone a long way in easing the situation I now faced.

That only made me feel worse. I had asked my lawyers several times about giving my side of the story to the police. The answer was always no, because Austin and Peter were concerned I'd incriminate myself.

Looking back, with the advantage of hindsight, I wish I had spoken to them. Nothing could have been worse than going to jail and having a criminal record for the rest of my life. Now, in his office, Peter Griffiths informed me that the Crown was asking for the same jail term for Marty Mendelow that I had received. After all, it was only fair, since his numbers on the grant were the ones we had used. He also informed me that after months of investigating Harold Green/Verdiroc, they weren't going to be charging Green.

I got up and walked over to the window overlooking College Street. There was a lot of construction going on, but I could see right down to the waterfront, where I had once dreamed of having an exciting and challenging career. Some of the men in this room had spent three years of their lives tracking my background and activities. I had read the verbatim transcripts of their interviews with witnesses and their questions were right on target in the direction they were going and their understanding of what really happened. They were a lot sharper than most people gave them credit for.

As a matter of fact, as the months passed, the focus of their questions turned to the complicity of the others. And it seemed that some of them were actually trying to get some of the girls to admit prior knowledge, especially on the reimbursed expenses, which would have eliminated the breach of trust charge. But the girls had obviously been well trained. "I don't remember" was their standard reply. I read one transcript in which the OPP investigator was questioning one of the girls who kept denying that she had attended a certain political dinner. Finally, with an impatient grunt transcribed on the record, the Inspector snapped that not only had she been there, but she had been reimbursed for her cheque. Others who had also attended testified to her presence.

"Well," she answered, "I don't remember how I got there."

"Perhaps the stork dropped you," was his response, though it seemed in the reading that this barb went right over her head.

So here I was. Nothing could change what had happened. How did I want to approach the rest of my life?

"Okay, guys," I said, still looking out the window, "I'll tell you my position on this matter. And after that, you can take me out for lunch, which will no doubt cause a sensation. I was the driving force behind that grant. The in-kind matching funds approach was my idea. The fact that it was common practice didn't mean diddly squat to any of you where I was concerned. But it has to mean something for Marty Mendelow.

"Once, years ago, he was someone special in my life. But his silence has changed all that. He's too old and set in his ways to go to jail. There's no point to it. Besides, it was always me you wanted, from day one, and it's me you got. The story's over. I want you to let him go." I turned to face them.

There was silence. "Don't worry, Peter, there won't even be a blip in the press about double standards, because I'm prepared to repeat what I've just said in open court. I'll do for him what he never did for me, or any of them did for me for that matter. I'm asking you to show him mercy in recognition of his years of community service. Let him go."

The looks that went around that room were hard to read. The police were still reluctant to waive the jail term and kept insisting that he was as guilty as me.

"No, he's not," I answered. "I'm the one who pushed them, and even though they went along with it, the penalty I've already paid should cover everybody."

Finally Peter agreed, but said he intended to make sure that Marty, through his lawyer Brian Greenspan, knew exactly what I'd done for him.

"Don't bother," I said. "I don't care what he knows."

However, the Crown would still insist on a $50,000 fine, along with a guilty plea to one charge of fraud so Marty wouldn't get off scot free.

Big deal, I thought.

I really didn't care what any of them thought anymore. It's what I knew that counted. I was free of them and soon I'd be free of the past.

With that, Peter Griffiths, along with some senior inspectors from the Metro Toronto police department and the OPP, took me out for a two-hour lunch. We had a ball — and it was an appropriate way to close this chapter in my life.

When I walked back to our store in Designers' Walk, I was free for the first time in three years.

Epilogue

Fall 1992. *Toronto Star* writer and columnist David Lewis Stein is launching a new book he has written. I've been invited to attend the party in his honour being held at the Jewish Community Centre, Bloor branch. There'll be a lot of people there I know, or at least once knew.

"Come on, Patti, I really want you to come. It's time you showed your face. You can't hide forever," he said.

I called up my buddy, Betty Disero, who had also been invited and asked her to go with me. For the first time in a long time, I wanted to schmooze with people — to gossip and talk politics.

When we got there, it was packed. Betty and I found ourselves in the middle of the room with people coming over to chat as though nothing had changed over this past three years. All eyes were on us. David Greenspan, former head of the Ontario Housing Corporation and former special friend of Toronto mayor June Rowlands, gave me a wonderful bear hug. I proceeded to give him a lecture on taking up with women who were too young for him, which I used to tease him about regularly after he and June split. David and I had become friends during the years we were involved in social housing issues, and we had come to respect each other's different perspectives on how best to deal with developers within the non-profit housing sector.

Our banter attracted a small group of others, who began teasing me on how my troubles hadn't affected my tact and diplomacy in light of how I was "harassing" Greenspan. Joanne

Epilogue

Campbell, chairman of the Metro Toronto Housing Company and a very respected senior bureaucrat within the current political power structure, joined us. Her husband, Gordon Cressy, had been president of the United Way when I was a member of its campaign cabinet.

"There are a lot of people who feel guilty about what happened to you," she said. "They should have come forward on your behalf, but they were afraid to speak up for fear of attracting attention to themselves. No one really thought what happened to you would. It was hard to believe, given the real criminals walking the streets. You didn't deserve it. But I thought you should know that many of us admired the way you handled it. I, personally, have a great deal of respect for you."

"Joanne, thank you for your comments. Coming from you, it really means a lot. I appreciate it," I said.

Just then Betty's face took on a dark look and she appeared to be glaring at someone behind me.

"May I join you?" a voice spoke, so well remembered and still missed.

I turned. We were face to face. Her hair was shorter, her eyes clear and direct, and her body still slim.

"How are you, Patti?" she asked.

We looked directly into each other's eyes. She hesitated, awkwardly leaning over as though to hug me. I grabbed her shoulders and put my arms around her. She responded enthusiastically.

"How are the kids and Jamie?" I asked.

"Great," she answered. "But I want to know about you, Jerry, and your family."

"Well," I answered, "Stuart is seventeen now and over six foot two. He plays a mean guitar and sings in a rock band after school. He's also driving. Can you believe it? Evan is in Sweden living with the girl he met in Israel when they were both working on a kibbutz. Brooke is working for a bank, and doing well. David is an executive with the World's Biggest Book Store, and Randy, the baby, is fourteen and taller than me. He's also an expert pool player.

"Jerry bought Reid & Lyons Inc. in 1990 when the owners retired. It's a business that specializes in better quality tassels and trims. We're both enjoying it, though sometimes I miss the action of the past. But things have settled down, and if we can survive this recession, we'll be okay."

"You don't know how many times I've thought of you," she said, "how many times I've wondered how you were doing, how badly I felt."

By now, Betty was really making facial expressions, mostly of disgust.

"I know you were thinking of me, and I appreciate it," I said. "But all things pass, in time. It really wasn't so bad, and I'm trying to move forward. I miss a lot of the people I once knew, but that's the way it goes. I'm just fine, though. Thank you for being so concerned."

Jane Pepino stayed with us as people continued to come over and make small talk for another half-hour. Then it was time for Betty and me to leave. Franco Prevedello had invited us up to Centro for a drink and Crème Brulée, which is almost worth dying for.

"How could you be so polite!" Betty whispered through clenched teeth as we were going for our coats. "She abandoned you — not even a goodbye. And that interview she gave to the press! Why didn't you just give her a blast? I can't believe this is really you. Are you getting old or what?"

"Betty," I said very quietly, "what would I accomplish by going on the attack? How many people out there have your loyalty and strength? Very few, believe me. Jane was a good friend for a long time. We had a lot of good times together. So she panicked. So did many others. Who knows if our paths will cross again? I made it easy for people to stab me in the back because of the very behaviour you're suggesting to me now. I could have accomplished more with honey than vinegar (where did I hear that before?).

"Besides, it took a lot of guts for her to come here tonight, much less walk up and talk to me, especially with you standing on guard. After all, she, better than most, knows what I'm capable of when it comes to retribution. No, it's time to turn the page, to close the book, and move on."

Betty just stared at me.

"Betty, learn from everything I did wrong. Don't make the same mistakes. You have the ability to reach the top. Don't waste your time with pettiness and revenge. Life is a circle. What goes around comes around. Things have a way of breaking even for everyone."

Once again, Jane walked up to us.

"Why don't you call me and we'll get together for a drink or something?" she suggested.

"That sounds terrific," I said.

With that she walked away into the clear, cold night. I watched her go. My eyes filled with tears as the memories of so many fun times, so many challenges and so much mutual affection and respect rushed over me, and then disappeared with her into the darkness. She had been such an important part of my life. But as great and productive as it had once been, that time was over. I was moving on.

Angelo, Angelo, I cried silently. I've finally learned. Too late.

INDEX

Aarons, Marilyn, 1
Aird & Bailis (lawyers), 67, 149
Allen, Duncan, 121, 140, 143, 145-147, 151
Andrew, Prince of England, 12
Appel, Bluma, 150-151
Applebaum, Martin, 42, 45, 47, 51, 63, 111
Appleby, Eleanor, 25, 213
Appleby, Ron, 53
Ariganello, Ottavio, 102
Arnold, Gita, 167
Aronson, Shirley, 169, 175, 214
Ashworth, Dyanne, 138-139, 202
Ashworth, Gordon, 121, 137-138, 150-151, 163; friendship with Patricia Starr, 138-139, 144, 220-223; and Patricia Starr Inquiry, 211-212; political association with Patricia Starr, 75-79, 81-83, 91-93, 97-99, 155, 161, 170-172, 174; resignation, 202, 203, 206; and Starr Affair, 192, 199-200, 220-223
Associated Hebrew School, 14, 18
Atkinson, Peter, 178-181, 184, 192, 195, 202, 203
Augimeri, Maria, 165
Avenal housing project. *see* Ridley housing project

Barbaro, Ron, 185
Bata, Sonja, 146-147
Bata, Thomas, 146-147
Bathurst Heights Collegiate, 19
Ben Gurion University (Israel), 54
Berger, Eveline, 185, 284; and NCJW Capital Fund, 114-115; and Ridley housing project, 164, 167; and Starr Affair, 178-182, 186, 198
Berger, Milton, 58, 59, 60
Beta Sigma Rho fraternity, 20
Beth Din, 15, 68
Bigelow, Bob, 274-275
Bitove, John Sr., 131-132, 143, 189
Bitove Corporation, 131-132
Block parents, 27
Blott, Alan, 67
B'nai Brith, 1; Camp (Haliburton, Ontario), 18, 21; tribute dinner for Patricia Starr, 75, 99-101, 180
Book, David, 14, 15-16
Book, Dora, 14, 16
Borg, Vince, 87, 101, 139, 161, 177, 199; political association with Patricia Starr, 120, 136; and Starr Affair, 190, 223-224; and Tridel Corporation, 92, 93, 205, 221
Brannon, Gina, 211, 222
Bratty, Rudy, 46, 95, 170, 171

293

INDEX

Brodski, Marek, 36, 37
Brorenstein, Sam, 161
Brott, Boris, 122
Burnett, Joe, 5, 205

Callum, Sue, 170
Campbell, Joanne, 289
Campion, John, 229
Canada Mortgage and Housing Corporation (CMHC), 45, 55, 62-64
Canadian Charter of Rights and Freedoms, 2, 206, 213
Canadian Council of Christians and Jews, 67
Canadian Jewish Congress, 34-35, 40, 50, 54, 176, 188; Ontario Region, 90-91, 111, 148, 189
Canadian Jewish News, 185-186
Canadian National Exhibition, 53, 116, 145
Canadian Occupational Therapy Association, 228
Caplan, Elinor, 59, 60, 66, 86-87, 185
Carman, Bob, 81, 120, 146, 147, 151
Carr, Donald, 182, 184
Chapley, Irving, 72-73, 74
Charney, Gerald, 143
Cherniak, Earl, 205, 211, 212, 214, 216
Chow, Olivia, 44
Co-operative Housing Federation of Toronto, 43-44
Cogan, Eddie, 115, 189
Cohen, Marty, 136-137
Colloleo, John, 106
Commission on Election Finances, 137, 222, 224, 225, 229-230
Cooper, Austin, 5, 205-219, 220, 226, 284-285
Cooper, Eleanor, 34, 56, 58, 59, 61, 63, 69, 164

Cooper, Sandler & West (lawyers), 6, 215, 232
Cooper, Virginia, 118-119, 129-130
Copeland, Clare, 120-121, 123
Corneille, Roland de, 51
Creative Living for Seniors, 27
Cressy, Gordon, 289
Crombie, David, 143, 146, 153
Curling, Alvin, 66, 157-158, 159
Cutts, Charlie, 76

Davey, Keith, 74, 138, 155
Davis, Bill, 83
Dawson, Ann, 229-230
Decima Research, 139, 161
DeGasperis, Fred, 170
DeLucca, Primo, 95
DelZotto, Angelo, 82-83, 98, 102, 170; association with Patricia Starr, 78, 94-96, 165, 204-205, 278-279; and Prince Charles housing project, 42, 45-48, 62, 64
DelZotto, Elvio, 51, 98-99, 162; and Liberal Party, 78, 79, 102, 104-106; and Ontario Police Commission, 83-88, 91-92, 94, 204; and Starr Affair, 205, 221
DelZotto, Jack, 46, 82
DelZotto, Leo, 51, 98
DelZotto, Marlene, 221
DelZotto family, 79, 81-84, 88, 97-98, 174. *see also* Tridel Corporation; and Starr Affair, 204-205, 221; U.S. operations, 91-92
Diament, Frank, 1
Disero, Betty, 102-103, 104; friendship with Patricia Starr, 200-201, 215, 218, 288, 289-291
Drea, Frank, 64
Dubin, Charles, 156, 212
Duffy, Al, 170

INDEX

Eakins, John, 66, 171, 172
Eggleton, Art, 53, 73-74, 153, 185, 194-195; and Toronto waterfront, 141, 143-144, 146
Eggleton, Brenda, 194
Elizabeth Fry Society, 282-283
Ellis-Don Construction Ltd., 89
Exhibition Place (Toronto), 141-145, 154, 174
Ezrin, Hershell, 36, 137-138, 155, 172, 189; political association with Patricia Starr, 76-80, 86-88, 97-99, 101-103, 146-147, 161

Famee Fulane housing project, 95
Feldman, Mike, 45
Ferguson, Derek, 58
Ferguson, Jock, 170
Fisher, Ralph, 54
Fleischman, Ivan, 86-87, 141, 143, 144, 185
Flynn, Dennis, 143, 173-174, 177
Foti, Joe, 103-107
Futurac Consultants, 163-164, 183, 190

Gardner, Norm, 128-129
Gentile, Mario, 142-143, 173-174
Giampietri, Mario, 78, 102-104, 106-107, 139; and Patricia Starr Inquiry, 206, 211-212; and Ridley housing project, 164-167
Globe and Mail, 158, 160, 162, 170, 171; coverage of Starr Affair, 169, 173-177, 181, 184, 191-192
Godfrey, Gina, 194
Godfrey, Paul, 74-75, 99, 122-123, 158, 171, 194
Goetz-Gadon, Sean, 161
Gold, Alan, 205, 206, 212-213, 214, 216

Goldband, Nita, 49, 55, 113, 134, 180, 284; and Futurac Consultants, 163-164, 190; and NCJW Capital Fund, 114-115; and NCJW renovation grant, 152, 169, 226; and Prince Charles housing project, 43, 53, 55-56, 60, 63-64; and Ridley housing project, 164, 167; and Starr Affair, 181-183, 184, 185; and Task Force on the Disabled, 32, 34-35
Goldband, Sam, 115, 284
Goldfarb, Joan, 155
Goldfarb, Martin, 74, 137-138, 155, 162, 171
Goldfarb, Stanley, 171
Goodman & Carr (lawyers), 182
Goodman, Eddie, 98, 180
Goodman & Goodman (lawyers), 180, 191
Gordon Capital (investments), 105
Gossage, Patrick, 162, 199
government grants: and matching funds, 37, 38-40, 152-153, 208-209, 227; and volunteer organizations, 38-40, 90-91
Graff, Barbara, 1
Grafstein, Carole, 74
Grafstein, Jerry, 73-74, 76, 138, 155, 221
Grandmaître, Bernard, 66
Grange Commission, 206
Green, Harold, 153, 169, 286
Greene, Barbara, 70-71
Greenspan, Brian, 287
Greenspan, David, 288
Greer, Tom, 143
Griffiths, Peter, 2, 233, 283, 285-287
Grossman, Georgina, 32, 34-35, 53, 60, 63; and Prince Charles housing project, 51, 53
Grossman, Larry, 64, 131

295

INDEX

Harbour Quay Developments. *see* Ramparts development
Harbourfront, 143, 146, 153, 154
Henderson, Paul, 173
Hosek, Chaviva, 67-68, 101-108, 109, 195; as Ontario Minister of Housing, 108, 157, 160-162; and Starr Affair, 192-193, 218
Houlden, Lloyd, 202, 205, 207, 210-214, 217-218
House of Chan (Toronto), 77, 117, 139, 177, 208
Huang & Danczkay (developers), 141
Hutzel, Ben, 229

Ianno, Tony, 102
Indianapolis '500, 194-195
International Fur Workers' Union, 17
Iseman, Seymour, 136-137
Island Yacht Club, 117

Jackman, Eric, 60
Jackman, Hal, 147, 151
Jackman, Sara, 60
Jackson, Jay, 36, 37
Jakobek, Tom, 77, 141, 145, 146, 200
Jewish Community Centre (Toronto), 36, 40, 50, 54, 77, 90, 152-153, 288
Jewish Federation of Greater Toronto. *see* Toronto Jewish Congress
Johnson, Ben, 156, 212

Kachuk, Connie, 61, 164
Keele Valley dump site, 75
Keyes, Ken, 66, 85, 186
Kids on the Block, 27
Kwinter, Monte, 53, 66, 117, 155-156, 194; and NCJW projects, 65, 83; political association with Patricia Starr, 86, 91, 114; and Starr Affair, 195-196, 206, 208, 221, 230-231
Kwinter, Wilma, 116-117, 155, 208

Lastman, Marilyn, 70
Lastman, Mel, 58, 59, 69-71, 158, 201
Laventhol & Horwath (accountants), 54, 112
Lax, Clifford, 180-181, 184, 191, 195, 198, 208, 229
Layton, Jack, 44, 177, 225
Lean, Marcelle, 194
Lean, Ralph, 53, 65, 143, 145, 158, 194, 196
Levy, Earl, 205, 207, 208
Liberal Party of Ontario: fundraising, 79, 88-89, 136-137, 179, 184, 227; involvement with developers, 81-108; Oakwood nomination, 101-106, 106-108; and Starr Affair, 190-191, 221, 223-224
Loretto Abbey (Toronto), 14
Lynn, Larry, 62
Lyons, Jeff, 158, 194
Lyons, Sandy, 194

MacDonald, Ross, 30-31
MacDougall, Cindy, 143
MacMaughton, David, 221
Mandell, Frances, 188-189
Marr, Helen, 25
Martin, Dale, 165-166, 225
McCaffrey, Bruce, 37
McDougall, Barbara, 54, 63, 99, 115, 153, 189
McGillvray, Bob, 230-231
McMichael Canadian Art Collection (Kleinburg, Ontario), 150
McMurtry, Roy, 83

INDEX

Meals On Wheels, 26
Mendelow, Martin, 90, 152-153, 169, 208-209, 227; charges against, 283, 285, 287
Metro Council, 73-74
Metro Toronto Convention Centre, 142
Metro Toronto West Detention Centre, 4, 6, 7-10, 246
Metropolitan Toronto Fraud Squad, 218
Metropolitan Toronto Housing Authority (MTHA), 84-85, 157-163
Metropolitan Toronto Housing Company, 45, 289
Metropolitan Toronto Police Commission, 52, 67
Metropolitan Toronto Police Services Board, 52
Michener, David, 148, 151
Midnorthern Appliances, 138
Midtown Properties, 115
Miller, Frank, 66
Miller, Lesley, 49, 111, 169, 284; and Futurac Consultants, 163-164, 190; and NCJW Capital Fund, 114; and Prince Charles housing project, 43, 56, 60, 63; and Ridley housing project, 164, 167; and Starr Affair, 176, 181-183, 185, 226; and Task Force on the Disabled, 32, 34-35
Miller, Ron, 114, 284; and Prince Charles housing project, 53, 55, 111; and Starr Affair, 182, 185, 196
Ministry of Correctional Services, 243, 244
Moldaver, Michael, 205, 212, 214
Molson Indy, 132, 141, 194
Molson's, 132, 171, 194

Moran, Hal, 194
Moro, Tony, 42, 45, 47
Moscoe, Howard, 51, 57, 164-167
Moss, Phyllis, 34, 61, 164, 214
Mulroney, Brian, 60, 131
Mulroney, Mila, 110
Munro, John, 148-149
Munro, Lily, 66, 147, 148-150
Murphy, Daniel, 229
Muzzo, Marco, 95, 97, 170, 171

National Action Committee on the Status of Women (NAC), 67, 68
National Council of Jewish Women (Toronto Section), 26-27, 32-38; Angels Ball, 29-31; Boutique Wearhouse, 26, 27; Capital Fund, 89, 113-115, 167, 181, 191-192, 195, 198, 227-228, 283; Casino Royale, 28-29; charges against, 225-227, 230; Charitable Foundation, 56; Conference on the Jewish Disabled, 34-35; Council House renovation grant, 112, 151-153, 169, 208-209, 222, 283; and government grants, 28, 36-38, 40, 151-152; Outreach Attendant Care program, 164; political donations, 54, 56, 65, 89-90, 112-114, 167, 169, 175-176, 186, 190-193, 196, 229-230; Prince Charles housing project, 42-65; Ridley housing project, 114, 163-168; staff, 40-41, 54-55, 69, 211-212, 213-214; and Starr Affair, 175-183, 184, 198-199, 213-214; Symposium on Violence against Women in the Jewish Community, 67-69, 102; Task Force on the Jewish Disabled, 32-33, 36-39, 42, 50; Thrift Shop, 26, 30; *Two Way Street*, 36-38

INDEX

Nelles, Susan, 5, 206
New Democratic Party (Ontario), 43, 84, 136, 165; city councillors, 173, 177; in government, 66, 159, 172, 225
Nixon, Bob, 130, 200, 221
North York, 70-72, 73
North York City Council, 58
North York Commissioner of Planning, 201
North York Committee of Adjustment, 71-72, 201
North York Mayor's Committee on Race Relations, 40
Nowlan, Nadine, 166

Office of the Ombudsman, 239
Office of the Public Trustee, 192-193, 199, 214
O'Keefe Centre, 73-74, 75-77, 145, 147, 166
Olympic bid, 141, 144, 145, 154, 173-174, 177
O'Neil, Hugh, 66, 194-195
Onrot, Martin, 76
Ontario Correctional Institute, 262, 264, 276-277
Ontario government: and Patricia Starr Inquiry, 206, 217-218; provincial elections, 63, 65-66, 135-137, 139, 223-225; and Starr Affair, 196, 199-200, 202-203, 221-224; York Region inquiry, 170-172
Ontario Housing Corporation, 288
Ontario Ministry of Citizenship and Culture, 36
Ontario Ministry of Community and Social Services (COMSOC), 62, 64, 165
Ontario Ministry of Consumer and Commercial Relations, 114
Ontario Ministry of Culture and Communications, 112, 147, 222, 227
Ontario Ministry of the Environment, 75
Ontario Ministry of Tourism and Recreation, 145
Ontario Municipal Board, 57, 65, 71-72, 142
Ontario Place, 76, 99, 115-133, 153, 195, 200; finance, 124-131; food services, 126-127, 132, 145; Patricia Starr resignation, 193-194, 199-200; staff, 118-119, 124, 126-127, 128; and Toronto waterfront, 140-146, 151
Ontario Police Commission, 82, 83, 85, 91, 204
Ontario prison system, 241, 262-264
Ontario Provincial Police, 88, 92, 192, 216; and Ontario Place, 127, 128-129
Ostry, Bernie, 148

Paisley, Hugh, 192, 195, 214
Patricia Starr Inquiry, 2, 177, 179, 202-203, 205-208, 210-215, 224; appeal, 206-207, 216-218; media coverage, 210-212, 214; and Ontario government, 206; terms of reference, 205, 206, 211, 212
Pearlson, (Rabbi) Jordan, 1
Pearson, Jamie, 100, 203
Pelligrini, Paul, 106
Pepino, N. Jane, 67, 77, 107-108, 148-150, 189; association with Patricia Starr, 97, 99, 100, 109-111, 115-116, 122, 128-129, 289-291; and Prince Charles housing project, 52, 55, 58-59, 63-66; and Starr Affair, 178-180, 192, 201, 202, 203

INDEX

Peterson, Clarence, 82
Peterson, David, 37, 64, 66, 131; association with Patricia Starr, 36, 76, 83, 86, 101, 102, 135-136, 148, 155, 177; and DelZotto family, 93-94, 97-98, 108; and Ontario Place, 99, 115, 119-121, 122; and Patricia Starr Inquiry, 2, 202, 217-218, 223-224; and Starr Affair, 169-170, 190, 193, 205, 222, 224-225, 233; Toronto waterfront plans, 144, 147, 173-174
Peterson, Heather, 83, 84, 86, 99
Peterson, Jim, 33, 36, 49, 65, 83, 84, 86, 99, 106, 189
Peterson, Marie, 82
Peterson, Shelley, 155
Peterson, Tim, 120
C.M. Peterson & Co., 49, 171
Porter, Julian, 205, 212
Prevedello, Franco, 290
Prince Charles housing project, 42-66, 84-85, 134, 157; lobbying for, 58-60, 61, 63-66; organization of, 44-45, 50-51, 53-56, 55, 60-61, 63, 96-97; opposition to, 51, 62, 65, 158; re-zoning application, 56-58, 61-62; sales tax rebate, 110-111, 113, 114; sponsorship of, 55-56
Prison for Women (Kingston, Ontario), 252
Project 50, 225, 283

Rae, Bob, 225, 233
Ramparts development, 141, 143, 145, 166
Regent Park (Toronto), 84-85, 158
Reid & Lyons Inc., 236, 269, 290
Reimer, Rudy, 195
Reingold, Rochelle, 61, 164, 185, 214

Revenue Canada, 112-113, 175-176, 190, 203, 283
Riccuiti, Joe, 104, 106-107
Richmond, Ted, 138
Ridley housing project, 114, 163-168, 186-187
Robarts, John, 88, 116
Robins, Appleby, Kotler (lawyers), 53, 111, 134, 143, 196, 284
Robinson, Kathryn, 89, 221, 229
Rotenberg, David, 51, 53, 57, 62, 64, 65, 66
Rowlands, June, 288
Royal Conservatory of Music (Toronto), 18
Royal Ontario Museum, 98
Rucker, Patricia, 185-186
Rudson, Dody, 181, 191, 213, 226, 284

Sandler, Gary, 61-62, 64, 96
Scheininger, Les, 1, 148, 187
Scott, Ian, 66, 156, 159; association with Patricia Starr, 84-85, 87-88, 101, 204; and Patricia Starr Inquiry, 205, 221, 223-224
Sewell, John, 51, 157-163, 225
Shea, Derwyn, 76
Silcox, David, 147-148, 150-152, 153, 209
Skydome (Toronto), 171, 200, 221
Slavens, Eric, 54, 176, 189-190, 284; and NCJW, 111, 112, 113-114; and Prince Charles housing project, 63; and Starr Affair, 185, 196
Slavens, Marsha, 55, 61, 69, 111, 180, 284; and NCJW Capital Fund, 114-115; and Prince Charles housing project, 54; and Ridley housing project, 167; and Starr Affair, 176, 181-182, 185
Smith, David, 158

INDEX

Smith, Don, 89, 90
Smith, Joan, 89
Sobel, Edith, 169
Sorbara, Greg, 66
St. Alban's Anglican Church (Toronto), 13
Starr, Jerry, 32, 100, 135, 139, 180, 201-202, 231-232, 235-236, 248, 269
Starr, Patricia. see also Patricia Starr Inquiry; Starr Affair. advice to, 111, 132, 178, 179-181; and anti-Semitism, 13, 19, 105-106, 123, 248-249, 267-268; B'nai Brith tribute dinner, 75, 99-101, 180; and Canadian Jewish Congress, 40, 50, 54, 90-91; charges against, 1, 218, 225, 227, 229-232, 232-236, 283; and Elizabeth Fry Society, 282-283; employment, 22-24; family, 13-18, 32, 201-202, 215, 235-236, 248, 289; fundraising for charities, 69, 90-91, 110, 151-152; and government grants, 36-37, 90-91; and Jewish Community Centre, 40, 50, 54, 77, 90-91, 152; on Judaism, 15, 240, 252; lawsuit against Ontario government, 223-224; lawyers, 5-6, 205, 212-213, 231-232; legal and accounting fees, 223-224, 231-232; marriage, 20-24, 25, 29, 32; and Mayor's Committee on Race Relations, 40; and the media, 157, 174-175, 185-186, 190-193, 199, 210-212; and Metropolitan Toronto Housing Authority, 135, 157-163; and NCJW, 25-31, 32-38, 50, 69, 134-135, 169, 178-183, 187-188, 190; and NCJW Capital Fund, 114-115, 181, 195, 227-228; and NCJW renovation grant, 152, 208-209, 218, 225-227, 286-287; and North York Committee of Adjustment, 71-72, 135, 201; and O'Keefe Centre, 73-74, 75-77, 135, 145, 166; and Ontario Place, 76, 99, 115-133, 135, 140-146, 153, 193-194, 195, 199-200; parole, 254, 269-270, 274-275; personal finances, 179-180, 203; police investigation, 2, 3, 201, 216, 218-219, 225-228; political activities, 54, 69-70, 75-80, 81-96, 101-108, 172-174; political fundraising, 65, 78, 79-80, 83-84, 88-90, 105, 136-137; on politics, 256-260; and Prince Charles housing project, 42, 53-54, 56, 58-60, 61-66, 157; prison experience, 3-4, 6-12, 237-255, 237-256, 261-275; prison sentence, 3, 233-236; professional career, 49-50, 109-110, 115-116, 204; and stock market, 23-24; and Toronto Jewish Congress, 54; and Toronto waterfront, 142-148, 151, 153-155; trial, 1-3; and Tridel Corporation, 78-79; and United Way, 40; Woman of Valour Award (State of Israel), 77; on women, 107, 259-260; youth, 13-24
Starr Affair, 132, 150, 184-197, 198-203, 220-222
Stein, David Lewis, 288
Stern, Rick, 5-6
Stone, Betty, 25, 27-28, 41, 54-55, 69, 134; and NCJW grants, 33, 36, 152, 191; and Patricia Starr Inquiry, 211, 213-214
Strom, Gloria, 25, 213, 215
Supreme Court of Canada, 2, 216-218

300

INDEX

Swadron, Barry, 223-224, 232
Swadron, Marshall, 223
Sweeney, John, 66
Switzman, Shirley, 164

Teeft, Roy, 218, 225, 284-285
Temple Sinai, 1
Thatcher, Margaret, 33
Timbrell, Dennis, 64, 131
Tobe, Joan, 164
Tonks, Alan, 173-174, 177, 185
Toronto ballet/opera house, 146, 147, 151-152, 153
Toronto City Council, 154; Land Use Committee, 145, 146, 166
Toronto Harbour Commission, 117, 153, 154
Toronto Jewish Congress, 35, 53, 54, 167, 186-187
Toronto Star, 58, 161, 288
Toronto Sun, 74, 122-123, 171, 194, 228-229
Toronto Symphony, 132
Toronto Transit Commission, 145, 146
Toronto waterfront: and 1996 Olympics, 141, 144, 145, 154; David Peterson plans for, 144, 147, 173-174; development of, 140-148, 154; and Expo 2000, 145, 154; light rapid transit line, 143-144; and Ontario Place, 151, 153; provincial control of, 140-147, 153-155; and Ramparts development, 141, 143, 145, 166
Tridel Corporation, 42, 65, 68, 132, 158, 162, 186. *see also* DelZotto family; and Patricia Starr Inquiry, 205, 206, 211-212; political donations, 65, 78-79, 100, 137; and Prince Charles housing project, 47-48, 51-53, 55, 57, 62, 64, 111, 113, 114; and Ridley housing project, 164-168, 187; and Starr Affair, 202, 204-205, 222
Trudeau, Pierre Elliott, 33-34, 79, 148, 162
Turner, John, 78
Two Way Street, 36-38

United Jewish Welfare Fund, 18
United Way of Metropolitan Toronto, 40, 60, 289
Urquhart, Carissa, 228

Valpy, Michael, 162-163
Vanier Centre for Women (Brampton, Ontario), 11. *see also* women in prison; anti-Semitism in, 249-249, 268; drugs in, 265-266; food, 254, 265; Hochelaga Cottage, 241, 262; Ingleside Cottage, 254, 255, 261-274, 276-281; Invictus Cottage, 241; Kon Tiki Cottage, 241, 262; lack of programs, 242, 262-264, 267; prisoners, 238-240, 246-248, 250-254, 265-268, 269-274, 277-281; regulations, 245, 247; sexual activity in, 250-251; staff, 237-238, 242-245, 248-249, 264-265; Temporary Absence Program, 244, 263, 269; Timberlea cottage, 12, 237-256; violence in, 245, 267-268
Varone, Toni, 106, 185
Verdiroc and Greenwin, 152, 153, 169, 209, 286
Volpe, Joe, 102

Waisberg Commission, 46, 81, 83, 84, 88, 98, 172, 204
Webster, Beth, 139

INDEX

Webster, John, 104, 139
West, Peter, 4-6, 205, 207, 213, 216, 218-219, 226, 232-235, 284-285
Windfields Public School (Toronto), 215
Wolfe, Helen, 61-62
women in prison: Lawrie Bemebenek, 7; Coco, 8-9, 246, 251, 269, 270-274, 277, 278-281; Isobel, 4; Katherine, 10; Lamb Chop, 243, 250-251; Linda, 252; Lori Pinkus, 238-241; Mrs. Li, 10; Victoria, 244, 247, 255, 265-266, 269-270, 277-278, 284
Wren, Ted, 1, 244
Wynn, Larry, 57-58, 65, 201

York Mills Collegiate (Toronto), 215
York Region Board of Education, 284
York Region inquiry, 170-172, 221

Zener, Donna, 34, 61, 164, 214
Zentil, Joe, 95

Fiction